RACING MECHANIC

ERMANNO CUOGHI
Mechanic to a world champion

by Jeremy Walton

OSPREY

Published in 1980 by Osprey Publishing Limited,
12–14 Long Acre, London WC2E 9LP
Member company of the
George Philip Group

British Library Cataloguing in Publication Data
Walton, Jeremy
Racing mechanic.
1. Automobiles, Racing—Maintenance and repair
I. Title
629.28′7′80924   TL236

ISBN 0–85045–329–1

© Copyright Jeremy Walton 1980

This book is copyrighted under the Berne Convention. All rights reserved. Apart from any fair dealing for the purpose of private study, research, criticism or review, as permitted under the Copyright Act, 1956, no part of this publication may be reproduced, stored in a retrieval system, or transmitted in any form or by any means, electronic, electrical, chemical, mechanical, optical, photocopying, recording or otherwise, without prior written permission. All enquiries should be addressed to the Publishers

Editor Tim Parker
Design Stephen McCurdy

Printed in Great Britain by
Butler & Tanner Ltd, Frome and London

Contents

Introduction	4
Preface	6
Acknowledgements	10
1 Modena 1935–56	12
2 Racing heritage	18
3 Racing without shoestrings	22
4 Trucking Shelby's Cobras	36
5 Preparing a legend for John Wyer	44
6 Working on the winning Porsche	70
7 Life at Ferrari	96
8 Back in Formula 1	112
9 Leaving ... Cuoghi's full account	134
10 Tough times at Brabham	138
11 Lauda on Cuoghi	158
12 Cuoghi on Lauda and others	164
Index	174

Introduction

I FIRST met Ermanno Cuoghi when he was working for Carroll Shelby during 1964 in Europe. The event was the Tour de France, which I followed in company with Shelby's chief engineer, Phil Remington. We were on our way out from Rouen to the circuit when we saw the Shelby transporter coming towards us in the wrong direction. It was driven by this cheerful little Italian who spoke little English and no French. He was completely lost, so we told him to turn around and follow us to the next circuit.

The Shelby team was based on Ford Advanced Vehicles at Slough; I was that organization's managing director. When the 1964 season ended, the cars and American personnel returned to the States, leaving us with the mechanics hired in Europe. We absorbed the best of them, including Ermanno.

At the end of 1966 FAV closed down and I formed JW Automotive Engineering, in the same premises, with the same staff. By this time the immensely likeable Ermanno had shown great mechanical ability and considerable qualities of leadership. Below me I had John Horsman as technical director and David Yorke as racing director, who shared an office. We made Ermanno chief racing mechanic with two leading mechanics, one for each racing car, below him. In the workshop Ermanno reported to John Horsman, while on the circuit he was responsible to David Yorke.

Each leading mechanic was assigned a team of mechanics and we tried not to change them around, so they could identify with 'their' car and drivers. The whole system worked well and very smoothly, which is a testimonial to the people concerned. All instructions to the racing mechanics went through Ermanno and it was left to him and the leading mechanics as to who was assigned particular tasks.

Ermanno was, I think, better and happier in the field than in the workshop. This is in no way to disparage his skill: he was very good at both. However, in the field he had more opportunity to use his initiative and powers of improvisation, and this suited him best.

His greatest quality, apart from his obvious ability, was his wonderful temperament. Ermanno was always cheerful, even at four o'clock in the morning. He could be very, very amusing: if he had not been a mechanic he would have been a born clown.

Ermanno Cuoghi brought his wife and family to England, where he was very happy. I think he truly loved England and was in tears when he left to return to Italy in 1971.

I will always remember him with great respect and affection.

John Wyer
Château-Tournon,
Var,
France
19 June 1979

Preface

TOP-LINE motor racing mechanics are a fascinating breed. Although Britain and Australasia seem to provide most of them, there are few industrialized countries that do not contribute to the truly international teams of today. The Italian love affair with fast cars is enough to ensure that nation's enthusiastic participation.

Ermanno Cuoghi of Italy stands out from his countrymen, and other international racing mechanics, because he has succeeded in working at the highest levels in both Italy and Britain, regarding either country as 'home'. Emotionally it has not been easy for him, or especially his family, being torn between the two camps, but Ermanno has still maintained a standard that perfectionist Niki Lauda simply regards as the best to be found.

It is very easy to overlook how hard it was for Cuoghi to climb to the status of World Championship sports car and double World Formula 1 Championship mechanic. Indeed one British driver rather dismissively said that Cuoghi had just always been with the right teams!

Wrong, oh so wrong! Cuoghi started his racing career with outfits that were frequently more concerned by the performance of the British legal system than that of their cars; outfits where enthusiasm far outstripped capital, but none of it mattered that much to Ermanno. The deft little craftsman from Modena still derived enormous pleasure from motor racing, even when his team were

fighting for a place on the grid, never mind beating the opposition!

Ermanno always worked upon a wide variety of machinery. He is still deeply enthusiastic when discussing either pedal-propelled or motorcycles, these first loves leading him into garage work. A chance meeting with the American-Italian Tony Settember brought him to sports and formula car racing, culminating in a first encounter with Formula 1—albeit on a very restricted budget—in 1962.

Cuoghi saw some of the top European circuits and teams in action during that period and Settember carefully coached the young Italian in the basics of racing car design. When that team collapsed it was some time before Ermanno reappeared and asserted his versatility by driving the Shelby transporter around Europe and helping out on mechanical chores with the team's brutal V8 American Shelby Cobras.

When the Americans returned home Cuoghi was absorbed within FAV, the Slough base that was to be Cuoghi's working home town until 1971.

By then his reputation as one of the world's best mechanics was recognized, especially in his race track speed at providing instant solutions, and for his team spirit in inspiring mechanics to work together slickly in routine fuel, tyre, oil and water pit stops.

Not surprisingly Ferrari hired him for 1972 after JW Automotive had been successful, winning Le Mans twice with the Ford GT40, and providing Porsche with twelve World Championship sports car victories to help them to their Championship titles in 1970/71 with the incredible 12-cylinder Porsche 917.

The Ferrari move was even more successful. The 312P sports cars won every race they entered in that

first season for Cuoghi! They were not so masterful in 1973, but Cuoghi had the chance to switch over to Formula 1 and a young Austrian called Niki Lauda arrived for the 1974 season. In 1975 and 1977 Lauda was World Champion, and Cuoghi was his mechanic throughout.

When this book was written Ermanno Cuoghi was still the chief mechanic upon Niki Lauda's Grand Prix machine, but by then the red finish was a little less searing than Ferrari red being that of the British-based Parmalat Brabham-Alfa Romeo team.

From space-framed sports cars on spindly wheels and one choice of tyre Cuoghi had travelled cheerfully to the summit of commercial motor racing as multi-million-pound teams battle for supremacy all over the world. Ground-effects, qualifying tyres, aerodynamic devices, these are the words that reflect a constant stream of technical progress which Cuoghi has absorbed and added to his armoury of knowledge gathered since he began his racing life in 1959.

This technical aspect is possibly what interests most readers, but Ermanno's story first interested me because he is such a likeable human being. I approached him about this book in his early days with Brabham. Ermanno shrugged in his best comic-Italian manner and said too much had been written about him in the specialist magazines already.

The idea to do the book at all was inspired by the story of the great Alf Francis (*Alf Francis—racing mechanic*, G. T. Foulis, 1957), a man with every bit as much character as Ermanno, who looked after Stirling Moss and his cars for many seasons. I read the Francis story before setting out on this project and found it thoroughly entertaining, but both Cuoghi and myself came to the con-

clusion that today's more sophisticated readership would be unlikely to accept a first person story in the Queen's English, so the narrative style was adopted.

Although there are a great deal of mechanical asides in the book, I hope that what will also come over is the story of a warm-hearted man with the gift of making others laugh whatever the circumstances; a man with a passion for motor racing, but no love of the outsize egos that often pass for character in that world.

Of course, Ermanno Cuoghi is an outstanding mechanic, but he is not the type of person to recite every nut and bolt detail of a delicate mechanical operation. A quick quip, born of drily observant humour rather than malice, and it is on to the next job.

Ermanno, like so many of the dedicated men who toil such long hours over temperamental grand prix machinery, seeks no limelight, no acclaim for what he does. He is happier fishing, cycling or simply being at home in Modena with his patient wife.

The financial rewards of his life, or indeed of this book, are negligible compared to the drivers he works for, but that misses the point. Ermanno Cuoghi and the other superb mechanics you see bustling over modern Formula 1 cars do so because they are rewarded inwardly by making the best possible job on 'their' racing car. It is the old-fashioned pride of a craftsman in a beautifully sculptured piece of 'furniture', but with the added zest of demonstrating (hopefully) its superiority over all the other four-wheeled works of art by beating them to the chequered flag!

It was a pleasure writing this book about a man who continues to make the most of his life. I hope you have as much enjoyment when reading it as I did talking to this witty genius with a spanner....

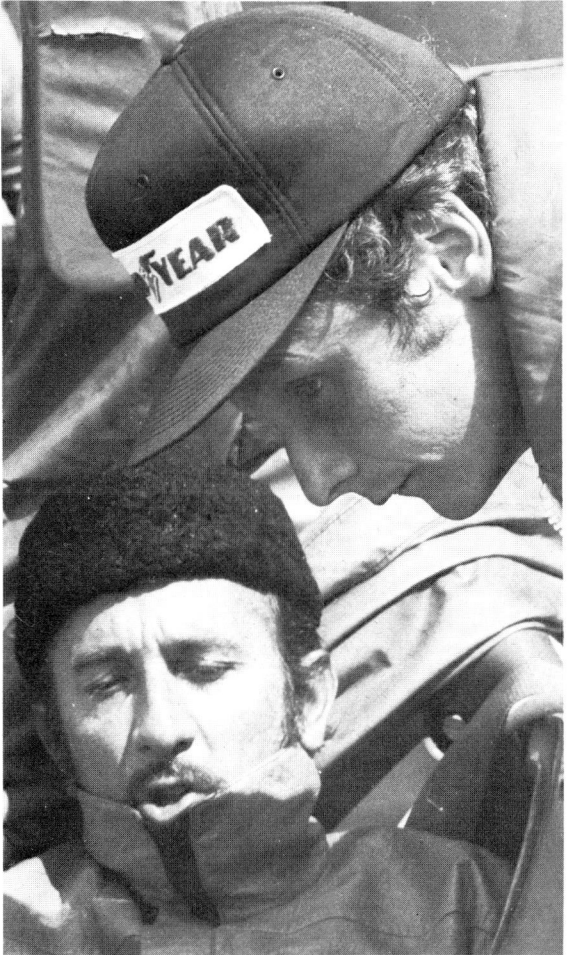

Acknowledgements

MY PRINCIPAL thanks have to go to the man who provided such a human story with a frankness that puts others to shame—Ermanno Cuoghi. Even when it came to the difficult section on his leaving Ferrari, Ermanno admitted his own shortcomings with a disarming speed that contrasts starkly with most racing drivers one interviews. The exception is Niki Lauda, who I must also thank for giving me a blunt insight into his working relationship with this extraordinary racing mechanic.

As ever, time prevented me taking full advantage of the generous help offered by fellow journalists to check the facts. However, Denis Jenkinson very kindly provided painstaking notes on the early sixties racing world, especially in the Modena region. For the same reason I would like also to express my gratitude to Pete Coltrin, 'the King of Modena motor lore'.

John Wyer, the management head of JW Automotive, provided a shrewd and moving letter on those years which gave me a clearer insight to that period. He also wrote the Foreword. I hope Mr Wyer continues to enjoy his retirement in the South of France for he certainly earned it.

Ermanno provided many of the pictures, but I am also happy to acknowledge the co-operation of London Art Tech and photographer Mike Marchant who worked hard on sports car pit activity during the sixties and seventies, providing some excellent material.

Also Maureen Magee shot a 1979 Silverstone test session for me. Many others in the grand prix world enthusiastically provided all the help they could for me on this popular pit-lane personality, a 'thanks' which applies with equal force to those who provided information too.

For reference I primarily depended on *Motor Sport*'s excellent coverage of the sport: I could not ask D.S.J. to check any more chapters in the book, or the debt would simply have been too large to call it my own work. If there are mistakes, and every written work is fallible, they are mine. Others who unfailingly answered my questions patiently were former *Motoring News* colleagues Alan Henry and Michael Cotton, the latter's current position with Porsche in Great Britain being no handicap in a work such as this!

The work of Jeff Hutchinson in *Autosport* was particularly useful for the 1973 season, and the co-operation of the publishers of that magazine is also gratefully acknowledged.

Reference books that proved helpful were Niki Lauda's own *For the Record*, published by William Kimber; *The John Player Motorsport Yearbook* from the Queen Anne Press and *The Racing Porsches* by Paul Frère, published by Patrick Stephens.

I should like to thank the Brabham team on Ermanno's behalf for providing such an enjoyable working atmosphere, and for myself for putting up with a temporary 'hanger-on' with humour and concise information.

As ever my greatest ally has been my wife Patricia. She has retyped most of it, read the manuscript twice (far beyond the call of conscience) and humoured others whom I didn't contact while this epic was in progress!

Jeremy Walton
Spa-Francorchamps, Belgium
July 1979

Dedicated to the memory of Pedro Rodriguez—A bighearted man and extraordinary racing driver

1

Modena 1935-1956

WHEN the mysterious forces that decide our destiny picked upon Modena as the birthplace for Ermanno Cuoghi, they picked precisely *the* place on earth for a resourceful motor racing mechanic to be born. The city is famous for the exotic machinery that has been produced within the region. The skills of generations of craftsmen in metal, especially in the fabrication and handwork of aluminium, have spawned most of the world's fastest and most exotic sporting cars. Lamborghini, Maserati and, most revered of all, Ferrari: all are the products of a fiercely independent region.

Today you can pass by the town in seconds on the *Autostrada del Sol.* You do not see the heart of this ancient town; a city that lies on a fertile plain full of flat arable land, peopled by slow-moving figures at odds with the image of the snarling high-performance cars produced in the area. The plain is fenced off by the Apennine mountains, peaks that stolidly watched as men hurled their cars against the challenging curves of the roads that straddle their backs, forming part of the legendary Mille Miglia road race; that extraordinary road race killed by the uncontrolled crowds which thronged by the roadside to watch the region defend its honour against invaders.

Modena lies at the heart of the Emilia-Romagna region, north-west of Bologna and well on the way to the industrial north, where the car-manufacturing giants of today reside at either end of the Milan–Turin motorway.

During Ermanno's upbringing the town's traditional good communications north and south—a railway line passes straight through, bisecting this provincial capital—ensured that the war came right to his door. Germans, Americans and the British all passed through during the Second World War.

This should be no surprise to any historian, for Modena was gripped by the Mutina Boii 218 years before Christ was born, a rebellion subdued by the Romans, who by 183 BC had colonized the area. Modena too has seen the ravages of Attila's Huns and the influence of the Lombards. In its time Modena has been controlled by many factions, including the Austrians and the French, so Ermanno's adaptability during the Second World War reflected a tradition of Modena citizens in coping with minor upheavals like war passing by the front door and over the roof!

Cuoghi's often hilarious memories of his childhood were given to me in surroundings far away from the atmosphere of the historic city. In 1979 Cuoghi was living with another Brabham Formula 1 mechanic in a tower block apartment, up there on the ninth floor and overlooking the struggle of south London suburbs that lay beneath his Sutton eyrie. Apparently unchanging, Cuoghi is quite self-conscious about his age and modest about the experience he has gathered by having the advantage of years over the many skilled youngsters now to be found in Grand Prix racing.

While he sipped Cinzano on the settee I wondered at the energy radiating from a man in one of the most demanding of jobs. He was then in the thick of constructing the new V12 ground-effect Brabham for Lauda's first race of 1979, a brand new design (itself a rarity in Formula 1, especially so with a new engine), and yet his shortish figure (5 ft 6 in) was charged with bonhomie at nine at night through to the small hours. I learned to recognize that a slight hair loss on top is compensated for by the luxuriant moustache and a range of gestures accompanied by flashing eyes that speak eloquently of the enjoyment he still derives from his working role in motor racing. Cuoghi may be far from home, with a full-grown son and his wife in Italy, but he still relishes his working life in what has become his second homeland.

He speaks English with a strong accent and a lot of humour. I have chosen to use his way of expressing things in many cases because it gives us the flavour and feeling of this extraordinary 'super-mech', a man who has looked after more of the world's fastest and most successful racing cars than anyone I can recall.

With Cuoghi almost at rest the recollections began....

'I cannot tell you when I was born,' he begins, 'it was too long ago! OK, I tell you: it was the fifth of May 1935.' There is a pause while Cuoghi looks suitably pensive at these years on earth before describing the house in which he was born and initially raised. 'It was a detached house, two floors. Very nice, just on the outskirts of the historic city part of Modena, and very beautiful. We live on one floor with five steps from one level to the next.'

He lived there until three years of age with his parents, whom he describes simply and with obvious love: 'My mother's name is Elmore and this is funny. You know, when she is nineteen she is being called to the Army! It is a very difficult Italian name....' A pause for laughter... 'because they spell it wrong! No don't laugh, my mother says, here is me I am not a man am I? I am a woman, no doubts. Now change the papers!'

Cuoghi's father was called Romeo and he was 'working in a factory, more a foundry, where they were making keys. The Corniff foundry in Modena is very old: the family are the same people who make the money to have a technical school, where you can study for a first degree in engineering. My father has work there practically all his life. In the beginning he was doing the tipping of the castings, pouring the metal, but after the war, when he has done many years, he is in charge of a section of the factory. It is quite big now, maybe 700–800 workers in all.

'I don't know exactly how my mother and father met. They lived quite close to each other on the outskirts of Modena, so perhaps it was in some ballroom... something like this.' Cuoghi then went on to illuminate age differential in Italian marriage: 'there is five years difference between my father and my mother, and it is the same with me and my wife. It is the average difference in Italy.' A twinkle in the Cuoghi eyes and some merriment in his voice became evident as he said, 'yes, it is important to understand this. The wife is always younger, naturally, because she's getting older quicker than the man! The younger you get, the longer she last....'

Recalling his childhood in Modena, Cuoghi notes that the family did move closer to his father's work for a while, but when the house was damaged during the war, they returned close to the place where he was born, this time in a three-storey house.

He has good cause to remember the layout, for the ground floor contained shops and small garage workshops. The house he lived in also contained the revered presence of a top-class motorcycle mechanic, who was to play quite a part in Cuoghi's formative mechanical years after the war.

Some of Cuoghi's earliest recollections are of attending nursery school, for it was during the

IN *1958 Ermanno was serving in the army. Typically he used conscription to learn something useful; how to be a chauffeur and dismantle lethal weapons*

height of the Mussolini era that the toddler began the almost irrelevant process (he is a great believer in education for others) of schooling.

'It was a pretty good school. There are only women to teach, not nuns, just qualified teachers. During this Mussolini time we all have uniforms, I remember they were mainly in white.

'We used to have a parade, and when I was young I was an actor too! This was in the first years at junior school, which I go to when I was six. Then we are on display with the blackshirts, all in their dress uniforms, and we have been in the theatre to make plays too.'

Cuoghi added quietly that he did about two full years at junior school because 'the bombing and so on make all the schools miss a year, you know?'

Modena itself was bombed regularly, but not heavily, in comparison to other Italian cities at the time. One might have thought that the racing car skills of the city would have been ideal for aeroplane manufacture, too, but as Cuoghi remembers it was the town of Reggio Nell'Emilia—'the next one up the road,' as Ermanno put it—that was famous for its Caprioni works. Some aeroplane parts were made in Modena, but the war action was down on the earth. 'In Modena is the main railway north to south and it goes straight across the town, which is surrounding like a river going through the middle. So they are bombing the railway, and all the houses in the area are being knocked down.'

Ermanno remembers it all quite well—he was five in 1940 and 'not even a teenager at the end of the war'—especially how they used to react to strafing runs from fighter planes. 'On the highway they would try to shoot *anything*. They were coming down using the machine guns, and we were running behind them picking up the cartridges! They were still hot, but they make good things to play with!'

Needless to say Cuoghi's mother was not impressed with her son's toys, but by the time he was eight she had other things to worry about. The most lasting was the birth of a daughter (Gianpaula) and the second was a three-month spell in bed for the infant Ermanno.

He had suffered in his early years with tonsillitis and the infection grew worse at eight years of age. Despite the doubts cast by some doctors called in for second opinions, the ministrations of their family doctor proved successful. The treatment was radical and hard for an eight-year-old to endure, composed of staying in bed on a diet of one spoonful of rice and a glass of milk every day.

Ermanno reports, 'I never had anything wrong since. Sure, a few colds, but nothing else. Doctor Romanini, I never forget his name, he says "trust me, keep it like that on the diet." And I tell you I never had nothing wrong with me since.' He subsequently did break a leg, also dislocated his knees, but on both occasions the cause was motorcycling rather than natural!

Back at the war in Modena, Cuoghi particularly remembers 'the Germans. We see them twice, first when they come through on the way down Italy in 1943. Then again in the following year when they are pushed back by the Americans and English.

'Modena did not suffer too much with the troops. The very big fight was down south, so we have a lot of troops just going up and down. There was no real fighting in Modena, just the resistance up in the mountains.

'It's funny really. When our house was bombed down and we moved back to the part of the town

CYCLING HAS *long been a Cuoghi passion. Even when I started this book, some thirty years after this photograph was taken in 1949, Ermanno had a racing bike stored away in the bedroom of his ninth floor flat*

ALSO TAKEN *in 1949, when Ermanno was still in his teens, this picture shows him with local enthusiasts in Modena. Ermanno is second from the left*

where I was born, our new home had three storeys with three flats. In the back was a big garden, because it was a mansion of some very rich people there, and there are many trees where the Germans can hide their trucks and jeeps and everything.

'I used to go and play in there. The Germans had occupied part of the house and the garden is full of tanks, trucks and stuff like that. Italy was in misery then: complete misery at that time. The Germans have everything, mainly food I mean, and I remember what we were doing to achieve a lump of bread from the bakery next door. There were always two or three of us kids and we used to take their donkey out for fire-kindling twigs, to be paid with bread. We were desperate and the German soldiers were always friends for us kids. When they have something left they always give it to us.

'The Germans were better than going without food, but the Americans were not like that. They were giving us nothing, so we were stealing chocolates from their trucks. They have their jeeps with a little trapdoor and cupboard, and they always keeping chocolate in there . . . but not for long! I was a very good runner by the end, I can tell you.'

Naturally all trace of merriment is gone from Cuoghi's normal jovial manner when remembering what it was like to be truly hungry, and he looks back with clarity on September 1943 with these words; 'in Italy the big stores they were always full of food. Flour, pasta, all these kind of things, even in this time of war.

'The people didn't have nothing to eat. So what they did, the poor peoples, one day they all came together. What they did? They knocked down all the store doors and took it all. I remember participating in that in Modena. Running through the stores, taking *anything* you could eat: stuff you could keep. Pasta, flour, cheese. It was the only

way to survive in those days.'

Such a background in wartime Europe, savouring the thrills of a childhood with unusually attractive grown war 'toys' alongside a real need for food at any cost certainly made a mark on Cuoghi's character. Alongside many of his Formula 1 colleagues his courteous way of answering even the silliest question and a cheery life-style, where many are dour perpetually, are not just attributable to his maturity. Partly it is his inherited character from a happy family—perhaps unusually fortunate and un-Italian in having only two offspring to feed in hard times—but a lot is because he has simply experienced things that are hard for a youth brought up in the fifties and sixties in the English-speaking world to really understand.

Cuoghi is certainly not one to dwell on the war period, but its effect on someone not yet ten years old, experiencing how it feels to be shot at, bombed out and strafed, seems to have been to leave Ermanno with a very strong streak of tolerance for humanity.

Just two years after the war ended in Europe, Italy was setting herself back on her feet, ready for the 'economic miracle' of the fifties and sixties. Ermanno Cuoghi was finding out the delights of motorcycle maintenance from the resident mechanic at home.

'Just before the war is ended, this mechanic and a friend went down to Rimini and they have bought a truck. It is full of English Army messenger motorcycles: Matchless, AJS, Ariel, Norton. . . . There are so many it is unbelievable!

'I was still at school, I was going to the elementary school at that time; me and another kid we've been helping the mechanic strip down the bike, take the paint off and so on.' By the time this work could commence Cuoghi was coming up to twelve years old, and it was his first experience of the delights of machinery repair and renovation.

The sight of the two children at work on these bikes was a fairly arresting one according to Cuoghi, for the pair had acquired some ex-American army goggles to ward off any stray paint stripper. Getting goggles designed for bulky Texans to fit tiny Italian children was the least of the problems to be surmounted when there was so much of mechanical interest to be learned.

'We took everything apart, the engine, gearbox. He showed us how everything was coming apart, and how to put it back together again. How each bit worked: the pistons, valves, everything. It was very interesting for me.'

Previously Ermanno had shown a fair curiosity and ability in drawing but his mechanical experiments were confined to 'making a little tank with a cotton reel, band and a match'.

However, there was mechanical influence in the family, even Ermanno's younger sister developing a talent for repairing, lubricating and generally looking after her own pushbike's needs. Now she is a tailor, 'a very good one', says Ermanno proudly.

With the war over and Cuoghi some twelve years of age he attended the local senior school, but he only went for two years as he explains: 'I liked school very much, but at some stages I could not follow it. I still don't know the reasons, but at some stages on the mathematical things, I just could not follow it. So this is the reason I give up. I was getting further and further behind.

'I was pretty good at drawing at that time, but mostly figures, not machinery. I was interested in some sport. Football was the major thing. I still support a team today.'

Asked who he supports in football Cuoghi laughed easily and replied, 'Milano, it has always been, all my life. Modena was no good for nothing!' Loud gusts of laughter before he described for me his first wheeled love from a participant's viewpoint. 'I always like cycling very much.

'I was fourteen years of age: after two months I stop school and go to work. My father has lent me the money to buy my first bicycle. I had told my father I could not follow school: he was upset, but he say, "OK—there are two ways. You go to work, or you go to school."

'So he has to find me a job: he didn't wait, he goes and finds me a job. It is a shop that sells general stores: salami, flour, that kind of thing. At that time you had to weigh everything, nothing was packed as it is now. All must be packed, weighed and calculated.' Italy was already out of rationing in 1947; Cuoghi's first job was two years after that. 'I liked working in the store very much, especially for one thing. It was on a Sunday morning—we were open until Sunday 1 o'clock—the lady wife of the owner of the shop, she like me very much, so every Sunday morning she was asking me at 11 o'clock "you want to go to the church? Or you want to stay at work?"

'I was saying "yes I am going to the church." I am never going! I used to go out with the bike training and did a few races later on too.

'It was a three-gear bike with two chainwheels, so six gears in all. It was a pretty good bike, by the Modenese firm Loris.

'This job in the store lasted about a year. I didn't

like a couple of little things. In the winter you had to go to the abattoir to kill the lambs and so on. We would go down with the sidecar with a live animal one way and come back with a dead one,' Cuoghi shook his head sadly at the memory.

The next job took him closer to a career as a mechanic, but did not lead directly to this.

'About 500 yards from my home there was a mechanic looking for a boy to help him. It was bicycles mainly, general repairs, so I went there to work. I enjoyed that, but when I came to sixteen years of age they had to pay me as if I was an adult. They could not keep me, it was a very small business.

'When we say you repair a bike at that time it means from a puncture to a complete rebuild of a pushbike: strip it down, repair it, grease it, chrome it and so on. We did some work on motorbikes, I remember we did quite a lot with a Guzzi, but I don't think I was taking the engines apart and things like this.'

When the job with the small cycle and general two-wheeler repair shop had come to an end, Ermanno was feeling pretty fed up with the mechanical life and decided to find something really different. He certainly succeeded, as he explained.

'I was a salesman for cheese. I quite liked it: they have three Lambrettas and two Vespas, all with a carrying space on the back. I prefer the Vespa and take this small van, fill it up with cheese and take it round all the local shops you can find, and sell whatever you can.

'I did this for quite a time, all round the local shops in Modena. Then I met a person who was selling biscuits, a very nice quality of biscuit called Calussi. They were chocolate, which I always like myself, even better than cheese! So I changed my job for this, but it didn't last very long, just a few months,' Cuoghi concluded.

Life as a food salesman was doomed to failure for a youngster so interested in fast and noisy machinery on two or four wheels. Especially in a town like Modena, where they made everything from sporting steering wheels to Colotti gearboxes and complete aluminium car bodies, besides their fabled fast-car industry.

Ermanno Cuoghi literally only had to walk from his doorstep to be part of the competition motoring world, either in a job on the same premises as those who prepared the cars (so near yet . . .) or to see some of the most exciting competition cars of the time in action. As we shall see, such sport concerned the Cuoghis long before Ermanno looked to Stanguellini for employment....

GREAT TO *be in Italy! A celebration at Padua, Cuoghi flanked by wife Maria Grazia*

WHEN CUOGHI *left Ferrari for Brabham Alfa Romeo, his wife Maria Grazia and (grinning with all the vigour of his father) son Roberto, remained in Italy for nearly two years before Ermanno could rejoin them more permanently in Modena. Even then Cuoghi's living would be earned in Modena. During that time Roberto also worked at Brabham briefly*

2
Racing heritage

'MY MOTHER she has friends, they are very rich people called Righetti; he was a racing driver. My mother, she went on a racing car even before I was born! They used to call him the mad Righetti as he was driving his Alfa-Romeo and cars like this on dirt roads—but she wins one race, I think, with him.'

With that kind of enthusiasm in the family's blood and Modena for a home it would seem racing was a natural destiny for Ermanno. He remembers watching some of the earliest post-Second World War racing in his home town thus: 'You practically look out of the window to see the road circuit they were using in that time. In fact it is the next crossroad up, and in 1948 and 1949, I went to see the races in the street.

'I think it was in 1949 that we see Righetti finish third. That was the year of the Delage, when Bracco went into the crowd and killed some people, very bad: later they are using the circuit in the park for these races in Modena,' Cuoghi recalled.

After his short spell selling chocolates Cuoghi was able to realize a long-held ambition. Very close

A NICE *change from chauffeuring army brass around during national service. Cuoghi poses on the Gilera 500 Saturno ridden by Italian champion Liberati*

to his home—'practically on the front of it' in his own words—were the premises of Stanguellini. By 1957 this Fiat agency was not only carrying on a thriving trade in Italy's most popular cars, but also 'they were converting the Fiat 500 into an overhead cam engine for the Italian sports car races. So it was my ambition to go and work for them. I tried to go and get a job there, but they were not employing people.

'So what I did was this. There was a petrol station on the front of Stanguellini, so I went and worked there on washing cars. I was about sixteen or seventeen, just before joining the army, something like that. After a while they did let me have a job in Stanguellini, but never on the racing side. I was doing repairing jobs all the time on the Fiats.

'At that time it was the 500 and 1100 Fiat, they were the kind of vehicles I was doing. I had learned to do a garage job. Upstairs they have the racing department, making the Formula cars, and they even made their own test-bench dynamometer. They were one of the first to make this kind of test in Italy with a water-brake dyno. In fact it was rather disturbing with the dynamometer running all day and night in the town . . . but at that time, the people, they were not complaining much!'

During his time at Stanguellini, Cuoghi made sure he became acquainted with the racing mechanics, admiring their white overalls and exciting life. Cuoghi particularly remembers Stanguellini's brother-in-law, Goldoni, as being very helpful, but was perhaps most impressed by the way in which the competition cars were all tested on the public road! 'They were really something. No silencers, and Stanguellini's foreman, he with light grey hair and a very important local person, he is always doing the testing with a U-turn on the main street! And the tyres, they were bending so much, the actual rim was touching the ground in sparks! Unbelievable, and the standard test route was much like that of the road race. . . .'

Cuoghi continued to work in this competition atmosphere without actually experiencing it first hand until his early twenties, for in November 1957 he was called up to do his national service in the army. Ermanno had resigned himself to this period and made the best of it in his usual resourceful fashion. 'I went to school as a mechanic for four months and then I drove the Colonel's car for a year.

'We were based at Spoleto, ninety-five kilometres or so north of Rome. I used to drive this commander into Rome once a week. This was very pleasant for me, as maybe we have some time there to relax. I think I scared him a coupla time in the car—it was 1957 Fiat 1100—but we get on OK.'

The rest of army life was quite appealing given Cuoghi's determination to 'make the best' out of his enforced service. He enjoyed shooting and the experience of finding out how to dismantle rifles and machine guns, though the anatomy of hand grenades and small bombs had understandably less appeal.

Emerging from the army there was the all-too-familiar prospect of unemployment. Cuoghi initiative put an end to this by hiring a car wash close to the Stanguellini outfit. That was soon after his discharge in March 1959—but he did have another three weeks' army training to get through in August of that year before the Italian armed forces had finished with him.

Cuoghi not only had his embryo business but a new partner to share it with as well. About five years earlier a ballroom romance had developed into a lengthy engagement and it was his fiancée Maria who joined him in 1959 in both marriage and some evening work at the car wash. That did not go on for very long as the Cuoghis had a son (Roberto) in February 1960. He was to be their only child and followed his father's footsteps to work in England for a British racing team (Brabham), but when this was written Roberto was back in Italy working at a Modenese factory and revelling in the dirty work, according to his father!

A frequent visitor to the Stantuellini's upstairs competition department during 1959 was Tony Settember, a southern Californian of Italian descent. His interest was in the pure racing cars, though his background was as a semi-professional driver with a strong mechanical talent. During the late fifties he was a well-known figure on the West Coast of the USA, *Road & Track*'s correspondent Peter Coltrin describing him as 'one of the very best in semi-pro road racing with Mercedes-Benz 300 SL coupés and, later, Chevrolet Corvettes'.

Settember had spotted a new development in sports car racing, that of mating a lightweight chassis to the powerful Italian engines of the period. As Denis Jenkinson of *Motor Sport* explained to me, 'Maserati and the other famous Italian names were used to building sports cars for the 1,000 miles of the Mille Miglia. They were powerful and strong, whereas Lotus and people like that in Britain made these light, fragile sports cars that went very well though they were desperately underpowered by Italian standards. Therefore it was worth putting a Maserati engine in a light-frame sports car.'

During Cuoghi's sojourn in the car wash trade he was reacquainted with Settember, whom he had first met while working at Stanguellini. The second meeting was entirely accidental, as Settember had brought his van in to be washed, but the chance meeting had all the impact on Cuoghi's future that chance meetings are reputed for in all the best novels.

'He wanted to make a sports car and I decided I would join him. So we went to another part of the town—up near the cemetery it was!—where he has rented a garage that is on a farm. They start in January (I could not work out until after March) and it is finished by the end of May, but the car is reasonably successful.'

The smooth result of their labours was called a WRE, which actually was meant to stand for World Racing Enterprises, though when the original backers dropped out most took it to refer to Wadsworth. Coltrin well remembers that, in 1957, a Willment sports racing car was imported to California with 'a chassis and a five-speed gearbox done mostly by an ex-RAF type named John Wadsworth.' The gearbox was actually made by a proprietary company. This car caused quite a stir in the States, though it was not an instant winner. John Wadsworth's expertise had been imported to Modena, where his welding skill was especially useful in the construction of the tubular spaceframe.

Cuoghi remembers, 'he bought a Maserati engine, gearbox and we start with tubes . . . no drawings, nothing like this . . . just some rough ideas, making a chassis. It had two big tubes for the main structure, drum brakes—but on the front they had bonded linings like on a Ferodo type now. They were very effective, compared to the Italian standard at that time.'

The four-cylinder, dohc, Maserati 200SI engine was mated to the usual Maserati four-speed gearbox and placed in the then conventional front position. What drew most attention were the car's smoothly flowing lines. Italian craftsmen, particularly those of Modena, constructed their cars by hand beating the thin sheets of metal into graceful panels. Wadsworth brought in the British roller method and the results were much admired.

After some preliminary testing of the all-independent suspension sports car, product of many sleepless nights' fabrication from its tubular steel spaceframe outward, Cuoghi recalls its impressive public debut in the early summer of 1959.

'We took it to the Naples Grand Prix on the Posillipo road circuit. It was the first time I have been with a racing car to the track. It was not exciting—it was murder, I can tell you! We left Modena in the evening with our funny OM 25 truck. It was a new truck, but too small to carry a racing car and all those parts.

'I have not done much truck driving then, so I drive all night. I arrive at Naples at 10 o'clock in

SPORTS CAR *designer and constructor John Wadsworth* (left) *and Tony Settember* (right) *beam proudly beside the sleek WRE. The picture was taken in England in 1959, before fitment of the Maserati engine. In the middle is mechanic Les Whitley*

the morning. Already they have closed the scrutineering. Somehow we get in and unload the car, but we were not organized enough even to have petrol! When we managed to get the car started up it was the end of the day and Settember could not do very much.

'I went down there with Wadsworth and Bruno—another Italian guy who joined a little time after me—and we did two days' practice. We have a few problems, some things on the car were not made strong enough, but in the race he is avoiding all the high kerbs and winning . . . but the seat is going from side to side in the car because the mountings of the seat are all broken.'

In fact it was a very fine debut win, for Settember's swarthy figure was a memory. Local heroes Bellucci and Boffa in their Maserati 200SI machines were left well behind, roaring their way through tree-lined roads, protected by the straw bales, the track set above that beautiful but often squalid Mediterranean port.

From Cuoghi's viewpoint that was the abrupt end to a promising new career, for Settember set off back home to try and raise fresh backing for the Wadsworth-designed sports car.

Ermanno returned to Stanguellini. . . .

3
Racing without shoestrings

WHILE Cuoghi returned to Stanguellini and the new-found responsibilities of parenthood, Settember and Wadsworth were busy men. Settember returned to America and started a successful search for a monied partner to finance a return to the pleasant and challenging world of European road racing. Though he found a fellow southern Californian to accompany him back to Italy, the process took a fair time and Settember does not enter our story again until late 1961.

Meanwhile Wadsworth's WRE design had certainly impressed the local Italians, who were beaten by Settember's Anglo-Italian hybrid in those May 1959 races at Naples. Neapolitans Bellucci and Boffa both decided that they would like one of these coil-sprung, spaceframe Maserati mongrels readied for the 1960 edition of the Naples Grand Prix.

The Italians purchased the original WRE prototype and raced that with success in Italian national

races, while Wadsworth built two more cars for the following season. Boffa used his car on the 1960 Targa Florio, but the highlight of his career with the car came when he did manage to win the up to 2000 cc race for sports cars in Naples that year, despite an accident and a heated battle with the then new Birdcage Maseratis for Govoni and Tedeschi, plus the older 200SI Maserati of Nino Vaccarella. The WRE also put in the fastest lap, but so far as Cuoghi was concerned, it just proved what a nice car he had been working on, nothing more.

Towards the close of 1961 Cuoghi and Settember had a second surprise reunion. Shortly afterwards, Ermanno went to Settember's premises and started work in the racing world again.

Settember's new partner was 'a pale-faced, short-haired American schoolboy', according to one contemporary describing Hugh Powell's youthful looks. However, he had a sturdy bank balance, one that was to be strained to keep up with the next few years of motor racing in association with Tony Settember, for they ranged through just about every branch of road racing and were to become a familiar part of the Grand Prix scene in 1962 and 1963.

For Cuoghi it was all to be marvellous experience, not only in car preparation but in the art of racing without visible means of support!

He recalls how the partnership developed: 'They came to Britain and bought two Formula Junior four-cylinder racing cars, one Lotus, one Cooper. Settember and Powell brought them to Italy for some races and hillclimbs, but one of the cars was lent to Govoni, the Italian driver, to use. He is from the next town up the road from Modena: they did a few hillclimbs, a few races, just as amateurs, and enjoyed themselves I think.

'So we 'ave been looking after these cars with just a few spare parts. Go out on the weekend and 'ave a good time!

'Then, in the beginning of 1962, they come back from another trip to England, where Powell and Settember have practically bought the company of Paul Emery—Emeryson Cars.

'At the same time they bought one Chevrolet Corvette. This was for some hillclimbing in Italy and long-distance races. So I was in Modena preparing the two Juniors and the Chevrolet Corvette. The Corvette was bought in America and parts of it were prepared there. It is an hardtop with a lot of spare parts which they bring for us (a friend of mine, Bruno, has joined us, as I mentioned earlier) to finish the car for Le Mans.

'The car has the 5.4-litre V8 engine and all drum brakes, but the drums they were of the latest type with bonded linings on top of the shoes. They work very well.

'We run the car in two hillclimbs, one of them in the Verona. Then we take the car to Le Mans.

'I tell you, they could not believe the capacity of this engine! So we had to take the cylinder heads out and check the bore and stroke and so on.' The Chevrolet V8 measured exactly what the makers claimed, 5369 cc.

'It was a good car. We prepared it so gently, so casually, but it was running *really* well. We have

TONY SETTEMBER *wheels the neat Scirocco-BRM V8 through the Belgian countryside at Spa-Francorchamps upon its belated debut. Settember was one of many to crash in subsequent heavy rain characteristic of the Ardennes circuit, but the car also suffered from fuel surge*

made the exhaust system in Modena, the Le Mans type running down the sides. Actually the first time we try the car in Modena, before the hillclimbs, it was fully prepared and we went to Modena race track. It was only 300 yards or so from where we were working... and everybody was very surprised to see such a *big* thing! The noise it was making, a kind of "blub, blah, blub, blub", it was fantastic. I always like the noise the big American V8s make for racing.' That was just as well, for there were to be an awful lot of years at an awful lot of race tracks, all over the world, for Cuoghi to listen to this particular American rhythm on wheels.

Of course the big American invasion of Le Mans was a few years away in the summer of 1962. When the Corvette arrived for *Les Vingt Quatre Heures*, it was a distinct oddity with an engine 1.3 litres bigger than the biggest Ferrari, Maserati and Aston Martin opposition. The American V8s had been to Sarthe before, of course, but that was back in the 1950s with Briggs Cunningham and his blue and white cars.

By a twist of fate Cunningham and Salvadori were at Le Mans that year, racing in the same class as the Corvette Cuoghi prepared, in one of three Jaguar E types entered that year, and the highest placed in fourth overall.

Settember shared the Corvette's driving with Englishman John Turner, the car entered by Scuderia Scirocco, which was to become the regular entrant's name for later Grand Prix efforts. The Corvette featured quite well in the class initially, but the prototype open V12 Ferrari from the works for Olivier Gendebien and Phil Hill set the pace. After an initial scrap with Graham Hill's factory Aston Martin coupé the Ferrari led most of the event on the way to victory.

The Corvette was forced to run for many laps with only first and fourth gears—cubic inches compensating for the enormous gap quite effectively—but the car was eventually retired because of gearbox trouble. Cuoghi was quite surprised how well the big, heavy car performed, and very pleased at its reliability outside the production gearbox.

THE EMERYSON *upon its first assembled appearance in 1962 with simple tubular frame. Note the size of the Colotti gearbox compared to the compact 1·5 litre Climax engine. And (above) Oulton Park, 1962 and the Emeryson is wheeled out to race in wider nose form to prevent the overheating*

ERMANNO (right) AND *colleague pose in a sports-racing Lotus during Ermanno's 1963 season with Tony Settember*

Settember and Powell had acquired three Emeryson Formula 1 cars. Cuoghi remembers: 'We had two of the 1961 type and one for 1962. They had the radiator on the front with a closed nose or the radiator underneath with a streamlined nose. Settember, he prefers the older one with the open nose.'

Paul Emery, later better known for his speed equipment installed upon various Hillman Imps, was one of many mechanic/drivers who decided that the advent of the new 1.5-litre/450 kg minimum weight Formula for Grand Prix racing events of 1961 onward (the present 3-litre F1 came in 1966) was the signal for privateers to join motor racing's élite. Paul Emery had been a racing special constructor since 1938, but this was his biggest project yet....

Britain had a history of small, light, rear-engined cars dating from the 500 cc days just after the Second World War. Cooper and Lotus had developed the idea in the Formula 2 category of the late 1950s, and had shown that it was possible for a relatively underpowered light car to stay on terms with a far more powerful, and heavier, front-engine design.

'All over Britain anybody and everybody built their Formula 1 cars on the kitchen table,' commented one eminent sports journalist, to the author, of this period in Grand Prix racing. When Emery found that he could not support F1 alone in 1962, the project passed on to Settember and Powell, who found they had cars very much along the then recently established practice in Britain. That meant a mid-mounted Coventry Climax four-cylinder engine. In good health one of these 1475 cc units could kick out just over 150 bhp at 7500 rpm,

but the double overhead camshaft fours (81.2 mm by 71.1 mm stroke) for the emerging Scirocco team had to be maintained by the team themselves, most of the time owing to lack of funds.

There was a spaceframe chassis, four-wheel disc brakes and—a throwback to Cuoghi's background—a five-speed Colotti gearbox, for which the machining, gears and design all came from the Modena area.

In fact that Colotti gearbox played a large part in Cuoghi's 1962 season. 'Just before the German Grand Prix at Nürburgring (5 August that year— J.W.] I am working in the garage in Modena where we are rebuilding the Emerysons. We need one gearbox collecting from the shop where they are making the casing and parts.

'All my life I have been motorbike mad and so I went up to this machine shop with my bike. I strap the gearbox casing on the back of the motorbike and come out of the gates of this small factory. It was all gravel outside and the rear end of the bike slip away under me.

'I fell inside a little ditch and felt lucky there was no water in there! The bike went on my leg and pulled the bones up [dislocated kneecap eloquently described!] . . . I was too far away to call some people out, so I slowly bring the bike back up again. I drive back to the workshop for our team, take the gearbox off, went to the hospital.

'The doctor say to me it 'as to be plastered up. I say it may be possible for the bones to stay in place if I just wear a bandage. I have to go to the Nürburgring and build a gearbox, I tell him! He has shown me the bones will not stay in place, Jesus it was bloody painful!'

The season for the inherited Emerysons was a bit painful for the team owners as well, but for Cuoghi it was an enjoyable introduction to the joys of Formula 1, and for him to develop an unusual passion for living in England.

He remembers his first Grand Prix thus: 'We go to Naples again. I was working in Modena and they have prepared the car mainly in England. Gordon Ross, the English mechanic, came down with their old Commer van.

'We drove all night from Modena and were very tired. They went off to rest and I took the transporter by myself to Naples. I drove through the night because the next morning, at 10 o'clock, it was the scrutineering. So I arrived there and had the car checked, took it to the race track and got it ready by myself. At 2 o'clock, something like that, it was the first practice.

'Tony [Settember] was doing reasonably well.

ERMANNO HELPED *out on Roy Salvadori's Cooper Monaco sports-racing car while at JW in the early years. Even a paddock rebuild of the tricky Colotti gearbox did not prevent start-line failure. Jo Ramirez took the picture of moustachioed Cuoghi in the V8 Ford-engined hybrid*

Then he went over one of the kerbs—and there are many of them to hit at this street race—and he has bent a rear radius arm. So we had to straighten that, which was quite a major job really.

'Second practice he was OK, but in the race he did the same thing and went over the kerb, bent the lower radius arm at the back suspension again. What we try to do is to bend it straight! Afterward he goes out and does a few laps, but it has collapsed again.' Settember was classified tenth, ten laps behind the winner.

'After that we were in Modena and prepared the car. It was funny when we run the car in Modena track. Stanguellini are there and they don't know much about the English cars.' Stanguellini had made a beautiful Maserati-style Formula Junior of 70 bhp during Cuoghi's 1959–60 spell with the company, but Cuoghi was not involved.

Cuoghi continued, 'Stanguellini have been on the race track with us watching the car. When we were towing it back, they were following us closely. Looking under the back, trying to see how the suspension works! At that time Ferrari was still running the trapezium type of suspension, with normal wishbones, not with the radius arms and so that the English cars are using. It was something new for them to see. . . .'

From spring to late summer 1962 the Emerysons struggled around the European circuits. Mainly they contested non-World Championship Formula 1 events, often on street circuits such as those of Naples and Brussels, but they also appeared regularly in Britain at circuits such as Crystal Palace, Aintree and Silverstone. In these non-Championship events the results were towards respectable for a private team soldiering along with the four-cylinder Climaxes in an era when the 185-plus bhp Coventry Climax V8 and the similarly powerful BRM had opened up a new British challenge to the Ferrari V6 motor. The Ferrari had ruled the first year of 1.5-litre Formula 1, producing inspiration for fellow Americans from their first World Champion in Phil Hill . . . a fact not lost on Settember and Powell.

At the start of the season there were actually three Emerysons to greet those attending the 1 April Bruxelles Grand Prix, the non-Champion-

ship event that brought many of the 1962 contestants together for the first time. One was the yellow hybrid of Lucien Bianchi, driving for the Equipe National Belge (ENB), this car also appearing throughout the year with a Colotti gearbox, but hitched up to a Maserati engine instead of a Climax.

Andre Pilette drove one of the Climax cars and John Campbell-Jones the other. Though they were about ten seconds off the fastest practice pace from the Jim Clark Lotus-Climax V8, the cars racked up a fourth and eighth place in their heats, Campbell-Jones taking fifth place overall, behind the Gilby-Climax of Keith Greene. Neither of the other Emerysons finished, but the mechanics had done very well to resuscitate the Campbell-Jones car when it failed to start on the line for its qualifying event.

Cuoghi was missing this race, like many others that season, usually because the team was so short of money! Winner of this dash around the sturdy houses and solid street scenery was Willy Mariesse's factory Ferrari V6. The Emerysons appeared at a surprising number of circuits with an equal variety of drivers, but Cuoghi best remembers tracks like Solitude. Now defunct, the track was set in the Stuttgart countryside and attracted loyal support in 1962 as Porsche were then making their Grand Prix effort with the flat eight cylinder 804 models. Dan Gurney had already given them their first Grand Prix victory at Rouen, and he then led team-mate Jo Bonnier home to a 1–2 result on their home track at Solitude.

Settember started from the fourth row in that 1962 race. The car's competitiveness can be judged from a time of 4 m 21.8 s versus Jim Clark's pole position 3 m 53.9 s in the Lotus-Climax V8. Settember retired after eleven laps, when he had got the better of both Count Carel Godin de Beaufort's and Gerhard Mitter's four-cylinder Porsches: an oil pipe broke, so Tony had to switch the engine off.

That was a lot further than John Campbell-Jones got, as Cuoghi recalled: 'He went off the road in practice on the back part of the circuit, where there is the large infield, and the car caught fire. He has burned his arm and the whole thing was very bad.' What made it worse was that the car was borrowed from Gerry Ashmore, but Campbell-Jones's injuries were not as severe as they could have been.

Ermanno's other very strong recollection of that season was of coming to Britain for the first time: by the end of the season he had actually spent more time in Britain than at home.

What were his first impressions of Britain and its circuits of the period? 'I liked it a lot, so much green and country space. I had heard a lot of talk about Crystal Palace, but I didn't know it was in London! It was very impressive to see a beautiful race track on a park inside a town. I liked Aintree very, very much too: I knew it 'ad a horse race, but not that you could motor race there too.

'When I first stayed in England, we were in an

hotel at Cobham. I don't remember the name, but is overlooking a great field. Huge it was, with the A3, or some big road like that, at the bottom. In the field I see a white dog with red eyes and a *very* strong nose. The dog is directing the cow with his nose! It is fantastically strong this small dog!

'... And that hotel, it is fantastic for me. I have ice-cream, pear and chocolate in every single meal! Jesus, that is so bloody good!'

For some of the 1962 season Cuoghi shared a flat with Settember at East Molesey, Surrey. The team were then based at Old Woking, not far away, and Settember, the designer, worked from home at Molesey, too.

The 1962 record was not a very happy one, Campbell-Jones and Settember providing the driving mainstay, but terribly handicapped by a lack of money. In late April they attended the Aintree 200 and Campbell-Jones finished sixth, Settember eighth, both two laps down on Jim Clark's V8 Lotus, which averaged nearly 93 mph. They did the British Grand Prix meeting at Aintree, too, and Clark won again in the revolutionary monocoque Lotus 25-Climax V8.

The Chapman monocoque was certainly a large step forward in safety, strength and competitiveness, but it was to be some time before it was more widely adopted, and certainly Cuoghi was not to grapple with the fabricated chassis 'tub' concept in a single seater until he joined Ferrari in the seventies!

The points-scoring Belgian Grand Prix at Spa-Francorchamps in June was a complete disaster for Campbell-Jones, for he damaged the gearbox on the Emeryson and had to borrow a friend's old Lotus for the race. The team skipped many of the World Championship rounds for understandable and obvious reasons, but they were one of those to fight for the twenty-two places on the grid of the Italian Grand Prix—which had thirty-one entries in September 1962!

The organizers actually reduced the number of places to twenty-one on the starting grid, but Settember still succeeded in getting the old four-cylinder racer on to the back of the grid in a field full of superior multi-cylinders: Clark's pole position time was 9.2 seconds faster. Conditions were cool and overcast for the race around the high-speed bankings and long straights of Milan's traditional home for the Italian Grand Prix. While the BRM V8s of Graham Hill and Richie Ginther screamed to their 10,500 peak rpm to score an historic 1–2 victory for the British marque, the four-cylinder Porsche of de Beaufort and Settember's Climax four were obliged to tag along at the tail of the field.

After nineteen laps Settember retired, and Cuoghi recalls the pit stop before the American was sidelined. 'It was funny: the car has double twin-choke carburetters, and on the intake of these Webers we have a sealed tube around the carburetter bodies. It came unstuck and Tony could not accelerate completely. So he came in the pit. We realized straight away the tube was stuck on the carb butterfly! We pull it out, throw it away, but it was no good.'

Summing up his first season in Formula 1 Cuoghi had the feeling, 'I enjoyed it despite all the troubles we had. I was driving the truck with Gordon Ross from Old Woking. And we 'ave been *really* enjoying ourselves around Europe with this Commer truck. We *never* have any trouble: it was an old Commer, but it was good and I really had a good time.'

Cuoghi remembered that Ross's eleven-year-old daughter was an excellent show-jumping rider and Ermanno was still meeting the Ross family in England seventeen years later.

So far as the cars were concerned and the management of the team itself went, things were not so bright. Cuoghi thought that the reasons for the poor placings were easy to find. 'The cars were cheap and badly designed. They always had secondhand tyres: it was difficult to run new tyres because of the money. When it was time to have the soft tyres on we had the hard ones and vice versa! It was always like that.

'We had the Coventry Climax engine, but we are preparing it mostly by ourselves. Perhaps a few services from the factory, a few parts, but we did not have much: not even the right number of carburetter jets to do the mixture properly.

'I think that, really, the basic problem was money.'

It looked as though things would be very different in 1963. Settember had persuaded more money from Powell and they were to start the season with a new spaceframe chassis, a new base and a new engine.

Paul Emery had been associated with the project during 1962, but for 1963 'we moved from Old Woking and Emery was not having anything to do with the Scirocco cars. During the winter they have found a place in Hammersmith, a very good place where Ausper were making Juniors before. It was right in Goldhawk Road, close to the Cliff Davis garage, then and now American car dealers. I cannot recognize it today myself! But I know we

moved in there and made the first spaceframe for the Scirocco. We make the first chassis with just a mock-up engine, Climax for the first one. The project was to have the same frame with a BRM 1500 eight-cylinder engine. We have one with fuel injection and another with carburetters.

'At this stage they have money, too. So they buy good Colotti gearboxes, the BRM engines and even some new tyres!

'For the BRM engine we make a spaceframe [Settember designed] with a welded-on tank instead of the carrier type of tank for the petrol. It was a bit heavy that chassis. In fact the tank was where it is put on Formula cars today, at the side. It was a good idea and ATS have copied the same idea.'
That ATS Grand Prix outfit has no connection with the Formula 1 team using the same initials in the late seventies, though both had some unhappy outings!

When this book was written, Cuoghi was again working for Chiti—though indirectly, as the bulky Italian (who left Ferrari for that abortive ATS project) was in charge of Autodelta and the Alfa-Romeo Formula 1 engine that powered the Brabhams from 1976 onwards.

Although work started in the winter it was not until the 8/9 June weekend of the Belgian Grand

THE SECOND *Scirocco with a four cylinder Climax installed and no fuel tanks, poses naked in 1963 at Shepherd's Bush. Note the complex framework above engine and down to rear*

AT SILVERSTONE *in 1963 for a test session, Ermanno poses with Arnold Stafford* (right) *and two neat Sciroccos. Stafford later team-managed at Shelby, so the association was renewed*

Prix at Spa that the 200 bhp Scirocco-BRM V8 could make its public debut. It attracted its share of attention, though the most publicized—and postponed!—debut was that of the ATS, though the car had been shown to the press in December 1962.

Settember and Powell had chosen the 90-degree, double-overhead camshaft BRM motor in preference to the Climax V8 after the latter company had temporarily ceased offering racing engines for sale: something they were eventually forced to do permanently before the advent of the 3-litre Formula, creating the British demand for the Ford-financed Cosworth DFV V8. The 1498 cc motor had a short stroke of 50.8 mm allied to a bore of 68.5 mm and, in works trim for F1 in 1963, it offered 202 bhp at 11,000 rpm. Scirocco had customer engines that were best left to rev to 10,500 rpm, when they probably had a little short of 200 bhp.

The spaceframe chassis broke some fresh ground with the extra strength provided by the boxed-in fuel tanks and extra tubing in the cockpit area. Strength where the driver/designer was to be glad of it!

Suspension at the front followed conventional practice of the time in having double wishbones at the front and a combination of links and parallel radius arms at the rear: combined coil spring/shock absorber units were a natural feature too. Cast Elektron wheels to their own design were featured, the cars finished in the white and blue racing colours that befitted the two Americans behind the project. Incidentally the Colotti gearboxes now contained six speeds and the fuel injection system was by Lucas—the carburetter car did not appear (for Ian Burgess) until the July British Grand Prix.

The first Grand Prix for World Championship points that season was at Monte Carlo in late May. As Cuoghi looks back, all the heartbreak of a small team trying to run a new car in the 'Big Boys' league is recalled. 'We were meant to go to Monaco. We finished the Scirocco overnight and took off in the morning from Shepherd's Bush. Instead of using the Commer they had bought a Cadillac car from Cliff Davis, and we put the racing car on the trailer. So we went to Dover and arrived in France. We are driving down France and stop. Then we get a telephone call from Powell and Settember in England: "Don't go to Monaco. It's not worth it, much too difficult to qualify a new car on this circuit. Forget it." So we come all the way home,' Cuoghi shuddered at the memory of the long and fruitless journey.

They did race in France that year. The four-cylinder was taken to the Pau Grand Prix, at the beginning of the season, in April and qualified just over six seconds off the pole position place on row three. Settember did six laps and hit the straw bales, retiring with deranged handling! Little better fortune at the Reims Grand Prix of France on 30 June either. The Burgess carburetter car was not ready and Settember again retired after six laps when a rear hub bearing went: he had qualified on the penultimate row.

The Scirocco V8's debut in neighbouring Belgium was to face the fantastic Francorchamps road circuit. Set in the Ardennes almost on the border with Germany, this eight-mile course on public roads contained the unique challenge of nearly three minutes' flat-out motoring in each lap for the 1.5-litre Formula 1 cars in the most skilled hands. Winner Jim Clark averaged 114.1 mph, including a downpour that reduced the twenty-car field to six survivors—and Cuoghi's Scirocco was not one of them. Clark's fastest lap before the rain set in was 3 m 58.1 s, exactly 132.5 mph average speed.

The Scirocco seemed to handle well enough, but the lowly grid position testified to a lack of power from the eight-cylinder unit. When the rain became really bad in the race Settember called into the pits for new goggles, while Tony Rudd, then of BRM, and Colin Chapman, the Lotus boss, pleaded with the Belgians to stop the race. They did not and Settember, like Siffert, Bianchi and Maggs, crashed needlessly. Settember careered down a bank after hitting an extra large lake across the circuit!

The July British Grand Prix at Silverstone saw Burgess appear in the second car with a narrower spaceframe, but neither was really ready to race and both missed the first practice session. Settember practised in a time that put him next to Mike Hailwood—then just learning his way in motor cars—and Burgess was a row from the back. Neither finished, Settember suffering ignition trouble and Burgess a multitude of debut problems.

Just eight days later Settember was again sitting next to Hailwood on the grid, but this time they were revisiting Solitude and their time put them half-way up the grid. Both cars failed to finish that

COOL MAN! *Ermanno gets into the feel of Americana as the Settember Corvette rumbles away, ready for the start of a local hillclimb. Cuoghi still likes the sound of big American V8s above most thoroughbreds today, but then he never wore ear plugs and 6000 rpm is easier to bear than 12,000 revs*

Racing without shoestrings

race and the official German Grand Prix at the 'Ring on the following weekend, Burgess suffering a steering arm failure and Settember crashing after six laps.

Things did not look promising at the 'Ring at all, the cars practising as the slowest two entries, but on 1 September at Zeltweg aerodrome in Austria, Settember scored their best, and nearly last, results. The start was disastrous for Settember and Burgess, as the American found the clutch refused to release and Burgess very quickly damaged the engine and had to stop.

However, Settember stuck at it and was soon circulating steadily. Up in front Innes Ireland's Lotus and Jack Brabham's own design fought for the lead. After thirty laps Settember was up to fifth with Ireland, Brabham, Chris Amon (Lola) and Jo Siffert (Lotus) ahead. All save Brabham hit some kind of engine trouble! Settember finished five laps behind Brabham, a gallant second, and brought a touch of cheer to the team around that warm airfield. The cash was much needed....

Just how much could be seen at the Italian Grand Prix on the next September weekend at Monza. The engine for Burgess had not been repaired. Settember qualified on 1 m 45.9 s, almost comfortably inside the 1 m 47.2 s qualifying time, but he did not line up for the start.

Giancarlo Baghetti's Ferrari had not qualified, but the Italians wanted their new hero in. Settember was one of four privateers who were 'encouraged' to step down for suitable compensation! An offer they could not afford to refuse.

They were out at the 21 September Oulton Park Gold Cup in England, where Settember retired with engine trouble and Burgess finished eighth, but Cuoghi knew there were bigger problems than that. 'We were spending much of the time preparing the cars and not knowing when we were going to race them.

'Hugh Powell went back to the United States. He was not sending any more money and so we 'ave reached the stage where we people must be paid. So Settember has decided to load everything on the transporter and keep moving! We even take the truck and hide it in a layby to stop the bailiffs getting all the equipment: it was a terrible time for us!'

Of that season in general Cuoghi commented frankly on another problem as the drivers struggled to get on terms with the BRM engine. 'The drivers

did not have much of an affinity with the engines: that engine was meant to go 10,500 rpm. Maybe you could go 10,800, it was perfectly OK, but at 11,000 the valves are hitting the pistons and the cam followers were disintegrating then because they are always overrevving them. This was a particular problem at some races, especially Oulton Park.

'It is difficult to say how Settember was as a driver or designer. In sports cars he was very good. In Formula 1 he could never prove himself, the car was never really competitive. There was money trouble, and he was overworking himself.'

Cuoghi remembers with particular affection one of the very first races he did with Settember in the four-cylinder Emeryson. 'It was at Pau in France. Trintignant won the race, we had trouble on the downhill swerves. The car is bottoming too hard and it ripped off a water pipe underneath. That was my real first race in F1 I think and it was a nice atmosphere, that street race. I enjoyed myself because the car was fully prepared that time and I had enough time to like this track and town very much.'

When all the trouble with Scirocco ended that racing team's activities, Cuoghi headed for Modena. 'I went to work for Stanguellini again! After just a month or so came Ian Burgess. He tells me he has money from BP and some of his own: he has bought a beautiful 250 GTO Ferrari and wants to fully prepare the car to do all the World Championship sport car races. Daytona, Sebring . . . it was a very interesting proposition.

'The car has been bought in Parma, and it is nearly fully prepared at the Lucci-Mazzetti place in Modena, the two partners who were working for Maserati and Ferrari before.

'They are making all kind of special cars there, so we took the car in and I joined Burgess to make this sports-car programme. We put in a new differential, the engine was rebuilt, there was a bit of tidying to be done on the body. Really check everything, the bearings, steering, wiring loom, wiring in the extra lights, lights for the numbers. In fact the full preparation for these kind of events.

'It was a *very nice* car to work on.'

However, that was not enough, because the Swiss-domiciled Burgess had run out of money. He could not afford to pay Cuoghi fully, but he made it a point of honour to do so when he could, and for years later Cuoghi felt the benefit in a sparkling green and white Mini Cooper S that did many fast journeys between Italy and England! The car was a present, and one that Cuoghi still speaks of with flashing eyes and a great deal of pleasure.

'So I never went to Daytona, or Sebring,' Cuoghi remembered of February 1962.

Meanwhile there was the problem of what to do. Cuoghi was told by Burgess in March that he could not afford to keep him working, and that there was no hope of racing the car, even in European events. 'Then he has told me that he knows Carroll Shelby. That he will ask him if he wants a mechanic when he comes to Europe shortly. But, by this time, Carroll Shelby don't need no mechanics!'

A little detail like that was not going to prevent Signor Cuoghi from gaining employment chez Shelby!

AT STUTTGART *for Solitude in 1962, the rounded nose Mk 2 Emeryson. Laughing is Hugh Powell, Settember donning his helmet behind*

CUOGHI'S FIRST *visit to Le Mans was with Settember's Corvette in 1963. Powell is to the right of Settember, in the checked shirt*

Over page: THE START *at Le Mans that year with the Corvette getting away to what was to be a brief class lead. It lasted longer than anyone expected*

4

Trucking Shelby's Cobras

BLAST OFF: *the magnificent spectacle of Cobra Daytona coupé versus Ferrari 250 GTOs at the start of Le Mans circuit race on the 1964 Tour de France. Only Maurice Trintignant's Daytona survived long enough to make some opposition for the Ferraris*

'AS I said, Carroll Shelby don't need any *real* mechanics at this time, but the project was to have an Italian truck. A Fiat bus chassis with a flat six-cylinder engine under the floor made as a racing car transporter with this nice big locker in the middle. It was prepared for Camoradi ['Lucky' Casner's team], but he never managed to pay it off, so when Shelby came to Europe and found it suitable he bought it.

'I met with Carroll Shelby through Ian Burgess at the Royal Hotel in Modena and he has employed me.' There could hardly have been a bigger contrast in the two men, one a typical long, tall Texan given to cowboy hats and fancy boots. The other slight, wiry and with typically fast Italian speech to punctuate the decisive drawl of his new employer.

Although it was a modest job, those who worked in other teams around the same period remember the determination Cuoghi put into getting the Anglo-American hybrids (some with Modenese-built coupé bodies) to their destinations on time. Cuoghi's humour and obvious aim to return to life as a full racing mechanic also marked him out, for he was drawn as if someone had displayed his favourite chocolate every time the American mechanics opened the bonnet!

Cuoghi respected Shelby management. 'What was he like? A big American! But a very nice person and a fantastic person to deal with. A straight through man.

'He says what he means: when he has to take a decision he knows how to take it. I mean he does not hesitate. For example, Le Mans time in 1964. It is a month or more before the race. We are supposed to prepare two Daytona coupés and one 7-litre Daytona coupé: that is to say the full-bodied closed cars compared to the open roadsters that are used for Targa Florio and hillclimbs.'

JOHN WYER (left) *looks on as John Etheridge and Ermanno* (right and centre *with hands on quick-lift jack*) *complete another tyre change, this one at Reims, during the Tour de France. Bob Bondurant chats from the open door of the Daytona coupé*

EVEN AS *the Tour de France thunders away, the Ferraris and Cobras mixing it for the lead and the Stuttgart Porches in class pursuit, Cuoghi and his massive truck rumbled off to another venue*

The 7-litre was the surprise weapon that Ford hoped to frighten the opposition with. The (near) 5-litre V8 in the coupé body was obviously quicker than much of the opposition—if not so reliable on many occasions—while the 7-litre might be just the job for the long Le Mans straight, the massive iron V8 Ford engine not such a handling handicap on a track which places the accent on top speed. Cuoghi resumed, 'Shelby came in Modena about a month before the race and he has realized we are too far behind with the car to make it properly for the race. Maybe we could just make all three cars, but he says, "no—forget it completely, we will not run that car at all." A thing like that makes you realize that he is a man who knows how to win.'

It was in the summer of 1962 that Henry Ford II had said words to the effect, 'let there be racing and all manner of motor sport and, lo, Ford shall dominate it!' At the time American manufacturers were officially abstaining from competition, but from ever-escalating bhp figures for their road cars to increasing participation in drag and stock car racing, it was evident the Detroit giants knew a good back-door sport when they saw it.

Ford were the first to break out officially and they certainly thought big. An effort to buy Ferrari was rebuffed, though that Enzo Ferrari needed more money to keep his scarlet cars in competition was never in any doubt until Fiat formally filled that role. For Indianapolis, Le Mans, the World Sports Car Championship, international rallying for . . . you name it, Ford would attack it globally.

Such a policy produced many interesting cars and engines. The Cobra, an amalgamation of the Thames Ditton AC tubular steel spaceframe chassis and iron Ford V8 engines from Dearborn, was just one such by-product of the main assault. At the end of May 1964 the Ford GT40 made its debut in the ADAC 1000 km at Nürburgring, but by that time five rounds of the World Sports Car Championship had already been held and the Shelby Cobra association was strong enough in the GT class to make it worth fighting for that title in Europe. . . .

The AC chassis dated back to the fifties, but it was March 1962 before the modified version to accept the V8 was sent to California for the original 4.2 Ford V8 engine to be installed in this chassis. It is said that about seventy-five such 4.2 Cobras were built, compared to nearer 600 of the machine that formed the racing base. This was the 4727 cc short-stroke V8; that 289 cubic inch motor, perhaps the most versatile competition base Ford ever produced, for it also appeared in GT40s, Falcons and Mustangs, besides other high-performance road cars.

For competition in 1964 there were two versions of the Cobra, both based on the 4.7 engine and tubular steel chassis. A pair of large-diameter tubes dominated the main structure, all-independent suspension attached at either end and comprising wishbones as the lower medium and transverse leaves—securely bolted together at the centre—as the upper 'arm' and springing. The basic idea had come from a John Tojeiro special, but it had carried six-cylinder engines by Bristol, AC and Ford.

In competition guise the 4.7-litre engines carried a bank of four twin-choke IDA downdraught Webers. Together with a racing camshaft in the body of the 90-degree pushrod block, bigger valves and a steel-fabricated exhaust system that exited abruptly under what passed for the driver's door, these modifications encouraged the production of approximately 350 bhp at 7000 rpm. Drive went through a four-speed Ford box and competition clutch to an open propeller shaft that transmitted it on to the chassis-mounted differential. Disc brakes were a standard feature of race and road cars on all four corners.

Perhaps the cleverest thing Ford and Shelby did was to make sure that the cars were homologated for racing in the Gran Turismo class, rather than as simple sports cars, for this cut down the opposition they would have to face from increasingly sophisticated mid-engine sports racers of the new GT40 type.

Because of the Americans' increased interest in long-distance racing a properly titled World Sports Car Championship was run in 1964, covering the classics at the Targa Florio, Le Mans and Nürburgring. Shelby's Cobra team started on the Championship trail in Florida's February sunshine and drivers Dave Macdonald/Bob Holbert were well ahead until a differential failure and a pit fire put them out. However, Macdonald in the Daytona-bodied version of the Cobra appropriately put in the fastest lap of the Daytona circuit.

At Sebring in March the Shelby Cobras beat the 3-litre Ferrari GTO models to win the category, though the Maranello machines scored outright victories in both cases, for at Sebring Ferrari fielded new 275P 3.3-litre cars. It was that Sebring category victory that encouraged Shelby to come to Europe with Ford backing, but Cuoghi was unfortunately not out on their first commitment: the Targa Florio.

On that Sicilian event there were five open Cobras, but none finished higher than eighth after the factory cars were literally shaken to bits over the tight twists of this rally-style road race.

Although that first Daytona coupé was fielded in America its sleek aluminium body, like those that followed, were made on the premises of Sport Car at Modena: today the site serves as a fitting restoration centre for Ferraris destined for life in the company museum.

Cuoghi recalled the work that went into the closed coupés: 'Whenever I was in Modena, I was working on the cars. At the races I must look after the truck and look after the spares and so on... but if I get the chance I help on the cars there too!

'In Modena we've been doing the panelling. A complete aluminium body, but not by hand in the normal Modena way. This is the good part of it, because one of the partners in Sport Car, he knows the English way with a rolling machine to bend the aluminium. I don't know if he made the equipment from experience in England and Australia, or if he bought it... but anyway, they make the Daytona coupé body this way. Most of the body has long panels, so they can be shaped on the roller: and everybody in Modena, they were laughing at us! But really it was better: beating panels by 'and take 'elluva long time, you know?'

The resultant body was typical of the time with fared-in headlamps, a long bonnet, and auxiliaries mounted either side of a narrower radiator air intake at the front. The rear had the usual GT style of sloping rear window, Kamm tail and rounded quarters in the general Italian exotic road car style of the period. There was still that brutal air of functional racer rather than sophisticated transport about this effective competition-only twist to the Cobra theme though. More of a boxing slogger than a dancing Muhammad Ali character. The American mechanics were augmented during the European season by the addition of three British racing mechanics who came from Willment, which West London organization was to run what amounted to a fleet of racing cars (usually Ford-linked) in its heyday. Jim Parton and Ernie Symons were to be Ermanno's partners in a number of trans-European trucking adventures that the former Willment men will hardly forget! Especially as the transporter had such good forward vision through its vast 'panoramic' windscreen.

Looking back at his truck-driving season Cuoghi recollected 'really we 'ave a lot of adventures. It was such a huge, big thing! There could be three cars on top and two below: yes, a five-car transporter ... and the cars, they were not small, light racers I can tell you!

'Shelby came back from the Targa Florio in late April and I was beginning my work at Modena. At that race the wishbones were pulling out of the chassis, so it was not a good race for them!

'So my first race with the Shelby Cobras was Spa, for the 500 kilometres in May. I took the big transporter there, but I was sharing the drive with another guy from Borletti, the people who had sold the truck to Shelby. It was such a bloody great thing this expert driver came along and show me how to drive this monster.'

What was it like to drive? Cuoghi said, 'It had only four gears with four low ratios too, but the gearbox was not synchronized. It was straight-cut gears, so you really had to rev it to get a gear in! But it was such a nice job to do properly, it was an enjoyment every time you change gear ... a challenge to your driving. I think, I beat you!

'We left Modena in very good weather, but I am expecting the rain as usual in Spa. No, it doesn't come and it was a beautiful weekend. For us it was a very, very easy job. Just take the cars off the truck, clean it, polish it; American style. Everything must be super-bright!

'I was not directly involved with the cars at the track, but I was working with an Australian and an American as the boy gofer; you know, go-for-this, go-for-that? I enjoy it all.'

Cuoghi was very impressed by his new team, as he was almost bound to be after the years in Formula 1 spent on a precarious budget. 'To be in there on a team like that, making so much effort with Carroll Shelby, it was marvellous for me. There were so many people, perhaps fifteen. And fifteen people at that time in motor racing was quite fantastic. Now is nothing! Considering we had four or five cars it was not so much, but it was quite a sight to see when we went to the races with our shiny cars, huge truck and a lot of people.

'Shelby didn't run the team at the track. John Bowes was the team manager when I started and Phil Remington—who was really good for this team—was the technical engineer. It was a really professional team, and a good way of working for me to see the way they did things. Nice systems to follow,' Cuoghi concluded carefully. It was his first encounter with a large, long-distance racing effort, and quite a surprise for their European rivals, particularly Ferrari, who knew they had yet to face the mid-engine Ford GTs besides the fierce class competition offered by the Cobras.

Cuoghi's first outing at Spa was for the 500-kilometre (319-mile) event run for homologated GT cars only by the local club. With no mid-engine

pure racers on hand the fight was simply between the beautiful GTO Ferraris, Protheroe's competition Jaguar E type and four Shelby Cobras, one the Daytona coupé making its public debut in Europe. Former Ferrari World Champion driver Phil Hill was a fifth of a second slower than Mike Parkes in the Maranello Concessionaires' Ferrari GTO in practice, the Daytona proving a handful on the flat-out swerves and swoops of the Belgian public road circuit.

The open roadsters ran in formation in the hands of Innes Ireland, Jo Schlesser and Bob Bondurant, but were simply not fast enough at the top end to support Phil Hill's efforts in the Daytona model. Unfortunately the Hill Cobra was suffering from fuel starvation: at the time it was thought this was due to a blockage, but today Cuoghi feels that the part played by a loosening Jubilee circlip on a fuel line had upset the carburation.

Whatever the true cause, everyone could see how fast the Daytona Cobra could be, for Hill turned in a lap record of 4 m 4.5 s, an average for the lap of 128.92 mph/207.61 km/h. So the big Cobra was reaching 160 mph or more on the straights, while the agile GTO Ferrari was lapping 2.3 seconds slower on the way to heading a 1–2–3–4 Ferrari result by Parkes, Jean Guichet, Lorenzo Bandini and David Piper.

The fifth round of the series was at Nürburgring on 31 May and Cuoghi drove the heavily laden Shelby transporter with pride as the man in charge, though Ernie Symons came along to share the chores too. Later the pair were also to share a flat in Britain, and all three British mechanics on the team—Symons, Parton and Bob Waterman—were to return to their home country the following season.

The ADAC 1000-kilometre event was massive in every sense of the word that year. The fourteen-mile Nürburgring attracted over 100 entries, of which eighty-one started the race in front of an estimated 300,000 spectators. Those were the days....

Unfortunately there were a lot of people without the skills needed to drive quick cars safely around the 'Ring and two drivers were killed in practice. The race start was equally hectic, the starter forced to implement the Le Mans getaway from half-way down the echelon of eighty-plus cars, so that everyone could see them. As Denis Jenkinson commented in a contemporary issue of *Motor Sport*; 'When the flag fell there was more excitement in the next few minutes than there has been in the whole length of some races.'

Bondurant's Shelby Cobra was clobbered in the start line mêlée by a class-rival's E type and Schlesser lost his first-lap ninth overall for the Cobra team when a low-tension lead broke. Bondurant's Cobra had to limp around for a lap with a flat rear tyre and was badly delayed by the time Jochen Neerpasch took it over, for it also had to stop (inevitably) for a new rear damper. Present-day Talbot manager Neerpasch didn't last long in the Cobra roadster because an oil pipe broke. The Schlesser/Dick Attwood Shelby Cobra did recover to win the class over a pretty standard Jaguar E type driven by two British privateers.

Better news was on the way. The most important race to the American team—and the new Ford GT, which had debuted at the 'Ring, failing to finish after suspension failure—was June's Le Mans.

A CHAOTIC *start to the 1964 Nürburgring 1000 km left Bob Bondurant's Shelby Cobra in this state for the race. The other picture, from May 1964, shows Cuoghi's converted Fiat transporter with Cobras on its back and some more miles for Shelby ahead*

The team took two Daytona coupés, Cuoghi working with the mechanics on the Gurney/Bondurant machine, which was new for the occasion. The Mulsanne straight proved much to the big V8's liking and the Cobras dominated the Ferrari GTO opposition initially, Gurney running as high as third overall in a race that was meant to be between the mid-engine Fords and Ferraris.

In the early hours there was a conference between Remington and the mechanics, for the Gurney/Bondurant car had to run with the oil cooler bypassed to avoid a leaking oil line, and there was concern over the future of the Amon/Neerpasch sister car, which had been running consistently until then. In fact the second Daytona was disqualified for infringing the rules on replacement batteries, leaving the Gurney/Bondurant car to finish a fine fourth overall, and a clear class winner by a lap from a 250 GTO.

This was some compensation for Ford, who finished not a single one of the three 4.2-litre mid-engined GTs of Lola ancestry in their first attempt at winning Le Mans, Ferrari managing a clean 1–2–3 sweep.

At Reims for the twelve-hour seventh Championship round two Cobra coupés appeared again, and there was lots more early morning briefing to be done as the Gurney coupé boiled and split its gearbox casing in separate incidents before Bondurant even had a chance to drive, while the coupé for Ireland/Neerpasch broke all the left-hand exhaust manifolding pipes at 5 am—the start was an exciting all-headlight affair at midnight!

Cuoghi commented, 'All the exhaust systems were made in Modena. They may have changed the material, but I think it was because the welds were overcooked! They split mainly on the weld, by the manifold. It didn't happen again after Reims.' At that race Neerpasch's car was repaired by fitting the exhaust system from the already retired coupé, but then the gearbox ultimately split its casing on that one too. That was effectively the end of the Cobra challenge.

Shelby was not beaten yet though. Cuoghi manhandled the big truck back to Britain and a place he was to become part of, Slough Trading Estate. There, next door to the Lola factory that was serving as HQ for the Ford GT effort (which had expired at Reims too after a good showing), the Cobras were tended in readiness for Goodwood's 312-mile counter in the Championship.

Ferrari won the race, but it looked as though Shelby Cobra might win the war for points as Gurney turned in another brilliant performance to finish third overall behind the prototype Ferraris, scoop the GT category, and record fastest lap around the West Sussex aerodrome circuit at nearly 100 mph.

The fate of the title was actually decided on the Tour de France, rather than the official last Championship round at Montlhèry, just outside Paris, in early October . . . but more on that later.

For Cuoghi the year had involved quite a few memorable drives and he remembered some of them for me with graphic clarity, for that was his primary job that year rather than working on the cars.

The first incident illustrated the importance of continental hillclimbing at the time, for the Cobras were proceeding from an early August date at Freiburg in Germany to a late August appointment with the AC de Suisse's Sierra Montana event at Sion, which, of the big towns in the area, is nearest Lausanne.

'In one of the towns on the way, I don't remember which, Ernie Symons and I are travelling along and meet a bridge, right in the middle of the town. We had the cars on top, and we couldn't go under the bridge—but not because of the bridge itself.

'No, there were two wires for the trolleybus hung underneath the bridge! So I was driving along and we manage to find two brooms for Ernie to go on top of the bus and keep pushing the wires up!

'We get under that bloody bridge all right....

'By that time we had another team manager, who was with us on the trip. After half the season John Bowes went out—I don't really know why—and Arnold Stafford took over. He was an Englishman who had lived in New Zealand for a long time.

'This was a funny thing for me, because Stafford had worked with me in my time with Tony Settember, as a mechanic!'

Racing is full of ups and downs, of course, but life in the truck held more excitements than sweeping away electricity cables. 'Another time we were travelling from Italy to England. We went through a small village in Switzerland, or at least we tried to.

'We couldn't get through with the truck!

'The streets were so narrow. I just bumped over one big block of rock and was practically stuck in the street. Could not go back, nor forwards either. Everybody out! Must 'ave been the Italian side of Switzerland, they were all out there shouting "go back, come forward!" It was such a small village, it was unbelievable. "This way, that way," they shouted at me, old men, small kids, everyone.

'I say "go back? Go forward?" I 'ave no choice, I go on and scrape past the side of a house!

'I am sorry I scratch the truck, you know. In all the time I drive it we do not have an accident with this truck. Once, it was raining I remember, when we come to a crossroad outside Lille. It was a ring road and, as you know, in France you have to give priority to the right. So I saw a car coming from there. I start to slow down, but as soon as I touch the brakes, they lock up.

'I go sideways ... all ways. But we didn't touch nothing at all. It was a big panic with all the Cobras on board, I tell you! Sideways completely ...' he roared with laughter.

The heroics on an event are still to come through. With a twinkle in his eye Cuoghi looked back on the Tour of France as, 'the most interesting part'.

The event consists of circuit races all over France, often venturing into neighbouring countries too, linked by non-competitive public road sections in the same way as a special stage rally. In fact British journals have always had the greatest difficulty in classifying whether it is a race or a rally; and when they have discovered that, the mathematics defeat them!

Cuoghi was 'on my own in the truck. To follow the event you have to have so many people servicing and following the races, there was no one to help me drive the truck. So I had a big truck with all the tyres, all the spare parts, moving from track to track. We couldn't change the axle ratio for the different courses (there were some hillclimbs too) on the road. So we were changing tyres, using the diameter to suit, more or less, the course.

'So I was driving day and night, changing tyres everywhere. It was murder ... but it was fantastic [Ermanno pronounced it fant*arsti*c].

'The last stage for me I remember pretty well. It was in Cognac. I am arriving thinking that I would be late. I was just on time as the cars started to come through. We have only one car left, which is driven by Maurice Trintignant. So I am there ... waiting ... and waiting ... it never turned up either! I enjoyed it, now it is all over for me. I had been going two days and one night.

'So we slept in Cognac: 'ave a nice drink and a nice, nice sleep!'

Over Tour de France tests at Reims, Rouen and Le Mans, plus the Col du Bramont on the first night, the four Cobras held the lead in the GT category initially. Three retired pretty quickly, Trintignant's later succumbing to wheel bearing failure, while the early retirement trio all suffered engine failure at Le Mans.

Mechanically speaking Cuoghi sums the Cobras up from his less direct experience as, 'to compare it to today's cars, there was nothing very much to do at the circuit. The wheel camber was set at home; the toe-in you could adjust, but you never 'ad to do this on the race track. You set the car up at base, but on the circuit what you do is the tappets, clearances of these, check over and see if there is any play in the wheel bearings: stuff like that.'

Turning to the early season wishbone problem at Targa Florio Cuoghi confirmed that 'they did strengthen up the wishbone mountings at Shelby. The year afterwards I was at Spa with Wyer and Settember. He was running a Cobra, and they ran into the same problem because they used the standard parts.

'They used to pull out at the inner end from the big main frame tube to the bottom suspension wishbone: in fact it was the attachment between the wishbone and the frame, not the actual wishbone itself, which used to pull out.

'I liked these cars very much. The engines sound like today's NASCAR; for me, this is a pleasant noise because I like a big engine in a sports car. I prefer the sound of a big engine V8 with Le Mans-type exhaust system to a thing like the Matra V12.'

Quite a surprising admission, but the reason is easy to understand when you learn that Ermanno never has worn ear plugs! 'The Matra is too acute

Above: CUOGHI CONTEMPLATES *the Cobra at Goodwood after early tests.*

when it's standing still for me, but I enjoyed it out on the track. Then it's fine!

'My wife say I am deaf a little bit, especially when she ask me to do work around the house!' I got the feeling that Ermanno thought the price had been worth paying in exhaust note enjoyment over the years....

Anyone who has ever seen the stubby Cobra roadsters in action must have wondered what it is like to drive them, and Cuoghi was no exception. He drove one of the team cars back down a hillclimb with more than a full load of passengers and found 'as soon as you step on the gas it is time to change gear or brake! Always something is happening very, very quickly! It is a *real* sports car....'

At the end of the season John Willment's Racing Division were advertising their 350-bhp Cobras were capable of 'top speed, 165 mph. 0–100 mph in under 8 secs. With £2500 worth of Race Development in each car.' For £50 less they would sell you the road version: today you could literally pay £25,000 plus....

For Cuoghi and his 1964 season English friends it was time to move on. The Cobras would not be run by Carroll Shelby in 1965. Ferrari had dominated the official Manufacturers' International Championship with nearly four times the score of Porsche, who were nine points ahead of the Shelby Cobra team. The Cobras had won the GT category four times in nine rounds against stiff Ferrari

Below: CUOGHI AND *Mrs Bondurant in high spirits at the Sierra Montana hillclimb, later that year*

opposition, so the result did not really reflect how close the fight was in that category.

Now Ford would rely on sheer numbers, both in cars and teams, concentrating upon the mid-engined GT40. Ahead for Cuoghi lay the perpetual problem that crops up in his life time and time again. Work at home in Modena, or where there were more jobs in Britain, perhaps this time as fully fledged mechanic?

But first there was a visit to Ferrari to make!

5

Preparing a legend for John Wyer

Wyer and Ford started to make GT40s to a fixed specification for homologation purposes from their Slough base.

The racing emphasis shifted to Carroll Shelby back in America, where designer Roy Lunn and staff had set up a similar plant to the FAV one in Slough under the name Kar Kraft, about four miles from Ford's main factories at Dearborn. Expatriate Englishmen Phil Remington and Ken Miles also aided the American programme with development work on the existing GT40s, as well as the Mk 2.

The FAV-Wyer operation (later JW Automotive) had a large number of staff, and a management who, like Wyer, had come from the Aston Martin racing department at Feltham in Middlesex.

'Shelby, Mr Wyer and his missus, came to the 1964 hillclimb at Sierra Montana in Switzerland.

1964

So, DURING this period when I knew Shelby must finish at the end of the season, I was trying to decide if I come and work in England, or find another job in Italy.

'I went to Ferrari to see if I could be employed. I fill in all the forms and say what I was doing, but I don't get an interview or a reply. There was not much other choice for a racing mechanic in Italy at that time. Alfa-Romeo were not running much from Milano—just some touring cars, while Autodelta was just beginning.

'Racing car work at home was difficult to find ... but I always like England from the first time I visit.

'In Italy you 'ave a town and there are houses and nothing else! It seems to me easier to breathe in England with all this green stuffs around you! The tower blocks spoil it a bit, but there is still a good lot of country left.

'The food I don't mind. I eat mainly Italian, but it never worry me to eat English. I like steak and kidney pie and fish very much—and there is a lot of good fish in Britain.' One of Ermanno's hobbies that developed in Britain was fishing, so this was all said with a chuckle, but he merrily added that, 'the weather ... that is what the English must change!'

Meanwhile Ford were getting the reorganization of their GT40 racing programme under way. The sports car racing season closed and Ford Advanced Vehicles (formed in 1963) under the control of

Shelby and Wyer had business things to discuss with the changes being made for the coming racing season . . . Shelby was a Ford man at the time, of course, and they were preparing the engine we would use in the future for the GT40: they had two engine men at FAV, experts to build these V8s.

'It was also practically arranged, though I still had to go and talk to my wife about it in Italy, that myself and the three English mechanics on the Shelby Cobra team would go to FAV.

'I had already been in this factory when we go to Goodwood with the Cobras, and I see Lola just beside.' Eric Broadley was leaving at the end of 1964 to go back to Lola, after a year spent on the GT Ford project that had sprung from his January 1963 exhibit of a Lola-Ford sports racing car at the BRSCC's annual Racing Car Show in London.

'So I came in England in September 1964 and spend a couple of weeks looking at the new place I would work. Then I go home to Modena for a holiday, pack a coupla suitcase and arrive in England again on my own.'

Cuoghi's early impressions of the Slough factory were: 'It was the same as a lot of modern factories, but the details were different. The way the factory was laid out impressed me . . . the machine shop . . . the big spaces . . . all white, bright . . . a really pleasant place to work, and very clean.

'There was all the equipment you wanted. For example, when I was working for Tony Settember, I had to go to the BRM place at Bourne in Lincoln-

OUTSIDE THE *Banbury Road, Slough premises of Advanced Vehicles in 1966 are* (left to right): *'Hug', Len Bailey, John Horsman, John Wyer, John Collins, Cuoghi, John Etheridge and Jo Ramirez*

shire. The machine shop, it was fantastic. To see all these tools laid out . . . but the actual working facilities of the mechanics, all those spread-out sheds, I didn't think they were very impressive. There were two fantastic building at FAV, so everyone had good facilities,' Cuoghi concluded.

Ermanno's new job was as one of a group of mechanics (about eighteen in all) who reported via a kind of unofficial chief mechanic (a post later formally developed) to Bill Pink, a very experienced racing hand with a strong background at Aston Martin. Cuoghi was also asked to drive one of two Ford transporters, 'not very big ones, but they carry two cars each, plus spares. They 'ave a permanent driver—"Billy Baldy" we call him!—and I was driving the other one all over Europe,' Cuoghi added.

When Cuoghi arrived, 'we were supposed to have run the Ford overhead cam engine, but we only have one there. It has been tried during that season, but it is a very difficult engine to run for a sports car, so they start changing to 4.7.' The cast-iron heads and block of the 289 did weigh more than the racing alloy Ford with its four overhead camshafts and 4.2 litres that proved so successful at Indianapolis and for many years in the back of A. J. Foyt's USAC machines. The 'but' was that the 4.2 demanded cumbersome dry sump lubrication with a front-mounted oil tank and associated plumbing in the GT40 installation.

The 289 demanded only a straightforward baffled sump for its production shallow wet sump layout and that saved 75 lb compared with the overall weight of the 4.2! The ex-Cobra V8 may have been rustic, but it offered more low-down torque, which was no bad thing when, as in its early appearances, it had to co-operate with a Colotti gearbox.

The 289 in full racing form with 12.5:1 compression ratio offered a quoted 390 bhp at 7000 rpm (officially another 40 bhp up on the same unit's performance in the Cobras), while the 4.2 four-cam was 'only' rated at 350 bhp on 7200 rpm. At Le Mans this was enough to push some 2500 lb of steel monocoque and sleek glass-fibre along at a little less than the 187.5 mph recorded there in 1964 because they then overheated at high rpm: later on 200 mph could genuinely be exceeded with these 'small' block V8 GT40s, as well as their bigger 7-litre cousins from the USA.

Incidentally the Colotti gearbox was dropped from the American Ford competition cars after the first two races of 1965, JW building the first open car with a ZF 5-speed that was to become synonymous with the Slough cars. However, Cuoghi remembers doing some races with the Colotti thus: 'It was a bit of a problem. The gearbox was heavy, unreliable and breaking all the gears: it was a problem to make the gears mesh, you had to do each one individually on assembly—hone it down and so forth. After they start using the ZF, it was a marvellous gearbox. Difficult to put together—you need special tools, but when it was together it was a beautiful change and very reliable. It was a double selector of course, so you had to change gear in sequence usually,' Cuoghi commented.

1965

In the closed season through the 1964–65 winter Cuoghi settled back into a British way of mechanical life and became increasingly accepted by his workmates as a colleague, though his English was limited at first. Still, as one of his former colleagues quipped recently, 'Ermanno couldn't speak a word of French either, but he can wave his hands about and people bloody well have to understand!'

A pair of men who worked with Cuoghi through most of his JW days are still working together now. John Etheridge owns a performance car restoration business in London's Chelsea and Bill Pink still performs the wiring tasks that he first did for GT40s fifteen years before while also doubling up as the senior man on the workshop floor.

Etheridge felt 'really Ermanno was a good mechanic before he came to us. Sure he learned a lot in Slough, but he was a good man in the first place.' Pink described him as 'the type of bloke who could improvise things quickly. Give him a bit of sheet metal and he would punch a couple of holes in it and make something useful out of it! He would put it on the car quickly, and it could come off just as fast if it didn't work!'

The first two rounds of 1965's Championship did not concern Cuoghi directly, but when the series returned to Europe from America and visited the fifth qualifier of the Targa Florio in Sicily, Cuoghi just *had* to go. To this day John Etheridge is convinced that they went down the wrong side of Italy in the transporter! Ermanno's story is a little different....

'We start driving down from Slough to Sicily and we know we could use a lot of motorway. We 'ave plenty of spare time, so Johnny 'as never seen the South part, you know the coast of Italy. Instead of driving through the easier way through Bari, then Messina and the boat, we drove from Salerno to Naples, slept the night there, and the day after

Preparing a legend for John Wyer

CUOGHI AT *work in Slough, September 1966. An engineless GT40 tub beside him, Ermanno obviously appreciated such premises after his Italian and British introduction to competition car preparation*

A PICTURE *which portrays well the neat, straightforward Slough premises in which the John Wyer managed concern prepared GT40s during the mid-1960s*

start driving down through the coast: right down to the toe. It was fantastic! Some of the corners we 'ad to back up because we could not go round in one turn of the steering wheel. It took us five days for this really nice drive,' Cuoghi chuckled.

Etheridge was convinced they were lost: 'Ermanno had never been to the Targa before, but he said he was Italian and *must* go. When we were going round endless corners, doing handbrake turns and 3-point manoeuvres to get round the real tight ones, I think his conscience got the better of him and he had to admit he was not quite sure of where we were going either!'

The pace was pretty hectic on the island too. The pale green GT40 prototype was an open car which suffered the confusion of being an FAV car fitted with Shelby-Cobra-style magnesium wheels as well as the new-to-Slough ZF gearbox. To be driven by Sir John Whitmore and Bob Bondurant the car enjoyed an exciting race: Whitmore lost a wheel at maximum speed on the sea-level long straight and Bondurant finally crashed the car on gravel.

Whitmore was travelling at such speed when the front wheel departed that it reputedly took down the overhead cables of the railway track adjacent, bounding off to the refuge of a field, with a trail of havoc behind! 'It was the first time we used these wheels and we dashed down from the start and finish area to the car. There was no damage to the car itself, just a bit of skidding on the bottom wishbones. We find the wheel and a good Italian find the spinner in the middle of a field, so it drives back into the race!

'After, Bondurant he was going *really* well, and the speaker 'ave told us that he 'as lost the car after Cerda. I think he just "lost" the corner—an easy thing to do on the Targa Florio, where there are so many!' Bob had hit one of the milestones and gone into a field, damaged the car this time all right. We got it out of the field with the expert tractor driver of the area.

Etheridge flew back, which was just as well, for Cuoghi and replacement partner 'Billy Baldy' swept along in the fastest possible time, trying to fight off the Porsche team's huge Mercedes transporter! It did get by . . . eventually.

Next on the list was Spa the following weekend, with the Nürburgring 1000 km a week after that, but Cuoghi's memories were of Le Mans in June, and the fact that 'the steering box of the transporter came loose on one corner in Switzerland! I remember it, but Billy was driving around this left-hander and he *just* manage to keep the transporter off the wall. We repair it, and back to England.'

THE OPEN *GT40* lines up at the 1965 Targa Florio. Just stepping out is John Etheridge while Cuoghi looks down on their handiwork from the other side of the car; Bob Bondurant is ready to go in Goodyear overalls on the right

THE REMAINS *are unloaded at Slough of the Bondurant GT40 after the Targa. The American, who today specializes in teaching others race craft with great effectiveness, simply lost the car on gravel. In practice partner Sir John Whitmore lost a wheel.*

ANOTHER FROM *the 1965 Targa file as Bondurant pounds the GT40 through a Sicilian village that has proclaimed its loyalties by painting on the road support for Bandini, Vaccarella and Ferrari!*

Le Mans was always a special place to John Wyer. His severe features would not betray his emotions regarding the scene of so many battles that he has overseen there with the loyal support of men like David Yorke. Equally special to the mechanics was the traditional Wyer accommodation in Le Chartre.

'I really enjoyed driving the cars to the circuit and back to Le Chartre. There we had the workshop and the transporter, so we could change an engine, or anything we needed to.'

In that first year with the Slough Ford team, and on his second working visit to Le Mans, Cuoghi came to appreciate the speed with which engine changes could be performed on the monocoque GT40. He was down to look after the Ireland/Whitmore car. 'In the practice we run our experimental 5.3 engine, but overnight we put in the racing 4.7 engine, which was a very quick job on these cars.' In the event the team's management had estimated a lap speed that was very close to that achieved by the winning private Ferarri of Jochen Rindt and Masten Gregory, but all the Slough-based cars had cylinder head water circulation problems and overheated. In fact, by midnight all six Ford GT derivatives, 7 or 4.7 litre, were out: only the failure of the factory Ferraris to complete the distance was any compensation for this humiliation!

For Cuoghi the other outstanding racing memory of the year was 'my first trip to a black country. This was my first Kyalami race in South Africa. Then the cars would go out there before us, and we—there were three mechanics—went to look after the car, which was a proper FAV one prepared for the job, though owned by Sutcliffe and driven by him and Innes Ireland. It was a very exciting race against David Piper and Richard Attwood in Piper's Ferrari prototype. It looked like our car would win, but the oil pressure was sometimes low and Sutcliffe finally had to slow down to let the Ferrari through when the wire wheels, they started collapsing!'

John Etheridge remembers that he and Cuoghi finished off the year by preparing a GT40 for the November and December races in Nassau, and how disappointed they were that they could not go along with the car. Smiling broadly, he also remembered that Ermanno 'went on his hols after they went testing with Whitmore at Monza later in the year.'

From a detailed development point of view the greatest amount of work was going on in America in 1965, but Cuoghi recalls that the job of assembling cars was made quite difficult because they were always changing things and the monocoques had to be virtually individually modified, even when building some of the single-carburetter GT40 road cars.

Before Le Mans the MIRA wind tunnel tricked Cuoghi and his colleagues as they cleaned up the front-end aerodynamics, following the removal of that front-mounted dry sump oil tank that was not required with the change to the 4.7 engine.

'We were often in that tunnel and we make a nose that make it one of the quickest cars on the straight, and one of the easiest to drive at night in difficult conditions. A lot of the work was overnight, because to make the big fan go there is not enough electric power in the daytime!

'It was very interesting, you learn a lot of things. It was not always that something which looked right really was the best aerodynamically. You don't really know what to expect; things are better now, but we are still far away from understanding what is happening to the car in the air.

'In South Africa the car is misfiring when we get out there because of the height and the temperature. Mr Wyer has a special box from Weber, a present they give to him many years ago, with a lot of carburetter jets. Some older jets, chokes, literally hundreds of choices inside this wooden box which he is carrying round with him the whole time. He gives it to me sometimes, when he was fed up of doing it! That was his job for many seasons until he just does the management only.

'In Kyalami we were in trouble and it is often the way with a carburetter engine when it is high up, like in an aeroplane. So the first thing we do when the racing car comes in off the aeroplane is take the carburetter top off and, with all these Weber gauges, we check the level of the float to see if it has risen, or has jammed. We didn't have the time to do the job properly in practice: we change all the jets afterwards, chokes, everything. That country is hot though, and the engine is running too hot, so we fill the radiator with cool water, just gives me time to do the mixture, before it gets really hot again. The result was so nice, you couldn't believe it, *but* it happens during the race'—he broke into laughter at the unfairness of it all—'during the race, the weather, he has changed! Suddenly it was *very* cold and the car started misfiring. The time was about nine in the evening and it was getting dark, just a few hours before the end of the race, so they came in the pit and we *stuff* the radiator with rag, newspaper even: bang it down and send him out. Then it runs perfectly again. I really enjoyed it.'

It was the close of the year. A successful first year for Cuoghi back in Britain, and he had made his mind up that his wife and son should join him in this new life. A few days back at Slough and he was off to Modena to sort out the details.

'In the beginning I was living in South Ealing with Ernie Symons. Then he left at the end of 1965 to join Jo Ramirez [former team manager of the Shadow Formula 1 team] and another guy at a flat in Old Windsor. I am living there too, until my family came over. That was in July '66 and we find a flat in Maidenhead, a very nice place in a quiet cul de sac. By 1968 I was able to get a mortgage on a house in Twyford: my boy is starting English primary school in Old Windsor, then he goes to Maidenhead and Twyford, where he finishes junior school and does a year and several months at senior school, before going back to Italy again when I went back in 1971.'

Ermanno's enthusiasm for fishing started at Old Windsor, when he used every scrap of spare time to get down to Runnymede with his rod. 'I was in there every evening catching things . . . eels, roach, a lot of fish I could catch down there.'

Today's passion for bicycling on super lightweight racers had not rekindled from his boyhood days then, but he was very proud of his Mini. 'Ian Burgess is coming to see me often at FAV and telling me not to worry, that he pay me the money he owed me. It was so long ago that I was not expecting it! One day he said he was off to live abroad again—"I give you my Mini instead of the money," he says to me. It was perfectly OK with me, it was a Cooper 1000 cc Mini, for the 1275S was pretty new at that time. It was British racing green with a white roof. I was *so* proud of this car, especially in Modena where only De Tomaso has one, Enzo Ferrari has one, and myself!

'At one time I left the Mini for my wife to use in Italy because she love that car, taking my mother and father out, and so on. I had to buy myself a Ford Popular and drive around in that! She loved that car . . . but it got old in the end and I bought a little bit bigger 1100 for the family.'

1966

The 1966 season started with another personal first for Cuoghi: a trip to America. The venue was the February Daytona Continental 24-hours and the Ford line-up betrayed another rethink by the organization. There were three of the revised 7-litre Mk IIs from Shelby American (Carroll Shelby sold the Cobra name to Ford in 1966) and expert engine tuners Holman and Moody were there with another pair of similar cars. David Yorke was then managing the Essex Wire GT40s, while Cuoghi and company were there to look after the customer GT40 entered for Sutcliffe and American Corvette ace Bob Grossman.

The preliminaries to the race were pretty exciting, with the JW boys—Etheridge, Ramirez and Cuoghi—being pulled up for driving with gay abandon on the nearby beach—'well they used to 'ave the racing there,' Cuoghi said in grinning justification. They were also stopped when Ramirez missed one of the unfamiliar traffic lights. In both cases the English suddenly found it impossible to speak their mother tongue and presented a startled Cuoghi as their incomprehensible interpreter! One of their number had a beard and earned himself a new nickname as an enormous policeman greeted him with 'Hel*lo* there, Moses!'

The racing was not so lighthearted for the team. Cuoghi explained: 'The car was running well in the race, in the top five I think in the closing stages. It had been a lot of effort through the night because the radiator kept getting clogged up with sand, so we keep on blowing it out with CO_2 equipment. Every pit stop we do the fuel, the tyres and so on, plus cleaning the radiator. The sand has blast away *all* the body paint, the glass-fibre was coming apart, the car it was *destroyed* by sand blasting I tell you. During the night it was *terribly* cold. To protect ourselves we take the cardboard of the fifty-gallon drums provided for the fuel and put the cardboard on to keep warm. You just freeze to death in the early morning waiting for the sunshine to come again.

'We had an oil leak as well as the blocked rad. This was from the sump: we jack it up and find one of the sump bolts is missing, so I was able to replace it.

'We had done twenty-three and three-quarter hours of the twenty-four when it came by and suddenly just stopped. For a while we did not know what had happened. In fact the engine had packed up, but to blow up in the last fifteen minutes, we were pretty shocked and the drivers, you can imagine after spending a day and a night with a good result ahead how disappointed they were.'

Cuoghi and a colleague went from Daytona to Long Island, where the enthusiastic William Wonder had offered them a garage to get the GT40 ready for Sutcliffe and Ireland to drive in the 12-hour race at Sebring in March. To make the return trip from a frozen New York they hired a 45-foot truck which started to have engine trouble as the atmosphere grew warmer. 'After a few troubles we arrived in Jacksonville. When the truck was fitted with new injectors it was good to drive down through Louisiana, North Carolina and Virginia. Really nice country. We even see a coupla small crocodiles in a swamp off a country road.' Although they had previously tested for twenty-four hours at Sebring with no troubles, the Slough team were out of luck for this race as the engine expired again, this time under not quite such distressing circumstances.

FAV were attending races in quite a low-key manner by the standards of their personnel. The 1966 season saw not only Holman and Moody brought in but also Alan Mann, the British saloon car racing expert, these two additional teams at the races emphasizing the JW responsibility to produce complete cars for customers, or rolling chassis to supply to the front-line organizations. In 1965 FAV had been charged with making fifty GT40s for homologation in group 4, a task successfully pursued and which led to Ermanno and his colleagues lending a hand in making all these cars and driving them on the road. Cuoghi confided that the GT40 was 'very impressive on the M4 [motorway],' but not at what speed!

Alan Mann had on their side the Ford America-employed Englishman Len Bailey and he oversaw the modification of five light alloy monocoque GT40s with slight suspension revision for the Mann concern. These cars, built through the 1965 winter and prepared to race in the prototype category, while Wyer and other favoured teams raced the steel-tub GT40 in group 4, first raced at the 1966 Sebring 12-hours with an array of driving talent that included Jackie Stewart and Graham Hill. They are important to our story because Bailey was to evolve the later JW Mirages from these first 4.7-litre machines.

Meanwhile the main American effort was going into the Holman and Moody NASCAR-engined 7-litre models. Kar Kraft made the Mk II a better proposition and then invested in the fabulous J-car design with its aircraft-style aluminium honeycomb-bonded tub. The revised Mk II won the Daytona 24-hour opening round (1–2–3–5) and the first three places at Sebring went to Fords too, but all of different types.

Monza was the first European round of the 1966 championship season and Cuoghi was there with the F. English GT40 for Ireland/Amon, but it retired before Amon could drive. Cuoghi remembers the weekend for what he thinks is a British 'All-comers' record. 'John Horsman is a chocolate-lover. We stay at the hotel St Eustorggio in Monza, which we share with the Ferrari team. They have profiteroles . . . they are simply fantastic! We've been pushing him to eat more and more. In the first year we stay there he eats fifteen profiteroles, something like that. The second year it is twenty-seven, really he has the record, nobody had beaten this.

'It was a golden tray, right to the top with profiteroles, and he was digging away . . . and away. And after a meal, a full meal . . . it was amazing!'

Cuoghi remembers how good Horsman was to the mechanics and recalled: 'When we working late: overnight perhaps, always the chocolate was coming "to give you strength", he say. Mr Wyer and 'is missus find us working one night in Slough to prepare the cars. They come to us with a basket of fruit, cakes, coffee. To see your boss coming with things like that is very good.' Certainly it would be hard to imagine Enzo Ferrari doing the same thing, but in the past, who knows?

'Innes Ireland remember the races we did together that year. Sometimes he is talking about it still when he see me working with Brabham.' Cuoghi also looked after the Belgian GT40 for Willy Mairesse—he vividly recalls trying to set the car up for level road on the sloping Spa start, and they might be called upon to work on the Ford France entries too.

The situation came to a head at Le Mans, the seventh and final qualification round of the championship that year. Ford had won the two American rounds; Ferrari conquered at Monza and Spa while Porsche were the winners on the Targa Florio and the intriguing Chaparral beat the Ferraris at the Nürburgring. It was Ford's third time at Le Mans as an official team: they had *eight* full factory 7-litre cars and the support of five 4.7-litre production GT40s.

That meant three cars came directly under the JW responsibility: Rindt/Ireland (F. English); Sutcliffe/Spoerry (Scuderia Filipinetti) and Ligier/Grossman (Ford France).

'We had so many cars to look after that what Mr Wyer had organized for everyone's benefit was a night shift to prepare the cars, and rested people to go from Le Chartre to the race track to do their duty. What I was doing was working all night through with the other guys, making improvements, doing all the jobs. Mainly at that stage the problem was with the Sylvania illuminated panels for the numbers. One night we were replacing one of these that had burned away and we had been working then for five nights.

'In the day we get a bit of fishing in! In front of the hotel there was a French shop to hire a rod for the day and we go down to the Loire: very good, that was the best part of Le Mans 1966! Driving to and from the circuit is good too, but very dangerous on French roads: Mr Wyer kills you if you damage one of the cars, so you 'ave to be careful and enjoy yourself. The road from Le Mans to Le Chartre is very small: lots of tractors and small villages. We go *quite* slowly . . .' Cuoghi laughs.

'You were not looking after one car, just moving round doing all the jobs on the list. We did not join in the Ford celebrations afterwards, but Mr Wyer gives us a really good, big, meal and there is plenty of champagne.' JW did not have any classified finishers, but Shelby and Holman and Moody had the first three finishers home with the 7-litre cars, also wrapping up the sports car title that year.

For Cuoghi there was a break back in Slough and at home in Italy, with some minor internationals to keep him busy before going to South Africa once more for Kyalami. This time the man Cuoghi described as 'a very nice English gentleman', Peter Sutcliffe, was sharing his Slough-prepared GT40 with Rhodesia's John Love. One of the reasons Cuoghi enjoyed South Africa so much was because Wyer booked them into the Kyalami Ranch: 'When we were there, there were just a few people, very nice entertainment. Now it is getting too big a 'otel. Too many rooms, not pleasant any more. The first year we went there we did not take the car down to Ford in town, but towed it back to Kyalami Ranch and prepared it in the open air. It was a nice way to work on this type of car, because there was not much to do anyway. The second year we did have to take the car up to Ford, but only when we were in troubles. They have the facilities there, but the normal checkover, we carried on at the Ranch . . . fifty yards from the pool . . . a nice drink . . .' his laughter returned at the memory.

In the nine-hour race there was no good result for Cuoghi labours that year.

Cuoghi's impressions of the GT40 at the beginning of what was to turn out to be a five-year career at JW were very interesting. 'Then we were building cars for the homologation, both racing and road cars. I was just assembling cars because we got the monocoques in from an outside supplier, but I remember we have been doing a lot of mods, though they were meant to be ready for assembly. Sometimes it was just parts missing—but there was already some development from when we start to build a run of cars. We are cutting and welding ourselves to start building the chassis up, but the main job is putting the car together.

'I remember we had an electrician [Bill Pink], who was making up the looms, which was quite complicated, because you have a normal car, plus the lights for night driving, door lights for number illumination and for that incredible dashboard—like an aeroplane, all the way across!

'From a mechanic's point of view it was a very nice car to work with, because it was a very advanced car for a sports car at that time. It was like one of the most sophisticated Formula 1 at times, even better in some ways. You could adjust anything on the suspension: camber, toe-in, ride height . . . *anything*. What I liked at Ford Advanced Vehicles was the surface plate, where you put a car up on blocks. When you take it out of there you know all the suspension setting are *perfect*.'

To Cuoghi the engine was a separate subject; it required only pre-race checking of the tappet clearances and so on, but what did impress him was 'the system of suspension geometry. I have never worked in such a sophisticated way, so I learned quite a lot in respect of setting up the car accurately. They 'ave the usual Dunlop gauges and so on, but it was the *procedure*. I work on sports cars and Formula 1 before, but never with so much detail for things like castor angles, so precisely.

'Every car was built to a job sheet and was coming along a production line in stages. The loom, the tank and so on. I was on one of the later stages of finishing the car, I never fitted the body to the chassis or anything like that. I would do the little details to make it *go* properly, especially the road cars. I drove them around the MIRA and Chobham test tracks, the skid pad and so on. It was a car beyond words, but I do remember it had a very big steering wheel.

'When Pedro Rodriguez came to drive for us the first time at Brands Hatch he has told me, "Ermanno, fit a smaller steering wheel, otherwise I feel, maybe, I am driving a lorry!"' It was an enormous wheel designed for anticipated heavy steering, which the car did not have.

1967

Motor Sport was able to announce in December 1966 that JW Automotive was to take over the FAV premises at Banbury Avenue in Slough. The JW stood for a partnership between two JWs—Johns Wyer and Willment, the latter well known for his Ford garages and racing team.

Every aspect of the JW programme was different, for the cars now appeared in the duck-egg blue and orange stripe livery of the Gulf Oil Corporation. The personal enthusiasm of Gulf's vice-president, I. G. 'Grady' Davis, carried the oil giant into the sporting arena, but they certainly knew how to capitalize on their racing investment through advertising and public relations.

Unusually the sponsorship extended to outright ownership of the cars and Cuoghi commented: 'It was a very good sponsorship from the beginning which allowed the best preparation. We did not worry about Ford going at all, especially for myself, we did not really notice the difference. Actually it was an improvement for us, as there was not so much politics. I was not personally affected by Ford politics because I understood only twenty-five per cent of the English language . . .!'

Cuoghi understood enough to be delighted when Wyer put him in charge of a car for the first time that year. They went to Daytona's 24-hour race with a rather special GT40 for Jacky Ickx and Dr Dick Thompson. 'It was a developed GT40 with a chassis made from lighter-gauge steel, relocated spare wheel and all the touring trim removed. We were virtually racing a road car in all that trim before,' Cuoghi said, 'now we make a racing car of the GT40. By the way, the car was in Gulf American colours of dark blue and orange stripe: the colours with light blue did not come until we go to Spa with the Mirage in May.'

Cuoghi was tickled by being in charge of a car quipping, 'considering I am a foreigner it is very good to 'ave work my way up like that!' Although it was a management decision to modify the basic GT40 into a lighter, simpler car Cuoghi remembers that the mechanics did play a part in the development programme via 'the English team's way of working with a suggestion box. They were taking notice of what you said; they were realizing the best out of every mechanic's ideas and using them. It must be more interesting for the mechanic to work in this way.'

The pace of development is such in racing that Cuoghi cannot recall the ideas today, but the emphasis at the Slough HQ was now firmly on the construction of the Mirage GT40 derivative.

The Gulf Mirage GT40 was good enough to finish sixth overall at Daytona and to lead the class until the engine blew at Sebring, but at the front of the field the 1967 Championship was an unusually exciting one for many of the rounds. This was because it had developed into a three-way fight, with the General Motors-backed Chaparrals of Jim Hall now sporting wings as well as the efficient Chevrolet V8 engine (a rather better unit than the Ford, to judge by ensuing CanAm success), besides the development of the Ferrari 330 P4 and revised Mk II Fords from Holman and Moody, and Shelby. These claimed some 500 bhp from 7 litres, while the lighter thoroughbred Ferrari V12 gave some 450 bhp from fractionally under 4 litres.

A pair of new P4s and a P3 led a Ferrari 1–2–3 at Daytona, but Ferrari skipped Sebring altogether, leaving the revamped version of the J-car Ford (known as J4 or Mk IV more frequently) to score an easy win from its Mk II back-up, which finished second while stationary in the pits with a broken camshaft.

Ford decided to skip Monza in April, but JW went along. On 10 April, 1967, two of the new JW-built Gulf Mirage machines had been put together and made their debut at Le Mans for the test weekend. Their lighter-running chassis was allied to narrower, sleeker top bodywork that allowed the Mirage (a name chosen for its international acceptance and ease of French pronunciation) a smaller frontal area. At Le Mans they had 4.7-litre V8s, but for Monza JW ran the pair with longer (76.2 mm v. 72.9 mm) stroke versions of the V8 Ford motor, which allowed 412 bhp at 6000 rpm and nearly 400 ft lb of torque.

Monza was on 25 April and the two cars showed they struck a good balance between straightline speed and fuel consumption. In the early stages the Piper/Thompson car ran fourth and the Ickx/Alan Rees (the Arrows F1 team manager) fifth. Ahead the Chaparral and the Ferraris matched their respective rumbling 525 bhp tenor and shrill V12 treble. Ickx/Rees had ignition failure, but Piper/Thompson were able to finish ninth after a long delay to repair persistent water loss.

1 May showed the pace of development that Cuoghi and the lads were having to keep up with. They had spent a frantic week screwing together a third twist to the Mirage GT40 theme for Spa, powered by a Holman and Moody version of the 5.7-litre/350-cu in Ford V8. This car was to be shared by Ickx with Rees, while Piper and Thompson had been moved together in the 5-litre model: incidentally the team was managed in the 1967 season 'on-track' by David Yorke following Wyer's successful support of the Essex Wire GT40s in the previous season.

With a record of fastest laps, and non-finishes, behind it, there was no surprise that the winged Chaparral was fastest in practice, but 3.4 seconds behind and 1.3 litres smaller, Ickx showed what a competitive car Cuoghi and company had built in that week's work. In the race, traditional Ardennes rain persisted and the fresh-faced young Ickx, then at the peak of his powers at Spa, simply hurtled away from most of the field, but not fellow Belgian

DAVID HOBBS *and Paul Hawkins shared this GT40 to finish fourth at the 1968 Spa 1000 km. Both in 1967 and 1968 the JW Automotive team won the event in pouring rain, utilizing the talents of Jacky Ickx—though he drove the slimmer roofline Mirage in 1967*

Mairesse in a converted P3/4 Ferrari.

However, Mairesse's co-driver was not so quick, and when Willy climbed back in he hastily shot the Ferarri off the road. Yorke had already anticipated that he would use Thompson in the Mirage to partner Ickx, for he was proving faster than Rees, and Piper had already crashed their 5-litre! Thompson was able to keep the car on the island long enough for Ickx to take his compulsory one-hour break and resume, the Mirage scoring a second race-appearance win by a lap from Siffert in a 2-litre Porsche, and Hans Herrman. The Mirage averaged 120.4 mph for the 5 hr 9 m 46.5 sec it took to cover the 100 kilometres. The Chaparral's fastest lap, in slightly dryer conditions, averaged 129.4 mph.

Cuoghi recalls that the first test of the Mirage was in the hands of that little-known driver but well-known Wyer management team member John Horsman! 'I think Mr Horsman just shake it down, see all the systems work, at the Military Vehicles test track in Chobham. Afterwards we did a little more testing at Snetterton, but the car was good from the start. Basically it was a GT40 with revised aerodynamics: the car was stable and we did not have to add any spoilers or tabs,' Cuoghi concluded, though they did have distinctive small 'ears' on the front wings.

At Spa Cuoghi crossed swords with Ferrari, for when 'I put the rain tyres on, they were not clearing the wheel arches. So we must chop away the body to make sure it will not cut the tyres. This is just before the race, on the front row, and we had never had the chance to fit the bigger-diameter, narrow-rim tyres on that Mirage before. So I am sitting there chopping away parts of our car and Ing Forghieri from Ferrari is telling me to get away because the race, it is starting!

'It is worth it though. Ickx is driving so well that day . . . those four-wheel drifts in the rain around

PAUL HAWKINS (left *in Gulf overalls and helmet*) *waits to see how Cuoghi gets on delving within the GT40 in 1968*

those fast corners ... I don't know how he does it. For sure, he must 'ave a big 'eart! So we win our first race for Wyer. It was a big celebration afterwards, but I don't remember what happened there!' Ford must have spared the odd corporate smile in Britain and the USA for Sebring, Daytona, and Monza had left the score at Ferrari two wins, Ford one; the defence of their title looked more hopeful. Ferrari tackled the Targa Florio and so did Chaparral, but the result was a Porsche walkover 1–2–3.

The Nürburgring 1000 km had no works Ferraris, but Porsche were there in strength with their 2.2- and 2.0-litre cars facing the Chaparral and two Gulf Mirages. Le Mans was only two weeks away, so the big guns of Ferrari and Ford were unsurprising absentees. Cuoghi's team had little luck. Thompson crashed the 5-litre car, while Ickx and Attwood in the 5.7 had been as high as second place when, after thirty of forty-four laps that were to be covered by the leading Porsche in another 1–2–3 for the Stuttgart concern, Attwood picked up two flat tyres after putting two wheels over sharp stones. Considering the size and varying quality of the entry, it was understandable that there should be many moments of this nature.

The penultimate round of the 1967 Championship was June's Le Mans and Ford attacked with open vigour, entering as Ford Motor Co versus Ferrari SpA, seven of the 7-litre Mk IIs and IVs supported by privateers in GT40s and the two Gulf Mirages, both in 5.7-litre trim. Gulf's drivers were Ickx with saloon car specialist Brian Muir (who had stepped very convincingly into the official Ford team at very short notice the previous year) and well-known British long-distance sports car privateer David Piper paired with Dick Thompson. Both Mirages had engine troubles and were retired: JW's Le Mans luck had to change soon! In practice JW tried 5.7 engines, but they overheated, so they had to lay on engines that were over 5 litres to correspond with the Mirages' fuel tank capacity. The faithful 4.7-litre motors could not be used because the tank capacity of the Mirage was too large under then current regulations, so 5.3-litre V8s were fitted instead.

'So far as I can remember we were back at Le Chartre early for us, having a good meal and a drink, instead of a whole night's work: sometimes, it does help not to be always working...' Ermanno said wistfully.

For Ford, the result, their last official factory fling at the French classic, had all the ingredients they could have wanted, save a three-Ford pile-up during the night. Indianapolis winner A. J. Foyt became the first Indy winner to do the double, the Texan paired with California's Dan Gurney. They were a long way ahead of the Parkes/Scarfiotti Ferrari, but the Chaparral had given both Ford and Ferrari a hard time until its automatic transmission wilted again and left them with their seventh non-finish of the Championship trail. So far Hall's GM-supported Chaparral 2Fs (there were two at Le Mans, the slower one didn't finish either) had just four fastest race laps to show their potential....

A new championship round formed the last event in the 1967 series, the BRSCC's BOAC 500 at Brands Hatch. For Cuoghi it was an unforgettable event because it marked his first working contact with the driver he idolized and could communicate with more easily than any other, Pedro Rodriguez.

'David Yorke knew Pedro was free and he has asked him to sell him a drive for the BOAC. It was very, very nice for me because we could speak Italian and understand each other perfectly and fast.

'When he drove the car in that first practice he came and told me all this business about the big steering wheel. No problem, we soon change that. He was very pleased about the car. Pedro says it was behaving so well you could set in any position on the track, no problem at all. A very neutral car, he liked it very much.

'Pedro had been driving Ferraris before, nearly always older type of Ferrari for many owners. I had talked to him before—I "knew him" in the same manner like Jim Clark through the reputation, but also through the Ferraris, talking with the mechanics, and through his brother, poor Ricardo [who was killed driving a Lotus—J.W.]. It was the first time we have any business contact with him.

'He was a fantastic person, driving with the heart the whole time. A lot of passion on the track and I admire him as a driver... as a person... very, very much indeed.

'Pedro knew what he wanted in a car. Mainly the little details like over- and understeer. He was not saying "look, it's understeering, do something." Pedro would collaborate to tell you and help you how to improve the behaviour of the car. He was an experienced driver and knew his way mechanically around the car too.

'Unfortunately this first time he is going like hell, but a few laps after his co-driver Thompson is taking over he is crashing it on Clearways! That was the end of the story, but we could 'ave finished pretty well there ...' Cuoghi finished.

He was absolutely right and so were the management when they decided to produce these modified GT40s, for the Gulf entry started from the fourth row of an 'all-star' grid yet was leading overall after one-and-a-half hours' racing. Pedro did not need to stop for fuel when the big Ferraris, Lola-Chevrolets and Chaparrals were forced to. Even with many of the top runners in their faster, usually bigger-engined, machinery still fighting it out at the end of the first hour, Pedro was still fifth overall.

As related Thompson crashed the car, but before he did, *Motor Sport*'s D.S.J. and some of his weekly contemporaries noted that (in Jenks's words) '... one of the few bright things seen in the pit stops was seen at the Mirage stop, for instead of pouring in oil from a can, the engine was fitted with a pipe sticking out of the tail, to which a flexible oil pipe was attached by a snap-connector, and oil was pumped into the sump under high pressure from a container in the pits. Other than this pit work was a bit vintage.'

Full marks for the suggestion box!

The race was fittingly won by Mike Spence and Phil Hill in the unique winged Chaparral 2F, a just reward for a season of providing a white 'dark horse' in the championship: this time they did not get fastest lap, but there was plenty of satisfaction at beating Stewart and Amon in their factory Ferrari 330 P4.

1968

The World Sports Car series over, JW went on to try new countries and drivers in some less serious international events. Ferrari had their revenge in that 1967 title fight, for they took the title by two points from Porsche (the result of the BOAC had been critical) with Ford third, a further ten points behind. But the Americans had what they came for, victory at Le Mans for the third time, and it would now be left to the JW-Gulf team and Ford of

Europe to fight for sports car honours with Ferrari and Porsche.

The regulations were to change for the 1968 season anyway, limiting group 6 (the premier league of sports car racing at the time) prototypes to 3 litres and the heavier group 4 cars to 5 litres. In time this latter regulation was ultimately to lead Ferrari and Porsche to the construction of the fastest sports cars seen in Europe—the 512 Ferrari 5-litre V12 and the 4.5/5.0-litre Porsche 917s—which were put into limited production to get around these regulations!

Of the remainder of 1967 Cuoghi remembers going for the first time to 'Sweden, which was very good. We took the transporter to Hull and got on a very big liner. A long trip, thirty-six hours, something like that. So we really had time to enjoy the crossing. Plenty of good drinking! I don't really like boats, but it was big and there was no rough weather, so everything OK.

'We arrived in Karlskoga circuit. It looked to me a funny place, but I enjoyed the weekend because there was a Formula 2 race as well. Ickx, Stewart in the Tyrrells [Matras actually—but it seemed that way at times!—J.W.] so there was plenty to watch. We had a Swedish driver in Jo Bonnier, of course, and he was second, so we were pretty popular. In fact we 'ad first place too . . .' he breaks off to laugh at a question asking about the opposition's quality . . . 'so it was a pretty relaxed weekend. Ickx was in the winning car.

'We took the cars to Copenhagen as well, visiting a Gulf refinery, and left them there when we returned to England. Then we went back to Copenhagen, cleaned the cars, you know just some paraffin on old overalls, and we have a race in Copenhagen that we win too. So it was very good for Gulf.

'That was the first time that we had Paul Hawkins in the car and he finished second to Bonnier. He was a very good this Australian driver. Always

58

Preparing a legend for John Wyer

DAYTONA *1968 and Cuoghi, back to camera, works on a Gulf promotion for JW in some nice company, including a now rare Shelby convertible Mustang. Not surprisingly such assignments were pretty popular with the mechanics*

SWOOSHING ROUND *the Daytona banking in 1968 with the Ickx/Redman pole position car (8) leading Hawkins/Hobbs. Both cars failed to finish, despite their double lucky horseshoes!*

he has been working on his own red GT40s. He cuts away all the unnecessary things, makes the car light; builds better engines, always working to make the car faster with his mechanic.' In fact John Etheridge was to help 'Hawkeye' in this quest to make the GT40 more competitive after Etheridge left JW *en route* to setting up his present successful business.

By early October they were at Montlhèry for the Paris 1000 km. Paul Hawkins was on a fantastic winning streak, having won two major races in Britain and the Austrian 1000 km. He shared the winning car in France with Ickx, who was having an even more successful year, for his international results were better.

The season closed at Kyalami in early November with yet another major victory for Ickx and JW. This time the young Belgian was sharing with Lancastrian Brian Redman, then on his way to a career as the most successful sports car driver save Ickx himself. Brian had been driving what Cuoghi described as 'a nice private GT40: always very smart in its British racing green.' That car belonged to Nick Cussons. Registered as GUN 805D it was still absolutely pristine, but now with a broad white stripe, when I went to visit Etheridge in 1979.

Redman reported: 'It was very early on in my times with the big teams and I had come to David Yorke's notice because of my outings in the Bridges Lola T70. I would say the whole team was exceptionally well co-ordinated to produce such excellent pitwork. Obviously the relationship between Yorke and Cuoghi was important, but it was the way the whole team worked together that impressed me.

'It was all rather embarrassing afterwards. I had virtually accepted the idea of racing for JW in 1968, but then I got this telegram from Porsche. I had a very good relationship with everyone at JW, but the GT40 was getting very heavy by comparison with some of its rivals and I thought Porsche offered a better chance of success in the following year....'

Cuoghi and Redman were to work together in 1968, but Redman's season was curtailed by unforeseen circumstances.

Development on the Mirage was always slanted towards taking weight out of the car, especially as the car would have to sacrifice its 5.7 engines in 1968, but Cuoghi recalls them as good cars to work on except for 'the fuel system and fuel tank. It is always involved in any racing car, but with them

ALSO AT *the 1968 Daytona race, a fine LAT picture of David Yorke at work as David Hobbs looks on*

either side in a steel frame and the use of CO_2 with continuous wire weld, it was very difficult to protect the tank itself. You need a lot of tank tape; plastic, wire and sponge. Really, you had to fill it all inside properly or it would damage the bag tank.' Of that South African win Cuoghi remembered: 'We had no trouble with the cars at all: just on the first day of practice we had to sort out the carburation again. After that we have solved the problem. Just clean up the car, check around and away we go,' was Cuoghi's happy conclusion.

'The cars, they were staying together forever. Providing there was nothing wrong on the machining or the casting they were really reliable. Sometimes the front casting did give us trouble, but when they went to blow casting everything was all right.' Those magnesium alloy castings did a fair bit of damage to the JW reputation for crash-free reliability before they were sorted out, but as Cuoghi said the cars scored primarily on their immense reliability, a by-product of conscientious preparation from a team who knew their steeds so well that mistakes became rarities.

For the 1968 season JW Automotive had to return to the GT40 rather than the Mirage, for that had been outlawed by the busy international lawmakers of Paris. Wyer commissioned Len Bailey to draw up a new Mirage prototype, one that this time would eventually use the 3-litre Ford DFV. Theoretically the GT40 would make way for the later Mirage when that was ready. In fact the later car was not raced in 1968. Of the three Mirages of GT40 descent one was sold, another crashed and the third converted to form one of the team's three regular GT40Ps for the 1968 season.

Hawkins and David 'Hobboe' Hobbs shared the JW GT40 converted from the Mirage, while Redman and Ickx were in the other car for the traditional February start to the season at Daytona. In practice Ickx and Redman were on pole by a large margin over the sister car and four Porsche 907s, these propelled by the fuel-injected 2.2-litre motors. An interesting novelty was described as 'the whistler' by Cuoghi, the Howmet turbine, but it was not destined to do anything as exciting as its specification suggested.

From the start the Gulf GTs pulled away, but the race was not to be a JW victory. Cuoghi's car suffered a rare ZF gearbox failure (the final drive?) while the other car expired in the puddle of fuel that Cuoghi has talked of as a design fault; its bag tank punctured in the dawn light. Cuoghi, and anyone else who was in the pits that year, will not forget one of the biggest accidents without injury ever seen in a long-distance race. Mitter skated the 907 on some oil, flipped over on to the roof and continued towards the next corner on his roof, pursued by showers of sparks and flaring magnesium. Masten Gregory punched the brakes hard on in his Ferrari, spun and hit Dieter Spoerry's 2-litre Porsche, which flew into the air at some 160 mph. 'It was exciting,' says Cuoghi nodding his head gravely, 'but thank God nobody was hurt: I just couldn't look!'

Sebring was no good to the team either. Ickx had practised *faster* than the 7-litre Mk II Fords at Daytona for pole, but this time he had to give best to one of the Porsches, the sister car down in seventh place. Cuoghi's face dropped a bit when Redman spun the Ickx car and burnt the clutch out trying to regain the track, but the team worked very hard on the Hawkins/Hobbs machine after it clobbered an errant backmarker, eventually rigging up a new front from the retired Ickx/Redman machine. This car had led at one stage and Hawkins even managed to claw back up to second before the front suspension failure occurred and gave the occupants of one marshals' post the closest view a spectator has ever had of an uncontrolled GT40!

Back in Europe things could only get better. The first week in April saw Jacky Ickx dashing between Le Mans, for the test weekend at which he set fastest time, and the BOAC 500, which he and Redman won for JWA, while Hawkins and Hobbs were third. Cuoghi was at Brands Hatch working on the winning car.

The Brands Hatch race was notable for two things outside JW's twenty-two-second win over Ludovico Scarfiotti's Porsche 907 (Ickx had a little trouble with gear selection in the closing stages), for the BOAC marked the first appearance of the Len Bailey official Ford-backed Alan Mann 3-litre prototype, and the terrible shock of Jim Clark's death at Germany's grim Hockenheimring.

Ferrari didn't appear, even at Monza, and JW won again, this time with Hawkins/Hobbs. Cuoghi had a chance to exercise his race-side ingenuity when the manifolding on the left bank suffered a severed pipe close to the exit from the cylinder head (the new Gurney-Weslake aluminium heads now homologated to provide well over 400 bhp). Using wire, asbestos sheet and clips, Cuoghi and company stitched it all together again. Unfortunately Redman subsequently spun the car on the unexpected loose surface then prevailing at Lesmo and damaged the tail section, unstitching the exhaust rig. It was too much to cope with as the hinge bracketry for the tail section was also damaged, so the car was retired as a consequence.

The fifth-round Targa Florio did not attract the cars from Slough (Cuoghi had only been there once), so Nürburgring's 1000 km in mid-May was the next date. Monza had marked the first appearance of the 3-litre Porsche 908 flat-eight design and 'at home' such cars were first and second at that year's 'Ring. Cuoghi was looking after Ickx paired with Hawkins for this race, as it had been decided that Redman's lack of Nürburgring experience would be a handicap. Practice hadn't been much guide in the damp conditions, but in the race it could be seen that this was an error: Ickx could threaten the Porsches, but Hawkins could not, so they finished a class-winning third, while Hobbs and Redman were sixth, a lap adrift.

The seventh round was the following weekend at Spa—just a short truck drive for Cuoghi this time, not that driving is a chore to him—'it gives you an extra couple of days at the circuit,' he commented simply! He carried on driving the transporter—for ninety-nine per cent of the time without accidents—but John Etheridge recalled just one mishap. 'One time we were going down through Belgium. We had dumped a car off, John Wyer's personal Mustang, at Brussels airport for the boss. We were both tired, I was driving and I think we were in a shooting brake of some sort. There was a junction to the right and I hit a car fair and square. It woke old Ermanno up all right. Unfortunately'—said with a broad grin—'unfortunately, Ermanno got the blame because the guy thought I was too young to drive!'

Next on the 1968 calendar was another of Ickx's fantastic performances around the Spa-Francorchamps. Brian Redman said Jacky 'put in the best opening lap I ever saw. Sure, he had just driven a Mustang to a win in the saloon car event and knew exactly what the soaking wet circuit was like—but it was a fabulous piece of driving. Do you know, he had over *40 seconds* on Vic Elford in that first lap, and Vic was no slouch!' Redman managed to maintain the pace and kept the one-lap lead that Ickx had opened on the opposition, many of whom had trouble with water on the electrics or simply spraying in through cooling ducts (the fate of the pole-winning Ford F3L prototype). Porsches took second and third places, JW fourth with Hawkins and Hobbs in their rather more troubled car.

14 July and Watkins Glen was the eighth round of that year's Championship, but JW were without Redman, for the likeable sports car specialist (who did not care for Formula 1, though he was to prove a match for many of their drivers) had suffered a broken arm when his Cooper-Maserati V12 crashed at *Virage Combes*. Ironic after his performance in the rain at the same circuit a fortnight earlier.

For Watkins Glen, Cuoghi and his colleagues fitted the long-stroke 5-litre versions of the Ford V8 complete with the Gurney-Weslake heads. Such a motor had been tried in practice at Spa, but the 4.7 was raced. Cuoghi recalled that the drivers were more impressed by the wider spread of good pulling power than in extra horses. A look at the torque figures shows the truth of this, for 396 ft lb was recorded at 4750 rpm, compared with 325 ft lb some 250 rpm up the scale for the smaller 4.7 unit.

At Watkins Glen, the first time the sports car series had visited the site of what was then America's only Grand Prix, Porsche could have taken the title, if they had won! JWA made sure they didn't, though Siffert gave Ickx a hard time for the first fifteen minutes of the six-hour event. Save a puncture for Ickx's co-driver compatriot Lucien Bianchi, the JW cars just ran as Cuoghi said 'forever', and faultlessly. They finished just eleven seconds apart, Ickx having averaged over 109 mph in the GT40 he shared with Bianchi, for he had been determined to unlap himself past team-mates Hawkins/Hobbs.

That brought the Championship score to four wins apiece for Ford-JWA and Porsche, the Germans leading by 2 points. Next was the Zeltweg, Austrian, round 9, but JWA did not attend as the event qualified for only half points. Instead they prepared for the task of attempting to win Le Mans, the track now with a chicane following the departure of the fastest Fords, Ferraris and Chaparrals! Le Mans was also rather different that year for it was not in June but September, as the traditional weekend was given to polling for the general election.

JWA brought all three cars into action, the team led by two replacement drivers required because of Redman's unhealed injuries and the Canadian Grand Prix practice accident that broke Ickx's leg in his Formula 1 Ferrari. 'That cost him the World Championship, that did,' Cuoghi commented. It was certainly true that the young Belgian was a thorn in even Stewart's side then....

Lucien Bianchi was drafted in alongside Cuoghi's favourite Mexican, Pedro Rodriguez. The other two cars were driven by Brian Muir with Jack Oliver and David Hobbs/Paul Hawkins. Cuoghi commented laconically, 'Muir wasn't bad, but on that Le Mans he must've forgot the Mulsanne straight has a Mulsanne corner and he went straight on the sand. It took him a long, long time to dig

THIS FINE *atmosphere shot captures all the drama of midnight toil as the JW boys renovate the clutch of the David Hobbs GT40 while the driver looks on anxiously with the others*

himself out. When he has managed to do so he has burned the clutch and 'as to retire.' Hawkins suffered an engine failure and this was interesting, for Rodriguez/Bianchi had a new dry-deck version of the 4.9 V8 and this led the team to adopt the unit. Later, it transpired that the cool of the night and lack of pressure on the car after the first four-hour scrap with the Porsches were more relevant. There were to be some expensive engine failures.

Cuoghi felt 'the dry-deck engine was a complex installation, really only successful on this occasion.

'Rodriguez was *so* confident of that race, you could not believe it. He really knew it, knew he was going to win his first Le Mans. He was never tired of driving. Never ever tired . . . Pedro did many

Opposite: IT WAS *worth it! Rodriguez sprays the champagne while Cuoghi grins and Bianchi tries to get out from the cockpit!*

LE MANS *1968 and Cuoghi guides 'his' GT40 for Rodriguez/Bianchi to the start with plenty of help from the rest of the team. It gave JW their first victory at Sarthe*

Preparing a legend for John Wyer

more hours than Bianchi, and he wants to finish the race as well. Yorke, he said "no. You started, Lucien will finish." Oh, Christ, Pedro was upset, he really *wanted* to do the finish!

'During the night we had one panic. We had to change the brake pads and they were very low. There was a special winding tool and on one side, I think it was the right, we could not put the tool in to force the pistons apart. We have to wiggle the piston back with a crowbar!

'We celebrate with Pedro afterwards: he wants us *all* to go on top of the car. He was sitting with his arm around my shoulder and the people were cheering as we drive to the line and round the paddock. The atmosphere at Le Mans is just amazing, it really is. The crowd, they were going berserk!

'Pedro liked Le Mans, but then he liked any kind of races. Even for a weekend entertainment race, he was giving everything.'

Whereas the winnning average had been over 135 mph the previous year, the changes to the Le Mans circuit and the lack of competition dropped the average winning speed to 115.29 mph. Pedro and Bianchi won by almost forty-six miles over a privately entered Porsche 907: there were no factory Ferraris that year.

The result ensured that Porsche won the title, 81 points to 62, but Le Mans was still Ford property and they conquered with a car much closer to the original design than the successful American entries of previous years.

Cuoghi remembers their Kyalami victory with the Mirage (the last win and race for the car in JW hands) not for the various bothers they had in practice, but 'for the major entertainment it was Ickx. He was limping everywhere because he 'as his bones kept together by a bar! The doctors kept him under supervision, we have realized that he will be safe to drive, but he just couldn't run. So Hobbs did the running for him, at the Le Mans type start.

'I like David Hobbs, I see he is now living in California and doing many things for television, but always he is coming to see me at the races and take the piss of me! "HellOOO ErmanOOO" he shouts. He is a very good man and his wife is sweet . . . but 'is kids are no kids any more, they are bigger than me.'

1969

The tail end of the 1968 season and the beginning of 1969 was taken up not only with running the GT40s again and experimenting with Tecalemit Jackson fuel injection, but also with a desperate try to get the 3-litre Mirage prototype ready. This was achieved early in 1969, but there was still a lot more work to do with that car, so the tried and tested GT40s went back into action ready for a try at Le Mans for the sixth consecutive year and the chance of a fourth straight victory.

Cuoghi looks back to the period: 'We built the whole car [the Mirage proto] at JW and I actually built some of the monocoque parts as well as working on the assembly in the final stages. We make the wishbones, everything we could on *that* car, so we were bloody busy. We did less races and more major work on *that* car. A lot of overtime hours on *that* car: pretty good for us!

'The monocoque was simple and very well designed, and we have all the facilities like bending and cutting machines. Easy enough, but the major trouble was fitting the dashboard and all the little panels and their strengthening parts. It was interesting because you could use all the equipment, argon arc machines and so on.

'Meanwhile, on the GT40 and TJ injection side they had tried it a few times, but they couldn't make it run properly. It was OK when you were using the car engine full bore, but when it came to a corner you had to be Japanese Kamikaze! So they went on racing GT40 much as before: quite heavy and quite reliable, though in America we had the liners shift on a dry sump engine and the suspension failures we talked about much earlier.'

Just how little had changed could be seen from a comparison of their 1968/69 practice times for the 24-hour 1969 opening round at Daytona. With the 1968 times in brackets the drivers managed as follows: 8th quickest, Ickx/Oliver, 1 m 54.5 s (pole position, Ickx/Redman, 1 m 54.91 s); 9th fastest, Hobbs/Hailwood, 1 m 55.3 s (2nd fastest, Hawkins/Hobbs, 1 m 57.0 s). Elford was fastest at Daytona in 1969, his Porche 908 3-litre recording 1 m 52.2 s.

However, the Porsche fleet had hit trouble and Hailwood was leading, but heading for the pits with what turned out to be a shifted liner in the V8 engine. That put the car out of the race after all the tricks of adding water and flushing out the cooling system had been exhausted. Ickx had the suspension front failure as he came off the banking on to the road circuit—'it singed Ickxy's eyebrows a bit,' said Cuoghi, 'but I was just glad it was not worse for Jacky.'

So neither JW nor Porsche were in the points, and Mark Donohue/Chuck Parsons had persuaded a Lola T70 to go for most of a twenty-four-hour race (the part that mattered anyway!), though even they had lost over two hours in the pits. Long-dis-

THE MOST *successful partnership of sports car racing, and the two most successful drivers in the category for many years, Brian Redman* (left) *and Jacky Ickx at Daytona*

tance racing is a unique branch of the sport. . . .

The Ickx/Oliver car received a new Gurney AAR-built version of the Ford V8 direct from their Santa Ana base in California. This engine was reputed to give 460 bhp, 70 bhp more than the original units of 4.7 litres had claimed! Both cars abandoned the dry-deck principle, leaving full water flow for the cylinder heads, which was thought to have led to the cracked liners at Daytona. Ickx opted for the older of the two cars and his seat and steering wheel were transferred by Cuoghi from the machine damaged at Daytona for the second marathon at Sebring.

The GT40s' competition age showed clearly, for they were twelfth and thirteenth in practice. Fastest time went to the new Ferrari 312 3-litre prototype, Amon and Mario Andretti marking the great Italian marque's return to long-distance events with a time 0.52 s faster than the 5-litre Penske Lola T70.

Neat pitwork and rumbling reliability brought pale blue cars gradually up through the field. Sebring's roughness collapsed the suspension upright again on the Hailwood/Hobbs machine: it was repaired once, but the second time saw the car stranded out on the circuit.

Luckily Ferrari were also in trouble, and the Porsches were suffering cracked chassis frames! Ickx overtook the Ferrari with one and a half hours to go and went on to win at an average of 103.36 mph, a lap ahead of Amon/Andretti's Ferrari.

Cuoghi has one vivid memory of the American races that year when 'one car lose the complete axle and wheels—you never see such shouting and running as they come hurtling towards the pits! Everything is OK though,' he shrugged dispassionately.

Of the cars that season Cuoghi summed up the team's feelings: 'Mechanically they are finished, really obsolete, and we know Porsche will have the 917 soon to go on top of the 908. Things did not look too good.'

Brands Hatch in April marked the debut of the JW Mirage M2-BRM V12 for Ickx and Oliver, while Hobbs and Hailwood took the now outclassed GT40. Despite a bag tank leak Hobbs and Hailwood took the faithful old chassis to fifth overall and a class win, but it was twenty laps behind the winning Siffert/Redman 908—which 'Seppi' had taken to pole position in practice at a time faster than his Lotus 49 F1 record lap!

The Mirage coupé, with its squared-off lines and general air of prototype (that does not mean it was

scruffy, the blue and orange paintwork was as smart as ever), was only finished on the Friday before the race. 'Jesus! we had to work all the nights to get the car complete,' Cuoghi recalled, adding, 'but it was too new and was not as fast as the Ferraris and Porsches. I remember when Jack Oliver try it he say it was undrivable and he was pretty right. The car was a cow at that time.'

It retired after two and a half of the six hours with a broken driveshaft, having held sixth to seventh overall.

World Championship rounds were now abandoned for the JW GT40s until Le Mans in June. That meant missing Monza, Targa Florio and even, with these cars, Spa, which was notable for Redman sharing the winning Porsche with Siffert at an average over 141 mph. It was also noted for the first one-lap appearance of Porsche's fearsome flat twelve-cylinder 917 model, then a very tricky beast to handle indeed.

However, JW did attend Spa with the first Mirage for Ickx/Oliver and the second for Hobbs/Hailwood. Though the latter was a brand-new car, both had BRM engines that were well down on power, for they were to 1968 specification with only two valves per cylinder. Ickx managed to slot the V12 Mirage on to the front row, but even he couldn't keep up and was no better than fifth when the engine died out on the circuit after ten of seventy-one scheduled laps: Hobbs and Hailwood managed to rack up a seventh place with the car. 'It was faster than the private GT40s, but not fast enough to catch the front-runners,' felt Cuoghi.

In the middle of the preparations for Le Mans and both 3-litre prototypes retiring at the 'Ring's 1000 kilometres Cuoghi received a telegram from his mother. 'My father was dying in Modena,' Cuoghi said starkly and simply, 'but he was dead before I arrived there.' Ermanno stayed on to comfort his mother and then found his way to Le

WHAT IT'S *all about for the drivers at Le Mans. The JW GT40 pounds toward 1968 victory through the rain. Contrast this lonely application of concentration with the crowded world of the mechanics working in the pits*

Mans by train. Mourning and work would be combined....

There the clock was turned back so far as JWA and Ford were concerned. The GT40s were lined up for Ickx/Oliver and Hobbs/Hailwood, Wyer and his management reasoning that the GT40s stood a much better chance of being in at the end than unproven Mirage prototypes.

The opposition was a phalanx of Porsche 908 and new 917 models, a pair of Ferrari 312Ps in coupé trim and entries from Matra and Alpine-Renault.

'Jacky said he could win before the start of the race,' Cuoghi confided. 'He does not run to the car, he *strolls*, just walking along! There was just a moment of hesitation, where he gets boxed in with the others, and then he goes.

'My job that year was to change left front tyres and pads, clean the screen and headlights, but we were all trained so that we could move around to any job. There were four people on each car and the refueller: it took 120 litres of petrol, and we still used the pressure oil feed system.

'Everyone stayed the whole time. Two of us might sit resting on our chins inside the pit boxes, but I don't remember sleeping at all: though I think I must've fallen off the chair sometimes because I got a lot of bruises!'

The race was a classic of the tortoise and hare kind, but at the end the tortoise had the spirit to sprint to win by less than a hundred yards after twenty-four hours! Even at 2 o'clock in the morning the two Gulf Fords were hardly challengers despite the carnage of a first lap that killed John Woolfe in the first £14,000 customer 917, and eliminated Amon's Ferrari. Even the subsequent failure rate amongst the front-runners had yet to bring JW to the front.

At 2 am the two GT40s were *eight laps* behind the leading but troubled 917. By mid-Sunday morning that 917 was out and the Ickx/Oliver car was in the lead: behind, Hans Herrman/Gerard Larrouse (now Renault's competition manager) were catching up in their works Porsche 908. At 1.30 pm, with no more scheduled pit stops, Herrman finally passed Ickx in the obsolete GT40, but with half an hour to go and Le Mans at stake the Belgian ace resorted to sheer driving nerve and skill to make up the deficiency on the technically superior, though smaller capacity, 908. Ickx used every wile of his successful career in Formula 3, 2 and 1 to out-brake, out-corner and generally harass the hapless Herrman, a veteran German sports and Grand Prix driver, but not in the same hungry league as the Ickx of that period. Even on the last lap it is reckoned that Ickx and Herrman swopped places four or five times, Ickx finally assuming a little control by his speed through the ultra-fast curve after the Mulsanne straight. 'I could not believe we win,' Cuoghi shouted in the excitement of recalling those closing minutes to 1969's classic Le Mans. 'When I see the car coming across the line ahead it is just too much, I just would start crying with the emotion. We bin awake thirty-six hours for a twenty-four-hour race and have to race the whole way!'

The crowd felt the same way and the event ended in chaos with the spectators running everywhere and the tired orange-overalled Gulf mechanics filled with emotion as they surveyed their equally grimy companions. Black trails of oil mixed with track dust tracing across their bright overalls as further evidence of 'a hard day's night'.

Porsche had already won the Championship with four outright wins that season, but JWA had won the war again simply by taking that most coveted win of all, their crews finishing first (averaging 129.4 mph for the 3105.61 miles covered), *and* JW took a fine third with Hobbs and Hailwood.

It was time to put the GT40s away and get on with the business of being competitive in other championship rounds once more....

CUOGHI WORKS *while Ickx studies* (right). *The scene at the Mirage-Cosworth's Brands Hatch debut in 1969 as Ermanno struggles to race-prepare the car. Cuoghi remembers that there were 'a lot of little troubles, especially the suspension bottom links, which kept breaking at first'*

Preparing a legend for John Wyer

6

Working on the winning Porsche

1970

WHEN THE the JW management team went looking for a competitive car to replace the now heavy and outdated GT40s, they tackled the problem two ways. The first was the construction of their own 3-litre Mirage prototypes. It looked as though 3-litres on GP lines was the competitive way to go, the 5-litre stock-blocks carrying a weight penalty.

After the Brands Hatch debut and disappointing performance at Spa, JW decided that the Len Terry Mirage design needed fundamental changes. They substituted the lighter and more powerful Ford-Cosworth GP engine and even chopped the roof off for Watkins Glen, saving a bit more weight. The car ran quite well, but had an engine failure while in fifth position.

That was in July. By August consistent hard development work had improved the Mirage considerably and it actually led the final, tenth, 1969 World Championship round at the Oesterreichring. Ickx and Oliver had secured fastest lap and practice time, but the steering column bracket broke and the Porsche 917 somewhat ironically gained its first victory instead; the drivers were Jo Siffert and Kurt Ahrens.

The Mirage was taken to a rain-soaked non-Championship round at Imola in September and

THAT'S LIFE *for a long distance mechanic. Cuoghi with 'lots of jackets on underneath to keep me warm', refuels the Siffert Porsche 917 at Le Mans*

Working on the winning Porsche

scored its only victory of the season after some slick tyre-changing and Ermanno's attention to blanking off the radiators to help overcome a worse misfire than afflicted many other damp rivals. 'In our case the water was not getting in, but the engine was running too cold, so I warm him up this way!' was Cuoghi's memory of the weekend.

However, the Mirage was not to become the JW weapon for 1970/71. The car that won at Oesterreichring in that last 1969 round was, for JW's second bid to find a competitive car had been successful beyond anyone's dreams. The idea was that JW and Gulf would run a factory-backed team of Porsche 917s. Having been beaten by the Slough-based team's GT40s in that classic Le Mans last lap epic, Porsche were exploring the true meaning of the phrase 'if you can't beat them . . .'

However, though the Porsche flat twelve-cylinder design had won at Oesterreichring, the exciting Weissach brainchild of a team led by Dr Ferdinand Piech was not without its problems, as driver Brian Redman told me. 'That Oesterreichring meeting was the only time I was temperamental about driving a racing car! I was classed as a good number 2 over the years to Ickxy and Seppi (Siffert) by not creating huge fusses: I just got in and drove the car the way the number 1 driver set it up. I got to Oesterreichring, which I had never been to before, to drive a car I had never sat in before, the Porsche 917 with Seppi. As usual Seppi did most of the practice driving. Now at that time the factory 917 was a *very* tricky car to handle *indeed*. At first nobody would drive it, and after my four laps only at that Austrian track I was all for going home. For the first time I just kicked up a fuss and they had to move all the partnerships around. I drove with Attwood in a 908 and that's why Siffert scored the car's first win with Ahrens co-driving!'

After the Austrian win for the 917, Porsche had organized a test session at the fast circuit which Cuoghi attended along with the JW team. It was time for JW to see what they would be taking on in 1970.

Redman recalled the crucial point in the sessions for me. 'They had Seppi's flat-back, open, CanAm 917 there as well as the usual Porsche bodywork closed 917 of the kind that was so unstable to drive. In the Spyder 917 I knocked off *four seconds* from our best time in the ordinary 917 over the weekend. To make the point about the closed car I went out in that and repeated our weekend time, just to show I wasn't mucking about. . . .'

Cuoghi takes up the story: 'We went down to see the car, to assist in the testing and hear what the driver impressions of that car were. If you remember the car was undrivable, and Le Mans has proved it. . . . Anyway Brian was very upset about the car and said he could not drive it. They have the 917 open, mid-tails, long tails, short tails—every tails! Brian just was not happy, so I was looking at the CanAm car against the 917 closed car. The front part was OK, the same in both cars. The cockpit, it didn't really matter: it was shaped like an egg, couldn't really affect either way the aerodynamic of the car.

'So I am looking at the tails and I say that the only thing we have not got to compare is the flat back of the CanAm car with the up and down body of the closed car. I suggest we put a big sheet on top of the car, to cover all the shape of the fastback to produce a closed CanAm car and see what he is like.

'Some of them 'ave laughed at me on the beginning, but considering we were in a bit of drama, they stop laughing and we make a big sheet. We cut round the shape at the back, just a flat sheet without even the hole in the middle for the back view. After an hour's work we have riveted and PK-it on. Tank tape, everything we got to get it on over the ordinary bodywork, it stretches right over the rear wing.

'Brian went out and he say it is a different car! Now you can *drive* the car. . . .

'Undoubtedly it needed a lot of work still to do on the body, but it had proved what needed to be done and they use this as the basis for the 917K (K for *kurz* in German, meaning short).

'So my first working encounter with the 917 was a very successful one. At least we have managed in a short while to make the car quick and safer. Not often you can do this. . . .

'Generally I was surprised at the enormous facilities at Porsche, and on the car. The machining was wonderful, but I was also surprised that the chassis was of an aluminium spaceframe. It was all done with big, thick weld and we never expected it would last very long.

'The chassis was not so advanced as the rest of the car with that super body moulded on top. The chassis was a funny looking thing, but very effective in strength.

'During the winter we, the teams of mechanics inside JW, went down to Stuttgart for a few weeks to learn all about the car, its assemblies, everything. That was interesting and enjoyable, because they told us every little thing we need to know about the car.

'WE SPEAK *the same language*', Cuoghi simply said of this picture. It depicts Rodriguez telling Alan Hern, David Yorke and Cuoghi how it is out there

RODRIGUEZ AT *the circuit he loved, in the car he enjoyed driving so much. Here he is on his way to leading the JW 1–2 at Spa-Francorchamps, 1971, in the 12-cylinder 917 with its little rear aerofoil. This is the slowest part of the track, La Source hairpin*

'We were studying this at Zuffenhausen, but we also went up to the Weissach test track, where all the racing people are working as scientists for the company too today. I spent a bit longer there than some people, doing things like two weeks on the gearbox, three weeks on the engine, weeks on the chassis all point-by-point. They were *very* thorough! Porsche had a very good way of telling you things too, very clear with complete co-operation so we understand how to strip and rebuild a gearbox, how to maintain the chassis in the smallest details. They took so much trouble, it's unbelievable.

'They even show us where they are going to move inside Weissach for the racing department . . . all the tanks they do for the Army . . . even the gearboxes for those tanks!

Of course, one of the test drivers take us around the track: it was a funny place like an English country road, but very useful for testing. Tiny, but they can reproduce anything there.

'The routine for us would be that we would have three cars altogether, two for racing and one spare. Our job was to do all the assembly and race track work, but the engines were sent from Stuttgart. We did the reconditioning of the gearbox at JW and, towards the end of the 1970 season, John Wyer had organized for us to do work on the engines at Slough. We did not do the race engines, but the ones used for practice and things like that,' Cuoghi concluded.

In fact the Wyer team, like the early factory cars, started with a 4.5-litre version of the fabulous air-cooled flat 12 and switched over to the 4.9-litre motor by the time this practice and test engine assembly routine came into play.

The Porsche 917 belonged to a generation of sports cars built specifically to get around some international rulings which provided the most spectacular long-distance racing seen in Europe. History will probably adjudge the 917 and its rival Ferrari 512 series in much the same way as Auto Unions and Mercedes-Benz of the thirties were spoken of by enthusiasts forty years after they had dominated Grand Prix racing.

This time there were no sinister political reasons behind the appearance of such powerful sports cars. Just the fact that the international controlling body of motor sport had decreed that 5-litre cars (or those over 3 litres more correctly) should be built in some sort of series production. They did not seriously think that the manufacturers would *each* go out and construct twenty-five of the most powerful racing cars ever seen to qualify.

Sure enough, they had reckoned without Porsche's desire to win outright after years of playing class or index of performance winner, while Ford and Ferrari slugged it out in the headlines. So Porsche took the controlling FIA body's words literally and constructed an initial twenty-five of the 917 model, all with over 550 bhp apiece, the most sophisticated cross-drilled disc brakes seen, space-frame chassis housing the mid-mounted 4.5-litre motor and accommodation that could and did serve two people when required.

As we have heard the original bodywork of 1969 was efficient enough at allowing the car its 200 mph head (on a circuit such as Le Mans with a three-mile-plus straight) but did not have the kind of predictable handling that Porsche drivers were used to from the fabulously light 908 3-litre series which had provided the bulk of Porsche's wins in their 1969 Championship year.

However, the Porsche 917 in JW Gulf colours was truly a different animal. For a start the blue and orange paintwork gave these massively powerful two-seaters a grace that they had lacked in stark white. The Formula 1-style wide wheels were hidden by the flowing lines, save from square-on at the rear, where the upswept tail exposed a wealth of tubes, wiring and menacing exhaust pipes that said Racer with a capital R and the assurance of Porsche power beneath.

Frequently you would see a master like Siffert or Redman just pottering around the paddock with the cars chuffing away as on a shopping errand. To see the same coupé snarling its way around the Daytona banking at over 200 mph in a four-wheel drift, or swishing through a downpour at Brands Hatch in bursts of sheer power and car control as Rodriguez added to his wet-weather repertoire, was to remember that the 917 was partially tamed by that revised body. It still took a driver of real talent to make it a front-runner!

Some people did convert them into road cars subsequently, demonstrating the sheer flexibility of the engine—but it was happier at the original near-8500 rpm redline, a masterful driver in the forward 'cockpit', and anything from a 1000-kilometre 'dash' (still longer than the usual Grand Prix!) to a twenty-four-hour marathon ahead.

JW's driving strength comprised three absolute sports car top-liners and one slightly unknown. Although they appeared in JW cars, Jo Siffert, the German-speaking Swiss, and 'our Brian' Redman from Lancashire, were employed by Porsche.

JW employed Cuoghi's Mexican hero Rodriguez and paired him to the comparatively unknown Leo

Kinnunen: like the rally drivers from his country, Kinnunen was quickly dubbed the Flying Finn, and the tubby little driver soon adopted the motto on his crash helmet.

'I was not too happy at the beginning about Kinnunen as co-driver, but he turned out not too bad. He had been driving well in Porsches in his own country and other places and looked as though he would be quick, so JW signed him up.' Communication was quite difficult with Kinnunen, as he spoke little English, but his performance in the Targa Florio round of the Championship (which Cuoghi did not attend, along with most of the JW personnel that year) was worth his retainer on its own. Leo was one and a half *minutes* under Elford's lap record for the 44.7-mile track!

And so JW arrived at the traditional Daytona Continental opening Championship round. It was a dramatic twenty-four hours that year, running from 31 January to 1 February, and some likened the race to the finish of the 1969 Le Mans. . . .

With Fiat's backing, Ferrari were able to get their 5-litre V12 512S into the fray. At Daytona three such works cars were entered and two for privateers: Porsche had four 917s on hand, including

JOSEPH SIFFERT *was the only other man apart from Rodriguez to really wring the utmost from the fearsome Porsche 917s*

SIMPLY THE *greatest in Cuoghi's estimation, though he could see the faults that made this generous Mexican a complete competitor. In wet weather only Jacky Ickx was in the same class*

one privateer, one for Porsche Salzburg (a season-long arrangement, Vic Elford as the principal thorn in JW's side), but Ferrari had a couple of basic problems. One was that they had started behind Porsche in the 5-litre sports car homologation race. The second was that they were a front-line Formula 1 team trying to beat Jochen Rindt in what was to tragically turn out to be the Austrian's posthumous World Championship year. The third major factor was the car itself. Some sources quoted it as weighing up to 200 pounds more than the Porsche 917, which is possible considering that the Ferrari had a four-valve-per-cylinder (forty-eight-valve) water-cooled motor and a steel space frame reinforced by alloy plates.

Cuoghi commented that the Ferrari engine was actually easier to work on than the Porsche, which had central power take-off via gears from the crankshaft and a massive air-cooling fan shrouding everything on top. Like the weight, power outputs quoted for the Ferrari varied from 560–600 bhp, while that for the Porsche 917 was said to be in the 600 bhp region after the adoption of the 4.9-litre engine, needed when it was realized how fast the Ferraris were on the banking of the American tracks. It seems likely that the Ferrari did have a little more power than the Porsche two-valve layout, which also had air-cooling, power-draining devices, but JW had proved before that good mechanics and drivers allied to a reliable car were *the* ingredients in long-distance racing . . . not bhp figures and talk of fabulous top speeds.

Other opposition at Daytona included a team of Matra 3-litre prototypes, forerunners of a highly successful outfit later in the seventies. Others to contest World Championship events with 3-litre cars during the season included Ferrari and Alfa-Romeo, but in 1970 the extra 2 litres was too much for the agile, often Formula 1-inspired machinery. Later on the 5- versus 3-litre equation would grow more even.

At Daytona JW scored their third twenty-four-hour race win in four starts (two Le Mans, one of two Daytonas 1968–70) with Rodriguez and Kinnunen getting off to a good start. 'We had only small problems on Pedro's car,' Cuoghi remembered, 'mainly of the bodywork—taping in the headlights like on the other 917s (the units were falling out) and so the car was covered in tank tape at the end.'

The sister car did not have such a restful event, as can be judged from the fact that it finished forty-five laps behind! At first Siffert was pulling away from a battle between pole-position man Andretti's Ferrari and Rodriguez, but after three hours Redman brought the car in with a brake line adrift after a Firestone had failed and disintegrated: almost certainly that failure was prompted by one of many track debris punctures suffered during the

THE 917S PARADE *at Brands Hatch in 1970. Rodriguez put in an amazing drive following an incident for which he was black-flagged, to win in the car he shared with Leo Kinnunen. The winning car is 10: Siffert/Redman's number 9 (second in queue) was classified twentieth though not running at the finish*

North American qualifying events at Daytona and Sebring. That cost seventeen minutes, the stop including headlamp replacement.

Inspired driving had the second JW car in second position again after three hours, Siffert coping very well considering he had only recently recovered from a broken ankle in a karting accident! In the early hours of the morning Seppi's car was back in to have a ten-minute stop to replace a broken Bilstein (it was *that* rough), but the real drama came just after seven in the morning when the car was brought in with clutch failure.

Ermanno lent a hand and recalled, 'It is an odd story. We have had the cars only a couple of weeks before the race and we are still a bit inexperienced with it at the track. We always had a couple of men from Porsche to help us and Siffert's car has this clutch problem. For my knowledge, our knowledge, the car could not finish the race. What we did, on Mr Wyer's orders, was start to push the car away into the paddock. Helmuth Flegl, the Porsche engineer, he says "you can replace the clutch". So instead we make a big U-turn and come back on the pit! Well, we did replace the clutch and it did

get back in the race, but to *our* knowledge at that time it would have taken too long.'

The 917 resumed the race in fourth place, having lost a good eighty minutes on the clutch change. Redman put in a typical hard-working stint and the retirement of a private Ferrari boosted them to third pretty quickly. The Porsche still had thirty-nine laps to make up on Andretti and Ickx in their 512S, but that Ferrari ran into such trouble, breaking part of the chassis beneath the gearbox (man it really is *tough* in the States!), that the Porsche was soon within five laps of second place. When Siffert took over he was really fired up, surviving one really hairy sideways moment on the grass before bearing down on the now-wounded Ferrari to unlap the Porsche repeatedly, until JW were back in number one and two positions with just a few hours to go. There was some confusion over lap placings towards the end that resulted in Siffert putting in some very rapid laps to overhaul the Ickx/Andretti Ferrari, but the lap-scorers decided they were three laps apart at the end. Mind you Seppi was probably just booting out the emotional fury felt when poor Redman had brought the car in with less than an hour to go and ruffled bodywork that required a five-minute pit stop and copious helpings of tank tape.

'Mr Wyer normally got us a place somewhere in the States to stay between Daytona and Sebring, so we spend six weeks in Pittsburgh with the cars at the Gulf place. We had all the facilities at Pittsburgh, and we needed them because we made some changes . . . not all good, I can tell you!

'We had hubs on the front with one retaining bolt, but they have realized that this titanium bolt might, perhaps, not be strong enough. Remember Sebring has a lot of old concrete and bad roads. So they put on four 6- or 7-mm bolts with a retaining flange instead of one big one in the middle. But they miscalculate . . . when the wheel was turning round, all the load was on one bolt!

'So, after six hours we start breaking the left front, where there is more load. Nine hours breaking the right front. About twelve hours the left front again! On both cars we had to replace discs, hubs, it was a disaster!' In fact the mechanics did manage to cope with this and what was to become a familiar problem—the engine cooling fan impersonating a helicopter and flying off vertically! Ermanno and the boys had a pretty busy race for they tried splinting up the tail section on their car when Kinnunen clipped a Mustang, eventually resorting to the complete tail section from the training car. When Siffert's 917 eventually ran out of spare bolts and associated front suspension parts it was retired and Seppi was put in to share with Rodriguez, this dynamite combination restrained sufficiently to limp to fourth place.

With twenty-two minutes to go the Gulf Porsche had been leading—Ferrari suffering catastrophe upon catastrophe—but then the bolts had sheared again. Despite changing the afflicted parts in eight minutes, Rodriguez and Siffert had to settle for fourth overall, while Ferrari celebrated victory in this tortuous battle.

Between Daytona and Sebring the JW mechanics had worked on cooling ducts for the drivers, and shock absorbers, plus wider wheels and the front suspension/hub change mentioned, but for Brands Hatch JW put the 917 on a diet that reduced it from a quoted 2003 pounds to 1900 pounds, the improvement credited by Cuoghi to 'the carbon-fibre reinforcement in the body and as many lightweight metals as possible—though the car was already using plenty of these. We also put it back on a stub axle arrangement instead of the Sebring bolts, and we make the wheel bearings a bit bigger.'

Rodriguez had a brand-new car, while Siffert and Redman took over an unraced test and development chassis. Practice was dry, but the 917s from JW had to be content with second and third row times, the open Ferraris and the Salzburg 917 up ahead. However, it did rain towards the end of practice and Siffert went out to make sure the car was OK on wets, something most rival teams ignored.

Race day saw the kind of weather for which Britain is famous, a heavy downpour, but it did not prevent over 20,000 sturdy fans turning out to watch the aces wrestle with hundreds of horses over a recently resurfaced track for six hours.

The conditions were diabolical enough for the powerful cars to spin on the straight and things were not going too well for JW.

'Pedro get a telling off from Mr Syrett, the guv'nor of the course,' Cuoghi recounted. 'They say he has been overtaking people under the yellow flag and is a *very* naughty boy: also he does not come in when the black flag is out. When they finish telling him, Pedro, 'e takes off all sideways with the back tyres on fire!' Siffert had also been early into the pits with a puncture.

The drive Rodriguez put in that day was not about to be altered by the pit lane argy-bargy. He just went faster and faster, 'making all the others look as though they don't belong out there,' in Cuoghi's words. Certainly, anyone who was there will not forget the moment when Rodriguez had worked his way up to leader Elford's Salzburg Porsche. The off-white 917 braved the pit straight with Rodriguez in the Gulf car, both billowing out long, high roosters of white spray, shimmering against menacing battleship grey skies above. Wriggling at 130 mph plus through the puddles on their broad tyres, the two 917s dived for the notorious Paddock Hill bend together. 'Pedro 'as the inside and there's no way Elford is going to get around faster,' Cuoghi chuckled.

'For most of the race Pedro is leading Seppi, but always Pedro is leading. Kinnunen gets about ten minutes,' Cuoghi reported. 'I think that race was really good for the spectators; Pedro and Siffert drove just a marvellous race. A few spins, but it was pretty good!' Siffert's car was eliminated when Redman spun at Westfield, but the Swiss had shown his class when taking thirty seconds off Kinnunen while the Finn was doing the legally required co-driver's stint after three and a half hours' racing.

Ferrari took three works cars to Monza Park in the suburbs of Milan to try and tip back the balance of winning that had tipped in the direction of the Stuttgart–Salzburg–Slough Porsche alliance. There were *seven* Porsche 917s there to meet them! Less than a fortnight had elapsed since Brands Hatch, but the Porsches were beginning to move into a new era, the works-supported teams from JW and Porsche Salzburg boasting Girling ventilated discs instead of Ate, these discs using GT40-style calipers from the same source.

'It was not the stopping alone we work on,' Cuoghi laughed, 'Siffert is taking pole position with the new 4.9-litre engine, but it is leaking oil so we take them out of that car and race the 4.5 litre.' The increased capacity came from an 86 mm bore instead of 85 mm, and a 70.4 mm stroke in place of 66 mm.

Cuoghi was primarily responsible for chassis 016, the new one Rodriguez and Kinnunen had shared to victory at Brands Hatch. In the States Pedro and Kinnunen had used 015 to win Daytona, and Cuoghi tended the same chassis to fourth at Sebring with Siffert doing a late co-driving stint. As a matter of interest Siffert's regular car in the States was 014 and the spare car was 013: at Brands Hatch Siffert/Redman had 004, so four races into the season JW had already made use of five cars and there is one training car unaccounted for. At that rate it does not take long to use up the homologation run of twenty-five cars—which were something of a customer bargain at £14,000 each, heavily subsidized considering the development costs and materials used.

Back at Monza Cuoghi commented of the 4.9-litre: 'They had realized that they needed the full capacity of the class and that engine was going pretty good. The oil leak was nothing really, just from an oil gallery not a basic part of the engine's strength.' In the race JW's pit work, especially on the refuelling, proved decisive to beat off a really determined and reliable Ferrari 512S pursuit. Rodriguez drove all but thirty-five of 174 laps and *averaged* 144.6 mph for the 4 h 18 m 1.7 s it took for victory—roughly one and a half minutes ahead of the best Ferrari after a race that virtually deserves a book to itself. The place-swopping amongst these fearsome Ferraris and Porsches on Monza's unfettered bankings and long slipstreaming straights was up to Grand Prix standards, and the lap times were faster. The record then stood at 1 m 25.2 s and Elford—who used the 4.9-litre Porsche engine in the Salzburg entry—managed a superb 1 m 24.8 s, a speed of 151.59 mph (244.103 km/h)!

'Unfortunately Siffert and Brian are badly delayed when Seppi 'as to spin avoidin' a slow car and damages the back suspension. But Pedro, I think it is typical of him myself, he stop by the pit and give us all a ride on our car to collect the prizes. That was *nice* of 'im to give us a lift!' That was Cuoghi on the finish of another JW performance that had earned remarks like 'stupendous' and 'matchless efficiency' from the specialist press and showed everyone else why Porsche, a name with a reputation for efficiency, had chosen two years' contract with JW in the first place.

Cuoghi felt that 'in that kind of a race, where you must get the fuel in, tyres change, oil in, *fast* sports car racing is very satisfying for the mechanics'. Staring at the floor he said quietly: I think the team just built up over the years. It was not that way at first, but after a coupla seasons we all got to know each other's way of working and the whole team really could work as one on a pit stop, or if there was trouble. Each man had his own job and *knew* what he must do. Yes, we were the best at the time, no question.'

Ermanno was not too keen on going back to the Targa, but JW maintained a watching brief and sent some help as Porsche took over. Ironically the JW pairing were first and second in special ultra-lightweight 908/3s, and it was by far and away Kinnunen's best performance in an otherwise rather lacklustre year for the Finn.

The sports car schedule of the time was pretty hectic, with nine rounds squeezed in up to July and an artificial extension to the season with Oesterreichring in October. April–May was a particularly crowded period with five races from Brands Hatch on 12 April to the ADAC Nürburgring 1000 km right at the end of May, a fortnight after the other 1000 km classic the other side of the Ardennes—Spa.

Having missed the Targa it was to Spa that Cuoghi next went for one of the most spectacular tests of sheer speed and guts in modern racing annals. In practice Cuoghi and his team worked almost as hard as their little Mexican driver for pole position in 3 m 19.8 s, putting on a slightly longer tail with the central 'valley' filled in to record that time, which was over ten seconds *under* John Surtees's record in the Formula 1 V12 Honda. Despite tyre troubles that afflicted the JW team all weekend, Siffert hogged enough of the driving to take second fastest on 3 m 23.9 s . . . but we really hadn't seen anything yet!

After one of those tyre failures, which occurred while Brian Redman was having a rare practice stint at the wheel, Cuoghi recalled Redman's laconic description of what happens when a tyre deflates suddenly on one of Spa's ultra-fast curves. He said, 'I just sat there with my arms crossed at over 160 mph and wondered if this was the right job for me!'

In the race Cuoghi's crew were able to play a vital role once more, for their refuelling equipment—an overhead gravity feed, while Ferrari struggled with churns and Siffert's crew had trouble with the rig—put Pedro in front. Up to that point it had been a magnificent three-way scrap between the two Gulf 917s (both running 4.9-litre motors now) and Ickx in the chunky Ferrari 512 shared with Surtees. After twenty-one laps Pedro suffered a chunking tyre—in practice the team had gone down from 12.5 wider front-to-rear to two inches less, with shot blasting to the rims to try and prevent the Firestones creeping at the enormous velocities the cars were reaching. It took Cuoghi's men about one and three-quarter minutes to change the cover, so Ickx took over the lead, being well matched in battle with Siffert.

When the cars came in for the second refuelling stops Surtees stepped into Ickx's shoes and Redman into Siffert's, but Pedro was still out there blazing through the valleys at close to 200 mph in his blue and orange ground-to-ground missile. Cuoghi's men had topped up the tanks when they had been forced into that early tyre change. That and a stupendous 3 m 16.5 s lap (an average of over 160 mph on closed public roads!) brought Rodriguez within striking distance of Redman in the other JW car. Redman pushed on to overtake Surtees and Rodriguez did the same, but only briefly. After driving half the distance solo it was time to pit and hand over to Kinnunen. The Finn lasted only until 'the input shaft on the gearbox broke', Cuoghi said mournfully. 'We never have that problem before.'

The Siffert/Redman car went on to win in 4 h 9 m 21.2 s, representing an average for that time of 149.33 mph. Consider that the 8.77-mile circuit had one first-gear hairpin and only two slower corners at that time and you see how fast places like the Masta Kink and Burnenville had to be tackled.

What aerodynamic tricks, apart from the revised tail, did JW and Cuoghi have to resort to on these fast tracks? 'To balance the car we would put a bigger or smaller flap on the rear at either side: a smaller flap for more oversteer, and so on.

'We had two basic spring rates: one for the bumpy type and the softer ones for smoother, faster tracks. The damping was the same Bilstein gas-filled unit.

'The gear ratios for these different tracks were not chosen at Porsche, but by learning in practice that first year. It was an easy gearbox to work on, like a Formula 1 Hewland, but not quite as simple to work on because it has the synchronizers. Still you could change ratios in half an hour or so. It was such a big-capacity engine though, that sometimes you forget to change the ratios for the absolute best choice! We had five gears, but many circuits, like Daytona, we would just run four gears.'

At Nürburgring there was a change in machinery for Cuoghi to work on. Porsche had shuffled around the 908/3s they had taken on the Targa Florio and come up with a brand-new chassis for Siffert and Redman (010), while Rodriguez and Kinnunen had chassis number 011, the car used by Dickie Attwood and rally ace Bjorn Waldegard on the Targa. Describing the latest versions of the open 908 series of sports racers with their flat eight-cylinder engines, Cuoghi simply said: 'It was a fantastic little machine, a smaller, lighter 917! To see the lightweight body and tubular chassis, and the car itself, he looks like a little boat!' The simple square lines certainly did look that way, hiding a gearbox between the engine and final drive differential, pushing the wheels to the extreme rear and the driver virtually between the front wheels.

In practice the JW team dominated the proceedings with Siffert half a second under the F1 record and Rodriguez less than a second slower. In the race it looked to be much the same story, with the JW team leaders driving the immaculate blue and orange machines—each wearing its own sign identification, Pedro's with one broad orange arrow and Siffert's with two. 'Unfortunately Kinnunen crash our car,' Cuoghi remembered, 'and we are in troubles with starting the Siffert car. We put jumper lead on for another battery. It was not enough, so we put 24 volts on. Still not enough, so we put 36 volts. I tell you it start OK!' Full marks for effort, but the engine seized on Seppi pretty quickly, so there was a good reason for the Porsche's disinterest in turning over on the starter....

That Nürburgring victory for Porsche was scored by Elford and Ahrens in another factory 908/3 and another such car secured second place, while Porsche themselves were sure of the Championship title of that year with three rounds remaining.

The race came next though, Le Mans. JW came armed with three 917s. The 4.9-litres went to the normal pairings and a third car with a 4.5-litre engine (026 chassis) to Hobbs and Hailwood. Instead of the tremendously fast but rather unstable long-tail bodywork that Porsche had developed—and with which Elford reached 227 mph on the Mulsanne while setting the fastest practice time (3 m 19.8 s, over 150 mph average)—Wyer opted for a little MIRA wind tunnel development.

'We make a little spoiler to fit in the centre section of the tail,' Cuoghi recounted, 'and this is easy to adjust so the drivers are 'appy with the car.' Detail changes on the Wyer cars included the usual cockpit ducting for longer events; separate oil pipes instead of the chassis oilways within the tubular spaceframe; two batteries; two alternators; and a larger starter motor from Bosch to increase reliability, and quick-change headlamp units within wings that had small internal alloy spaceframes and sheets of alloy protection. The titanium coil springs of extra hard rate that had proven worth while at Daytona were also incorporated in the Le Mans JW specification.

Porsche had made up some heavier-duty gearbox parts, including first and second gears with no radial lubrication oilways and special input shafts with narrow oilways and uprated material specification: these were intended for the 4.9-litre cars.

According to the Le Mans weighbridge the heaviest 917 weighed 1887 pounds and the heaviest Ferrari (and there were four factory cars pitted against six directly factory-backed 917s and two more Porsche-prepared 917s for privateers!) was 2094 pounds. That sounds quite convincing, but since the lightest Ferrari and Porsche examples were each a good 100 pounds lighter than the top weight, the weight question was not as straightforward as many believed at the time. Get a light Ferrari with a top-grade engine and you were on to something, as Roger Penske and Mark Donohue were to later prove!

None of this mattered too much to the JW personnel. They concentrated on making the cars reach the finish, but the 917 was not as kind to them as the GT40 had been. After starting third, fifth and tenth on the grid not a single JW car made it beyond ten hours. 'Pedro's car blew its engine when the shaft to the cooling fan failed. Hailwood he has a crash with Facetti's Alfa while trying to sort himself out! Mike come back and say to Mr Wyer how sorry 'e is and Mr Wyer tell him not to worry: don't ring us, we'll ring you! Siffert is leading for a while, but then that bloody thing come in with a lotta revs on the counter and oil leaking from his exhaust pipes ... it was a bloody disaster this race!'

Cuoghi was a lot more cheerful in 1979 than he could be at the time. Porsche were happy enough though, for at last the 917 had won at Le Mans, the only race that counted with many in business and publicity.

On the surface the penultimate 1970 Championship round was of little importance, Porsche having won both the series and Le Mans, but the North American car market is big enough to pull anyone interested in selling expensive cars, so it was not surprising to see two JW 917s face a pair of factory Ferraris and the Porsche-Salzburg 917 duo at Watkins Glen.

Cuoghi remembers practice best: 'Siffert was not happy with his car, it just was no good compared to Pedro's. So we put Pedro's car in one flat concrete bay and take all the suspension geometry readings off that car. Then we push Siffert's car on the same spot: check everything out—especially bump and rebound settings—and it was quite a long way out. So we put Siffert's car in exactly the same trim and Siffert was very happy with that car. He was going like hell and, during the race when they were just running away from all the others (Siffert having already nudged Andretti in the opening lap), we were waiting for the two cars and they were a bit late. Then Pedro's came by with a big wheelmark on the door, alone! They had been banging each other....' The two Gulf Porsches actually collided when lapping a back marker and zooming together afterwards, Siffert had to pit for a new tyre before he and Redman could get going again, finishing on the same lap as the winning Rodriguez/Kinnunen machine after six tough hours.

Such fierce inter-team driver rivalry would have

worried most equipes, but the JW people from top to bottom seemed remarkably unconcerned about controlling such a passionate pair of drivers as Siffert and Rodriguez. Cuoghi thought, 'It is difficult to say if they liked each other. When they were sitting on the track they were full enemies, like all drivers, they want to win the race. John Wyer was a pretty strong team manager, but at a certain stage the drivers do not listen. I don't recall either of them being given signs to slow them down, but I don't think it would 'ave made any difference at all if they had been told! Siffert was a strong character and driver: Pedro was temperamental and just as good driver . . . what can you do? Just let them do the best they can, and say bye, bye!

'There was no bad feeling afterwards, just the usual driver teasing about what the other 'ad done wrong. They used to spend some time together off the track too, so there were no real bad feelings about it all. I don't think it happened again like at Watkins Glen, but Pedro did once get in contact with the Penske Ferrari; you know that was a very, *very* competitive car!'

There was a long gap then until the final Championship round at Oesterreichring in October. The JW cars arrived with the subtly modified bodywork that they had sported since Le Mans. Distinguished by that rear centre spoiler, the new back, 'gave us less downforce on the centre of the car and more on the back'. Rodriguez took pole position in his last championship round, but the car was in within a few laps of the start with valve gear failure—'then all we can do is push the car away, make sure all the photographers are cleared away and push all the newspaper people out,' Cuoghi said with a grin.

The winning car for Siffert and Redman (then intent on retirement to South Africa, thus leaving the team after this race) was similarly afflicted, but still crawled home at an average of over 120 mph, laps clear of a depleted field. Incidentally the opposition provided was notable for the first appearance of the M-bodywork for the Ferrari 512, Ickx setting fastest lap with the car before electrical troubles sidelined it.

So Porsche had won their title convincingly once more, suffering only one defeat by Ferrari in ten rounds. It was a victory that Cuoghi and colleagues directly benefited from in direct win-bonuses for their fabulous pitwork. The JW team had won seven rounds, including the Targa Florio, which was more of a Porsche effort in truth, and established clearly that their refuelling techniques and tyre changing speed were unmatched, even by the works mechanics working for Porsche-Salzburg on many occasions.

Cuoghi talked about how the bonus scheme had arrived at JW. 'Ickx has introduced this system because all the English mechanics in Formula 1 and 2, they get some percentage of the prize money. Ickx talked to David Yorke about it, and we got five to six per cent because of Jacky's initiative. Very good, we think!'

I asked with my tongue slightly in cheek if being a mechanic had ever become reasonably well paid. I was surprised by the straightforward frankness of the reply. 'It was very poor for a long time. Even now it is not very good. The average racing mechanic now [June 1979] is making about £100 to £110 a week. Take the taxes out of that and you realize a bus driver make the same amount of money. There is no overtime: perhaps you get a day off, or you get the travel, but there is no way anyone will pay for all those hours.'

For Cuoghi there was the additional factor of living away from home and family for so many years, though Lauda once told me that he thought the life satisfied the Gipsy in Ermanno's soul—but in rather more direct speech than that!

Ermanno recalled that 'when Ickx won Le Mans in 1969 the bonus money was £150–£170 a person. That was good money, but unfortunately it does not happen too often! Mind you it's true that it was quite good with all the winning we did at JW, but today [he was in the middle of a rather barren Brabham Alfa season at the time] it's getting worse. *If* we ever win the mechanic get about £200 a person, but most Formula 1 mechanics are paid by points at the rate of some £20 per point, so a win is worth about £180 for the nine points.'

However, Cuoghi was at great pains to point out what Brabham boss Bernie Ecclestone had done for the mechanics' working hours. 'Practice would finish at eight or nine in the evening with an early start needed in the morning too. Mr Ecclestone, 'e has reduce the practice time where it is still more than enough, and there are reasonable hours, where you have time to re-prepare the car properly.'

1971

The 1971 season did not promise so much interest. In the last year of allowing the 5-litre production sports cars there was not a great deal of interest in taking Porsche on directly, Ferrari promising indirect support to those who ran the 512 series in its lighter and better-looking M form, while they got on with developing their flat twelve 312P prototype in readiness for a serious title assault under the new 3-litre 1972 regulations.

However, Alfa Romeo decided to have a real go with their 3-litre cars and Matra also appeared. Pennsylvanian Chevrolet dealer and racing entrepreneur, millionaire Roger Penske, fielded a beautiful blue Sunoco-sponsored Ferrari 512M that came to Europe, as well as injecting much-needed interest to the American rounds.

Porsche and JW altered quite a few things in their bid to take a fourth successive title and send the 917 into the history books with yet more victories to its credit. The Porsche-Salzburg team went, though some of the personnel went along with the cars (three 917s) to Hans-Dieter Dechent's Martini-Shell-backed team, the cars looking a lot more appealing in silver with Martini striping than they usually had in 1970.

JW had lost Redman to retirement and decided to drop Kinnunen, many observers at the time feeling that the Finn simply had not been up to the job in the majority of rounds. After a typically thorough search amongst the prospects, the Gulf-backed seats were filled by two Britons. Jack Oliver, then recovering from the experience of being a Lotus number 2 Grand Prix driver and a spell at BRM, and Derek Bell, who had caused a great stir in the sixties by attracting a Ferrari contract: alas it didn't work out in the Championship way that Mike Hawthorn's once did.

The 917s for JW were externally little changed, but Porsche pushed on with mechanical developments on the engine, gearbox and braking side during the season. The nett result was that some engines were out to the full 86.8 mm bore on the usual 4.9 version's stroke. This provided 4998 cc (4907 cc previously and up to 620 bhp), crankshafts made from one solid steel billet instead of two-piece built-up construction. Carbon-fibre was used more extensively in the bodies and beryllium disc brakes were made or cast-iron discs made even lighter by the cross-drilling process.

The season started on a confused and tragic note, 'and it was one of the worst we ever had for drivers being killed,' Cuoghi reminded me. The series began in Buenos Aires with a 1000 km race attracting a very full entry, including JW Automotive Porsche 917s in Gulf colours for Rodriguez/Oliver (the latter having an accident that delayed its practice little: it still took pole for Pedro!) and Siffert/Bell. Incidentally none of those drivers was with the team at the end of the year, except Bell.

On the front row with Rodriguez was Ignazio Giunti in the new 312P. The Ferrari proved very quick in the race too and was actually leading again on lap 37 after the bigger cars had made their refuelling stops. Then the young Roman works Ferrari driver pulled out of the slipstream of Mike Parkes in the bigger Ferrari 512 and was confronted with Jean-Pierre Beltoise pushing his Matra unsteadily in search of fuel....

'I knew of Giunti as an Italian driver of course. I had talked with him a couple of times, but I was not a close friend. We have heard a bang and seen a car on fire coming toward us. It was not very far from us at all. It has happened so quick, but as the cars slow down I run with many others to see what we can do. The car had been on fire a long, long time... too long, so we see what we can do. There is nothing. It was a terrible thing, a complete and total disaster....' I have not told Ermanno's full account; it is too horrible. We sometimes forget what careless organization and a moment of rule-breaking can do when added to the dangers of motor sport. Nobody seems to remember the grim lessons.

The second round, at Daytona for the twenty-four-hour annual thrash, was really hard on the JW mechanics and drivers, for the Penske Ferrari in royal blue was gleaming in the Florida sun. The twinkle of sun from the body was echoed in the engine bay, where Chevrolet V8 specialists Traco had allegedly built the most powerful Ferrari engine of all. Shared between Mark Donohue and David Hobbs this hybrid proved a really worthwhile opponent, practising over a second faster than Pedro to take pole. The opening laps of the race were a fight between Rodriguez and Donohue. After thirty laps, fifty-four minutes' racing, the duel switched to the pits. The American crew on the Ferrari, specialists in long-distance saloon car racing, had their car fuelled, screen wiped and tyres checked in 12.5 seconds! JW's boys took 20.5 seconds: this was serious stuff! Another hour's duelling with Donohue ahead and the Penske car was in for forty-four seconds, refuelling going well but baulked by the need for rear tyres and two Penske men diving for the same air wheelbrace! Cuoghi and company trimmed their car service to thirty-five seconds, but needed no rear tyres. That left the situation of Siffert leading, but about to stop, and Pedro leading Donohue by three seconds ... now you see the role pit staff played in the JW success story. The point was emphasized when the Ferrari lost its lead and suffered over ten minutes in the pits when Penske's team had to rewire the alternator: JW cars carried a spare ready to switch into the system.

At little more than a sixth of the total distance

Bell found the Siffert car dumping all its oil from a split crankcase and that was most definitely that.

Cuoghi takes up the story, 'a few hours from the finish with Pedro and Oliver well ahead I thought I would be clever and change into some clean things: the Ferrari had crashed and lost over an hour, and Pedro was miles ahead of anything else. So I get a nice shirt on and laugh at the other boys in the dirty overalls. Hell! Rodriguez comes in with the box in top gear only. It was a cow to work on, really hot inside and with all the synchronizer hubs jammed on the shaft. While one of our teams strip out the spare gearbox we get this broken one apart [the rules forbid simply changing the gearbox—J.W.] with pullers and a big 'ammer!'

Some ninety-five minutes later the Porsche rejoined in second place. Three-quarters of an hour later it had overhauled the private NART Ferrari 512M of Ronnie Bucknum/Tony Adamaowicz, and there Rodriguez and Oliver stayed to finish a lap clear, having covered over 2600 miles in twenty-four hours at an average of 109.203 mph, despite being over one and a half hours stationary in the pits! But without mechanics like that. . . .

'I THOUGHT *I'd be smart'*, *Cuoghi stands with his JW compatriots towards the close of the 1971 Daytona 24 hours, his nice clean pants and shirt assaulted by the need for late-race gearbox work on the leading Rodriguez 917. It was worth it*

Right: CUOGHI SPRAWLS *on the front wing of the winning Porsche at that Daytona 24 hours. Ramirez supports the door while Pedro unfurls the flag*

Working on the winning Porsche

Cuoghi simply said, 'I don't ever change into something clean before the end of the race again!'

The third, Sebring, round was a tough race too, Ferraris from Penske and the works filling the front row with the JW cars a little off the pace in practice. In the race Siffert recorded the fastest lap seen thus far at Sebring, averaging over 124 mph on the bumpy airfield track that threads its way against a background of parked and operational aircraft. Then Seppi ran out of fuel and was penalized four laps for accepting a lift on a motorbike to go back and get some more! After five of twelve scheduled hours Donohue was in firm command of the race and coming up to lap Pedro on a tight right-hander that led on to the main straight.

The two collided and damage was pretty heavy—enough to cost both cars a chance of victory. The mechanics managed to tape and cut the heavily damaged front portion of the Porsche into a semblance of order, but the bitterly upset Penske protested that the car should not be allowed to run with so much bodywork missing. Derek Bell recalled that Cuoghi had pretty well made up a replacement front side by the time the race ended!

Working on the winning Porsche

PITWORK WAS *at the very heart of the JW team's success and here this shot from 1971 shows the team in full cry. Despite the damp conditions Cuoghi encourages his fellow workers on the Rodriguez 917*

Recalling Siffert's fuel-less state Cuoghi commented: 'He had been driving hard and the warning light was on. We also had a reserve tap, but that must have been switched on too.'

Sebring brought them a fourth and fifth. Brands Hatch had its share of disappointments, Rodriguez actually having to abandon his car when the petrol was not getting through and Siffert being badly delayed by both gearbox troubles and wheelnuts that would not come off. Today Cuoghi is not convinced as to what caused their problems. 'On the Siffert car the wheelnut had simply seized up. I don't know if some dirt had got inside, but we could not undo it; we had to practically chisel it off! On Pedro's car I think there must have been something wrong with the refuelling system of connected churns that we used. You have to tip it over, and I think some glue that was used on the connections must have got in, and probably blocked up the pumps.'

JW were represented at the Le Mans tests that year, with Oliver and Bell staying rather longer than Siffert (who was committed to the Spanish Grand Prix for BRM) to assess the latest Porsche long-tail body. Oliver managed a lap in 3 m 13.6 s (155.53 mph), phenomenal speed by any standards.

JW gathered a great deal of data using Girling recording equipment in the training car—which was 016, winner of three Championship rounds for JW the previous year.

For Monza the Gulf Porsches had modified bodywork again. 'We try two or three tails by now. This one is more or less the same as the K, but it accelerates the air better toward the rear, where it has these vertical stabilizers. We found these pretty useful, even on slower circuits. There were two different types, the longer one for faster tracks.' They had few problems running away to a convincing first and second overall (Pedro's car ahead), averaging 146.21 mph for four hours. Rodriguez put in a fastest lap equivalent to 153.12 mph. There was one unusual problem associated with the high refuelling towers they were using to dump fuel into the car at a rate faster than they could clean the windscreens. Cuoghi explained: 'When you refuel with these high rigs, you hear the car *creaking*! The pressure increase between the top, inside the tank, and the bottom as you dump a full fuel load down a 100 mm-bore pipe is terrible. You can see the car expanding! I think that is why the Martini cars cracked their chassis in this race, we were just lucky. We did once have a 917 chassis crack, but it was not a fundamental thing, just at the rear end, I think.'

However, they did have another refuelling drama during this clockwork 1–2 Monza performance when the fuelling juggernaut pipe—which allowed 110 litres to flow in within four seconds—actually split. 'Everywhere is fifty gallons of fuel, and we are swimming everywhere with definitely no smoking,' said Cuoghi. The split was repaired with Gulf's help, for it was they who had helped provide these high refuelling facilities which speeded pit stops so much from Brands Hatch onward.

The cars ran at Spa-Francorchamps in their original short tail K-guise, though the training car was equipped with the vertical stabilizers, and completely dominated the weekend. Rodriguez and Siffert were committed on the Formula 1 front during practice. So it was that 'new boy' Derek Bell got a chance to show what he could do with a 3 m 16 s lap (a little under Pedro's 1970 record) that was enough for pole position for Siffert/Bell.

In the race it was obvious that Pedro was not going to settle for second to anyone and the two Gulf Porsches motored into history slipstreaming each other, smashing the lap record and leaving any trace of opposition trampled, especially as the unlucky Ferrari 312P prototype had once again found a slow car to fall over. To this day Derek Bell maintains that Rodriguez and Siffert collided again in their fight to take fastest lap and victory, but neither Cuoghi nor some reporters of the time recollect it. However, co-drivers Bell and Oliver were drafted in for the closing stages of the race because Yorke felt he had a better chance of controlling them!

The Rodriguez and Siffert battle had motored into history, via the *Guinness Book of Records*, as Rodriguez and Oliver recorded the fastest-ever winning speed for a road race. In 4 h 1 m 9.7 s they averaged 154.765 mph (249.070 km/h) around the daunting Belgian track. To Siffert went the honour of recording the fastest-ever road racing lap at 3 m 14.6 s, an average of 161.98 mph (260.842 km/h). Those who saw the pair running up to 200 mph through the hills and valleys of the wooded Ardennes countryside are unlikely to see a finer motor racing sight. Spa itself was forced to adopt chicanes, the sports car formula changed the following year, and finally the old course was dropped in favour of a shorter circuit in 1979. However, a 3-litre Matra did break the 917 lap record in 1973.

Once again the Porsche factory masterminded the Targa Florio operation, JW's senior management attending with two mechanics looking after refuelling. For Cuoghi and the majority of the staff it was a welcome respite as there was the Nürburgring 1000 km to attend at the end of May with Le

APRIL 1971 *and Rodriguez in the leading Gulf 917 battles with Ickx in the agile Ferrari 312P. Siffert looks on; he and Bell finished third while Rodriguez suffered a fuel line blockage*

Mans a fortnight later.

The Targa had not been a success. Alfa-Romeo's ever-present 3-litre *Tipo* 33 prototypes had burst through to finish first and second after a spate of accidents and breakages had put the Porsche 908/3s out of the running, poor Brian Redman suffering burns that scarred his cheerful face having returned from his South African 'retirement' quite rapidly!

At Nürburgring Porsche again lent JW and the other favourite private team (Dechent-Martini), the Targa 908s, but JW still had less fortune than usual. There was also the problem of Jacky Ickx/Clay Regazzoni in the Ferrari 312P: it was simply in a class of its own at this circuit with Ickx at the wheel.

While the Ferrari battled away from the Alfas and Porsches easily in the opening stages, neither of the JW-coloured 908s was giving the usual race-dominating performance. Siffert did fight his way into the top three, but then his car developed a handling problem that later affected Rodriguez too ... it broke the chassis! Cuoghi reported, 'Siffert's car dropped its gearbox virtually on the track with the wheels at the back going every way. So then David Yorke put Seppi in with Pedro, but this car too had the problem. It was not the most important part of the back chassis, but by the end of the race the body was collapsing over to one side and he practically lost the engine! We could not repair it, so they just had to drive on.' That they did very effectively, Pedro blocking out Austrian Dr Helmut Marko and Dutchman Gijs van Lennep by yards to take second place, with the car wobbling its way all round the demanding Nürburgring!

The stuff of which legends are made....

In fact Gerard Larrousse and Vic Elford had won and Porsche finished 1–2–3 after the Ferrari developed an unquenchable thirst for water, so Porsche had achieved that fourth straight Championship title at the Nürburgring that weekend.

There was still Le Mans to win though, and Penske were bringing their famed Ferrari 512M for another crack at beating JW. The Slough-based team had two 917L models (L for *Lang* or long bodywork) which had partial enclosure of the rear wheels for Rodriguez/Oliver and Siffert/Bell. A third JW-Gulf entry was for Richard Attwood and Herbert Muller, the latter deputizing for the injured Redman. Attwood and Muller used the normal K-body with vertical stabilizing fins: incidentally the car for Rodriguez and Oliver was the one that 'Jack O' had been timed in at a reported 241.1 mph on the Mulsanne in those April trials; the other car was brand new. Although the long-tailed cars were harder to drive, a large aerofoil across the rear had removed the worst of the instability that always was the complaint with more aerodynamically efficient Porsche 917 bodywork. Incidentally the JW cars in L form carried no extra weight penalty, but the third car was the heaviest 917 at Le Mans that year. It registered 2073 pounds, compared to 2111 pounds for the Penske Ferrari 512M.

In the race neither of the 917Ls had any luck, though both led at some time in the first eleven hours. As Cuoghi remembers it their problems were set off by 'the bloody driveshaft. We change the uprights and hubs too, for the shaft had led to a seizure in the hub. We 'ave find it very difficult to work on the car because of the long tail. The rear axle is so far up the car that you have to lay yourself in the middle of the body, change the halfshaft, hubs and stuff like that. I remember that during the night, it was a terrible job. Disconnecting the shaft was bloody uncomfortable—on the shorter tail you do this job in a minute!

'It was a shame you know, because they were 1–2–3 at 10 pm, and then the troubles all start! Elford has one of our old problems on the Martini car, I remember, the fan flying off into the fields again. The reason for this to keep happening is because it was such a small coupling with two bolts retaining the thing that sometimes the bolts were shearing off!

'Because of the handling problems on both cars—at first thought to be because the shock absorbers are failing—we change the back suspension, complete corner. Of course it was a terrible job to get past the complete undershield and all the tubes everywhere. Impossible, but you 'ave to do it!

'At 3 o'clock in the morning, or so, we are all standing around feeling pretty cold when Pedro's car is in again with a split oil pipe on the engine oil gallery: in fact it is the blanking boss that has split. We have tried everything to try and stop it leaking with Araldite and so on, but it is still leaking: we 'ave even tried to make another catch tank for that oil to return it to the main tank because you cannot add oil when you like at Le Mans.

'Then, when we try, and try again, the engine would not go. It would *not* go any more, for some bloody reason it 'as seized. I know it was leaking oil, but I think the real reason is because of the long

Opposite: SIFFERT IN *the tail-finned, 5-litre JW 917 at Monza in 1971. It was the scene of another JW 1–2 victory, this car finishing second, even though winner Rodriguez suffered gearbox trouble in the four speed unit they used for the race*

BRUTE BEING *tamed! Siffert and Bell shared at Spa for the 1971 edition of the 1000 km, following Rodriguez/Oliver home, but having the compensation of a new 162 mph plus lap record on the public road circuit*

tail and the air-cooled motorbike-type engine, it is just getting too hot under there.

'At virtually the same time we are visited by the Attwood car—and this one 'as no fifth gear. That is useful at Le Mans (!) so we must change that.' It took them twenty-seven minutes, but it was well worth while....

Oil loss was also the problem on the Siffert/Bell car. It lasted until daylight, but then expired, for they just could not keep oil inside the gearbox.

However, there was a reward for JW as the Attwood/Muller 917K performed steadily after its fifth gear replacement and finally finished second, two laps behind the winning Martini Porsche of

NOVEMBER 1970 *and Cuoghi (his finger bandaged) talks to Rodriguez at a Gulf party in England. Ermanno's wife, Maria Grazia, completes the conversationalists*

Marko/van Lennep. Rodriguez also went into the history books again, recording the fastest lap seen at Sarthe to date, 3 m 18.7 s (151.81 mph).

Incidentally the Penske Ferrari retired in the opening stages of the race with suspected piston failure and the race that year was notable for the lack of opposition to the 917s as neither Ferrari nor Alfa-Romeo bothered to venture their 3-litre machinery upon a race that reduced forty-nine starters to thirteen finishers.

There were only two more rounds of the Championship left, and only two more 917 World Championship outings therefore. At Oesterreichring the 3-litre Ferrari was nearly as fast as the big Porsche in practice and led the race when Rodriguez had to pit after twenty-nine laps to fit a new battery. 'You never tell the precise cause,' said Cuoghi, 'sometimes the current had just dispersed, another time the alternator is dodgy: all the electrical systems seemed to ask for different amounts of electricity.'

Rodriguez then put in one of his classic comeback drives, chopping back to within a minute of the Ferrari and the second place Martini Porsche before he had to come in and hand over to Attwood—who was driving because Oliver had apparently broken his contract and gone off CanAm racing.

'Pedro was always so *impatient*. He can see he is losing places with the co-driver, he wants to get back in straight away. David Yorke 'as to stop him for the actual time allowed. Pedro would get out of the car, comb his hair, washing his hands and face and sittin' on the pit wall ready to jump in the car again! He was fantastic, driving always with so much human effort,' Cuoghi recalled of this and many other races where similar situations arose.

In Austria Attwood did just twelve laps and the Mexican was clambering back into that wraparound cockpit, his silver and black crash hat framing alert eyes, restlessly flickered over the track through that deep windscreen. Some rain helped him on his way, and the Martini Porsche was retired with the aftermath of crash damage. With thirty laps to go there was a 2 m 5 s gap to close, Pedro reeling off 1 m 39 s (right in his best practice time bracket!) as Regazzoni in the Ferrari did his best on 1 m 43 s.

Then Regga crashed and one of Pedro's hardest and best race wins was the inevitable result—the more welcome as Siffert had been forced out with clutch failure. Pedro had driven 158 of the 170 laps and had returned a new lap record of 1 m 39.35 s (132.95 mph/214.09 km/h).

It was to be a fitting epitaph for the 917 in European sports car racing, and for Pedro Rodriguez.

'I was driving from the seaside in England. There was no major race for sports car that weekend, and Pedro had asked David Yorke to find him a drive. They want him in Norisring and he goes there to drive Müller's Ferrari 512M in one of those Interserie races. On the Friday we go testing with the Mirage (we just keep developing it ready for the 3-litre formula the following year) and Pedro 'as been driving his CanAm BRM. Everything is OK.

'So I have nothing to do this weekend. So I take my family down to the seaside. I am driving back to Twyford and we are listening to the wireless. We heard that Pedro 'as killed himself in that race. Just a funfair race, not worth anything.

'It was a disastrous year for drivers, but for me the death of Pedro was the saddest thing. We had worked so hard together. I jus' could not believe it, for some time I would not take it in.'

Cuoghi was left with the memory of victories they had shared together—four World Championship rounds in 1971 alone—but perhaps his most moving memory of the mild-mannered Mexican who turned into such a formidable competitor every time he went out on the track was of the evening spent after Giunti's death in Argentina earlier that year.

'After the race Pedro takes us all out to forget that terrible day. We go to a very nice place and there is enough wine so that I don't remember anything 'til I wake up the next morning.

'He was a big-hearted guy. Always he is giving the mechanic presents, and nice presents too. After Buenos Aires we had not only the evening but also 'e gave me some very good cuff links.'

A great man of small stature was lost and, because this was real life, it was not to be the end of the terrible losses of 1971.

The JW line-up with the usual 917Ks at their last appearance—the 24 July 1971 Watkins Glen 6 Hours—contained Siffert/Van Lennep in one car and Bell, promoted to number 1 driver, sharing with Attwood. The Penske Ferrari beat them to pole, but the race was a bit of an anti-climax, punctures from nails on the newly resurfaced and substantially revised track amenities ruining JW's chances along with a throttle pedal that actually broke off on Bell opposite the pits. After swinging into the rear compartment in an effort to jury-rig the throttles, Bell eventually managed to get the remains of the inside accelerator to work and limped the car back for repairs.

Bell had just recorded the race's fastest lap at that point, but in a long, wet, miserable five hours of remaining racing the team, led by Siffert, could only haul themselves back to second and third overall on their farewell appearance.

Cuoghi is not one for remembering anything but wins, so his chief memory of the weekend was staying at the Glen Motor Inn with the Ferrari boys 'and a super swimming pool. The daughters of the owners at the hotel were nice too and it was an enjoyable weekend, despite all the rain. Usually I like to go to Watkins Glen better in July than at the end of the year with the Formula 1.'

Of course Porsche had wrapped up the title again. JW had contributed five race wins in 1971 and seven the previous year: twelve victories in twenty-one races covering thousands of hard racing miles under every condition short of standing ice and snow.

Sadly Jo Siffert was killed after his great contribution to the 917 story was finished. He died at the wheel of his Grand Prix BRM at Brands Hatch in October of that year. Joseph Siffert was thirty-five, just four years older than Pedro had been, but like Rodriguez he still had a lot more to give after years of entertaining the public with the kind of courageous driving that warms spectators on the coldest days.

That both Siffert and Rodriguez should die in the year that the 917 and the other big sports cars were eliminated from international motor racing was ironic. Neither as sportsmen nor human beings could we afford to lose them. Their deaths truly marked the end of an era.

For Cuoghi there had been six years at JW and a host of other experiences since he came to live in England. He had even driven a 917 'at Silverstone for a film company. I spin it when it has oil on the back tyres and Mr Wyer gives me my own roll of toilet paper!'

Cuoghi preferred the Mirage-Cosworth V8 sports prototype, but his future did not lie with that for 1972. Waiting for him at home was a telegram from Italy.

David Yorke had been talking to Peter Schetty.

PRACTICE FOR *Monza 1000 km, 1971, was this wet as Rodriguez demonstrates in the 5-litre 917. Run without chicanes in strong sunshine the race produced a new absolute record lap of over 153 mph for Rodriguez and a 1–2 result for JW Automotive. Cuoghi and crew contributed with regular sub-30 sec refuelling stops*

Working on the winning Porsche

7
Life at Ferrari

The sports cars 1972–73; a fantastic first season, but in 1973 ...

'I KNEW Porsche were not continuing in racing for 1972, they have their own programmes inside and JW will not be involved. My father died in June 1969, so I have my sister and my mother left in Italy, asking me when I was going to go back?

'One day I was talking with David Yorke. He is asking me what I intend to do in the next season? Am I to stay with JW, because they have only the Mirage programme with the Cosworth engine. It was not a very interesting thing to me.

'So David Yorke must have talked with Peter Schetty, the Ferrari team manager at that time, and they have sent a telegram to my home in England asking if I was interested to go back to work in Italy? It says really, come and have a look at us ... see if we can talk together about a job. When Yorke and Schetty were talking, it must have been said that they would give me a job if I intended to

return to live in Italy.

'It was fantastic! I knew nothing about this. To receive a telegram like that from Ferrari . . . Jesus Christ! I have tried so many times to work with Ferrari, all unsuccessfully. I had applied twice before and then give up because I did not have the qualifications. At that time it was harder than now, you had to be an engineer, or with a diploma of some kind. I had nothing.

'The interview was with Schetty and Ing. Caliri, whom I had met before at sports car races and thought it would be good to work with. I did not meet Enzo Ferrari for a while.

'When I joined, Mr Ferrari was pretty ill for a while, so I did not meet him until two or three months after I joined. When we met it was not a meeting of strangers . . . he knew me! Of course I knew of him.

Charges to pay
s. d.
RECEIVED

POST OFFICE
TELEGRAM

No.
OFFICE STAMP

TS 15/106 LN Y29 GTX14/80 ce Instructions. Words.

At BOLOGNA/TELEXE/DE/MARANELL 27 7 815 m
From To
By By

ERMANNO CUOGHI 55 HERMITAGE DRIVE
TWYFORDBERKSHIRE/UK
PLEASE COME ON OUR EXPENCE TO MARANELLO POSSIBLY
NOT LATER THAN SATURDAY 9TH OCTOBER STOP
CONFIRM STOP PETER SCHETTY / FERRARI RACING

COL 55 9TH
...oubtful words telephone "TELEGRAMS ENQUIRY" or call, with this form
...hould be accompanied by this form, and, if possible, the envelope.
B or C

TS 15/106 LN

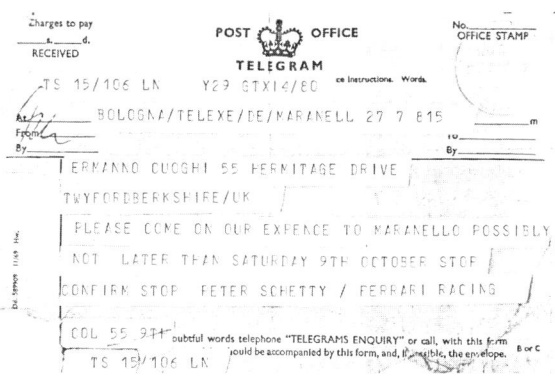

THE TELEGRAM *that started the Ferrari story for Cuoghi*

Below: CLAY REGAZZONI *at work in the 312P he shared with Brian Redman, Brands Hatch 1972, when the Ferrari sports cars were in devastating form all year*

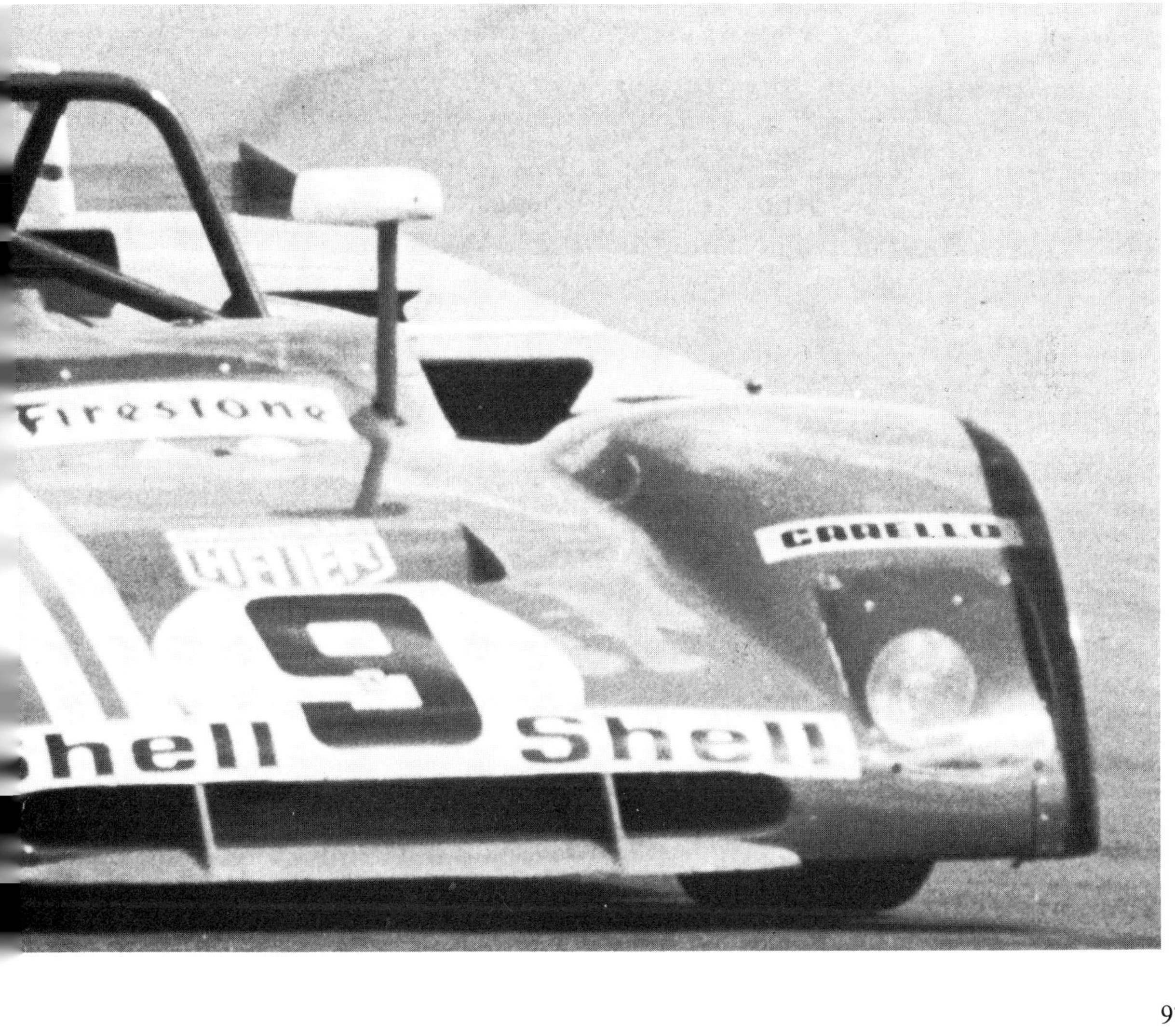

'Then I see him every day, every *single* day, he comes round the workshop asking how the job is going? Looking at the car, saying hullo. He *knows exactly* every single movement: all the engineers on the racing department report to him every evening before they go home.

'Mr Ferrari is there from eight or nine in the morning up to seven o'clock or later in the evening ... he is always in his office. A very active person while I was there,' Cuoghi recorded.

Ferrari were preparing for their most professional attack on the World Sports Car Championship. In January 1971 they made their first racing appearance with a new Ferrari 312P. For that Buenos Aires opener to the title hunt, the flat-twelve Ferrari was quoted as weighing 600 kg, over 100 lb less than designs from Matra and Alfa Romeo at the time, and providing 450 bhp from an engine in nearly the same stage of tune as the Formula 1 unit for the 312B (for Boxer or flat, opposing, cylinder layout). This led a lot of people to dub it a Formula 1 car with a sports body on it. In Cuoghi's opinion that was very far from the truth, the wide spaceframe chassis being totally different to the Grand Prix design, having the appearance of a full monocoque, thanks to riveted-on alloy sheets. Many other essential components were unique to the sports Ferrari as well.

At the close of the 1970 season Ferrari offered Basle-born Swiss Peter Schetty the job of managing both the Formula 1 and Grand Prix team. A businessman and an academic with a degree in economics and social history, Schetty had won the 1969 European Mountain (literally hill, in sense) Climb Championship in Ferrari's original flat-twelve design before appearing in their 1970 sports car team. Although he had four languages at his disposal and a business mind inherited from the family textile business, Schetty said he was not really ready to retire at the time. He eventually resigned himself to thinking that he was not going to be one of the very best drivers and 'unless you can be best I think there is no point in doing something'.

By the end of 1971 the 312P was recognized as the coming force in sports car racing. After that tragic start at Buenos Aires the car seemed to have little more luck—fortunately subsequent crashes did not bear the same dire results. However, as Cuoghi told me, 'the chief rival for our 5-litre Porsche in 1971 was often this little Ferrari, so I was very interested in this beautiful red car.'

In 1971 the best result for the 312P had been the British Brands Hatch round of the series, where Ickx/Regazzoni were second. For 1972 Ferrari pulled out all the stops in the first year of the new 3-litre Formula (remember how they did the same when Grand Prix racing first went to 1.5 litres?) and put together an incredible team of drivers allied to eight cars. These were deployed as one test-cum-development model, and two chassis per driver, pairing alternating between race and rebuild use with another car left over from those built in 1971 (three in all) raced as well! Occasionally crashes rudely interrupted this attractive alternate race, switch car, theory, but it usually worked to great effect.

In charge of both aerodynamic and general sports car development, Ing. Giacomo Caliri also supported Schetty in the team managing role, both unusually calm men by Ferrari standards.

During the year Ferrari relied mainly on a three-car race-day team, but for the Oesterreichring they brought four of their all-conquering sports cars and finished 1–2–3–4! It was that sort of year, the JW Mirage-Cosworths often promising in practice but pushed to turn in a race result in the face of the red squad. Matra stuck to fighting for Le Mans honours, Ferrari himself saying that the 3-litre cars would not run in races of more than six hours' duration, while Alfa Romeo and Lola were also overwhelmed, the Lola-Ford Cosworth V8s being rather disorganized, though potentially quick enough to win. Porsche were conspicuous by their absence after four straight Championship titles.

The Ferrari driver pairings changed frequently during the season, men like Clay Regazzoni and Mario Andretti flashing in and out, while Jacky Ickx, Brian Redman, Ronnie Peterson, Tim Schenken and Arturo Merzario formed a constant pool of drivers. Carlos Pace appeared in Austria as did Sandro Munari (the rally man also appearing on the Targa with a lot more success) and Austrian Helmut Marko.

Although the curved sheets and flat bulkheads in aluminium sheet convinced any onlooker that this was a monocoque chassis, triangulated tubing visible particularly on the floor showed it to be the usual Ferrari mixture between the two types of construction at that time. Each side to the hull carried a water radiator in front of the rear wheels with

Opposite, left: RONNIE PETERSON *in unfamiliar Ferrari jacket studies the neatly constructed cockpit of the 312P at Monza, 1972, in company with Clay Regazzoni, who had a lot more experience with the Ferrari 3-litre prototype*

'plug-in' access for speedy refreshment of both water and oil systems: the oil level could be read off from a side glass visible through the side of the car, both features to speed pit stops.

The four-wheel ventilated disc brakes and wishbone suspension went to normal practice at the time, though the outboard rear brakes may have been in the interests of service at a time when inboard back brakes were popular. Firestone tyres were still used by Ferrari, Goodyear appearing on the Formula 1 Ferraris from 1974 to 1977, superseded by Michelin. For the sports car 10-inch-wide front rims and up to 15.5-inch-wide rear were employed.

The bodywork came in two large sections of glass-fibre, the front half hinging upwards and incorporating ducts for the side radiators. The back 'half' of the body would be in either a short fenced form, as at the beginning of the year, or a slightly longer layout with vertical outside fins, and a transverse wing. I am told a longer tail was tried for testing at Le Mans, but the car did not race in this form.

In racing form the 312P was later quoted as offering 440 bhp with little short of 11,000 rpm as the rpm limit. In Grand Prix racing different camshafts were principal among changes that allowed 12,500 rpm to be slightly exceeded and a reputed extra 20–25 bhp. The engine had an extremely short stroke—78.5 mm by 51.5 mm for 2993 cc—and is remembered very affectionately by Cuoghi for 'the beautiful workmanship of the castings. Everything on this side was superb.'

The five-speed gearbox was right at the back of the car surrounded by megaphone exhausts. Ferrari's transverse gearbox did not appear until the F1 cars of several seasons later.

Refuelling was naturally a high priority on a long-distance racing design and the 26.4-gallon tank on one side of the car was replenished via the Avery Hardoll system. A large gravity hose supply of petrol would be slotted into one side and a transfer pipe would take it over to the tank on the left (looking from the rear). When the tank was full, petrol would swirl up into a transparent container placed on an outlet above the tank itself. The air in the tank was expelled through the transparent container. The Avery Hardoll plug-in points for fuelling and venting were self-sealing and could only be opened by a deliberate twist as the equipment was inserted.

That was the anatomy of Ferrari's crushingly successful design, one that was to last until the close of the 1973 season. 21 July, 1973 was the last time Ferrari raced a sports car officially.

Remembering the weekend that took him to Ferrari Cuoghi said, 'sometime in October 1971 I went to Italy. There was a club called *Amici di Volanti*, and they were giving me a prize for the season, something for the mechanical work after all the success we had at JW. The presentation was not far from Turin, so I put the weekend together: went to the prize-giving, had a very good time and then went to Modena to see my mother. There I contact Peter Schetty and go to see the Ferrari people, including the finance men, the lot. We reach an agreement: it was very suitable for me to go back to Italy!

'I go back to England, take my son out of school, pack all the things and return to Italy. I started work the 27th of December 1971.'

In Modena Cuoghi returned to the same area and resumed links with all the old familiar people and places, but with the exciting bonus of his Ferrari job to look forward to. In such a region, the man who works for Ferrari is a man amongst the menfolk!

The routine of daily life comes to Cuoghi vividly as his dream that came true is relived. 'I rented a flat in Modena for all of us: matter of fact I kept it right up to the beginning of the summer in 1979. It was very convenient and the cost was right, just on the outskirts of the old town.

'I am born in that area and it is close to my mother, to all my friends and not too far from Maranello. To get there every working day is about fifteen kilometres and I drive in most days. It was a pleasant drive, but I had sold my Mini some time before I went to Italy of course (a shame, he could have compared notes with Ferrari!) and I had an Austin 1100: you should have seen that 1100 come back to Italy with three of us, plus all the rubbish of living in England all that time! We had to send some of the big boxes by rail....

'So I started just after Christmas. Just before Ferrari had employed me they had made a man up to head mechanic, so I started between head mechanic and ordinary mechanic in my status, but I had overall responsibility on the sports cars. Considering that I spoke English, I was working mainly on the Peterson/Schenken car, but I was generally looking at all the cars in collaboration with the

Opposite: THE FIRST *and last time with the 312P at Le Mans. The year was 1973 and Ferrari were forced to fight Matra on home ground in order to defend their World Championship. Cuoghi (with Prancing Horse tee-shirt) oversees operations on the Merzario/Pace car*

other head mechanic, Antonio Bellentani. Most of the time we used the six cars made for that year and rotated them, but not all the time if an accident got in the way! Still there was always a car at home being prepared.

'So I set off to work in the morning and ten minutes or less later I am there. We did not have a pass to go in, but I have a time card with my works number on it. The guard knows you anyway! Usually I get there about eight o'clock in the morning, but in the beginning I did a few days like that finishing at half-past five, six o'clock, something like that to get to know everybody.

'Then to help with the preparation of the cars we were working shifts (because of the difficult industrial situation in Italy at the time: not even Ferrari were immune), and that would mean a morning shift from six until two. The other week you would do from two in the afternoon 'til ten at night. I never became a union member, but you 'ave to follow them. . . .

'Even when the racing season it was the same, and we find the two-shift system is better for preparation. We called it "the changing of the guard" and always there was a person in charge and three mechanics explaining where they had got to on each car. There was one such team per car, but there was also help from some other mechanics in the shop. Altogether there must have been twenty-five in that department—and there was a separate Formula 1 preparation area, plus those for the engine and gearbox to take into consideration too!

'Lunch hour was just that, but it was nice in Ferrari because you have proper metal cutlery in a beautifully clean self-service cafeteria with three types of pasta or antipasta, three or four choices of main course, wine, water, what you will. Afterward some nice cheese or fruit, very much local in food or drink . . . which means Lambrusco!

'We also had two breaks in the working day for fifteen minutes for black coffee, not tea.

'At the beginning I had nothing to do with the Formula 1 people in their separate place, but pretty soon I find excuses to go over there as often as I can get away, but mainly you are too busy with your job.

'For testing I remember we had the Fiorano track and especially the presentation of that track, including the improvements of TV and corner-sensors were built-in toward the end of my first season.' That bank of ten TV monitors plus all the other digital readout equipment to precisely monitor and record car behaviour was reputed to have cost £270,000, a bargain if true, for the later improvement in Formula 1 was worth at least four times as much! *Pista di Fiorano* was opened earlier in 1972, had a lap length of three kilometres and squashed in fourteen varied corners.

'We were sharing the testing, the other head mechanic and myself, alternating like the cars! By road it was about one kilometre from our works, by crow some 200 yards. We could not drive the cars across the *Stradale 12* though; it was too busy and we must spare the clutch. So each time we load up on the transporter or a trailer.

'When I arrived the car was pretty well sorted in a wider track specification than they had in 1971: at Kyalami one older 312 and a newer one had finished first and second, so they were winning cars already,' Cuoghi chuckled.

'The 312P was very easy to work on. The chassis was basically made by the other non-team mechanics, then it would go to the machine shop to be bored for the wishbones, welded and made straight according to the drawings. I was concerned again in assembly, not manufacture. Sometimes we make up a few brackets, bits and pieces like that, basic jobs.'

The engines and gearboxes are made on site, none of this buying a Cosworth and strapping it on to a Hewland gearbox with some individual modifications that characterized British competition cars after the demise of BRM as an effective force. Such Ferrari engines and boxes, with their associated transmission parts, were made in the same building as the sports car work was undertaken in Cuoghi's employment. That building is in one of the oldest parts of the Ferrari factory, separate from the now heavily Fiat-linked road car production, and once visited is totally unforgettable. On the floor are red ceramic tiles, outside a courtyard of cobblestones, the building washed in an ochre that seems to blend with long, hot days.

'On the left-hand side there are a few offices and the whole building is very long, as you can imagine, to hold all those cars and building activities.

'Everything was really clean, a fantastic place to work.' Compared with the English way of competition preparation Cuoghi said he had to 'settle myself to the Italian way of working. That is a different atmosphere, different feeling, a bit more relaxed in some ways. However, it is Ferrari, and you feel more responsible: if something did go wrong . . .' he stopped talking and slit his throat with a joking grin! 'Now if that was Porsche, they put you against the wall and boom, boom with the firing squad!' Cuoghi's sense of humour knows no nationalistic boundaries, but he stresses he is joking for the benefit of company lawyers.

What were the differences in protocol between the Italian organization and the British one? 'The mechanics have respect for the people they are dealing with in Italy. If the head mechanic is doing his job properly they are happy enough: they don't need to talk to anyone higher up. In the evening or when relaxing, all are sitting together, engineers, everyone, Ferrari is a very friendly team. When they are working, to avoid chaos, they just take one order directly from the head mechanic and bye, bye.

'The other mechanics were perfectly friendly to me after so long in England. We knew each other from race meeting to meeting so we were friends. Some of them I knew before they were mechanics at Ferrari, perhaps even at school.'

At the race meetings themselves Schetty and Caliri, perhaps because of Cuoghi's arrival, adopted an English system of working on the cars as Cuoghi expounded: 'At that time six person were allowed to each car in the pit. The refuelling man [often that was him], four for the tyres, one each, and the oil-man. He was carrying a pressurized container of oil on his shoulder ready for to plug it in, stopping when he could see on the level glass that it was full, through the side of the body.

'In short we have adopted the one man, one job system. Before Ferrari had their own way of doing things, but Schetty has seen and I have learned at JW this way of making certain each man knows what he has to do. We also made it so that each mechanic had a helper in normal times, now everyone does it.

'At Wyer's I think there was no doubt that we could do the fastest pit stops on the 917 or GT40, and that helped everyone see there was a better way of doing the pit work.

'For Ferrari stops I was happy to work on the refuelling until they had the overhead type: for myself I prefer churns. Later on I would change tyres, or brake pads.

'The atmosphere in the pits was very good. Mr Schetty has such a strong personality that the organization is better than the attempted chaos, whatever is happening! We knew exactly where we were, how many laps we had to do; what was to happen in the next few laps. Peter Schetty was putting up a board in our pits, how many pit stops? What lap? It was all there on the wall so you could read what was needed to do *now*,' Cuoghi finished his description of their activities.

The racing record in 1972 for Ferrari SEFAC was perfect in respect of wins: twelve races entered, twelve won! In the total were ten World Championship qualifying rounds, all giving them a win. The only race missing from that Championship tally was Le Mans, and Enzo Ferrari had decided they would not go there, though they were present for the test day.

Of their World Championship results, six wins came from Ickx—paired with Andretti on four victorious occasions, once with Redman and once with Regazzoni. Peterson and Schenken contributed two victories, Munari and Merzario one, while the unusual and ill-matched Redman-Merzario duo finished a lap ahead of Ickx and Regazzoni at Spa for the tenth World Championship win.

The measure of Ferrari's dominance in that period came from the fact that it was not until the fifth round of the series that Ferrari took anything less than first and second places in a Championship round! In the end the score was seven 1–2 results.

Cuoghi's outstanding memory of the season is of a race where they had only one car entered and nobody fancied their chances against four Alfa Romeos.

'The 312P was a marvellous little car to drive. The drivers, and we had quite a few, all said what a good car it was. To dominate such a season needs some luck, but it must have been the strongest sports car team ever from Ferrari.

'The race I remember was the Targa Florio. We take a rallyman like Sandro Munari, fine to work with, but we knew him as Lancia's rally driver. He came to Fiorano for some trials to get to know the car before we go down for the Targa. His progress on the Fiorano lap times did not prove very much.

'So when we were preparing the car for the trials and race in Sicily we are going for a small chance. Start one day, cover a few miles, we were behind with a truck and van, and we are following to see how the car is behaving on these "stages!" Check it out, alter little things, so a few more miles, so it took us a day to do one lap practically! However, it was interesting making small suspension changes and see if the car goes better. The following days they do full laps in traffic, and the times are competitive.'

Ferrari had taken the decision late to attend the Targa Florio, so only a small crew (without manager Schetty) went along with a single car. It had the feel of Enzo Ferrari psychology: if they lost against such a strong Alfa turnout, well at least it took all those Milanese motors to beat him! If they won, it would be an unexpected bonus on top of the six championship wins they had already put in by May.

So far as the car that Arturo Merzario would share with Munari was concerned, Cuoghi said 'we had no problems at all with the strength of the car on rougher roads. Basically it was a strong car from the beginning with that chassis. The engine was the same as for sports car racing, but they have made a different exhaust to give better torque on the bottom end. Mind you, the Ferrari engine was *very* flexible and would pull from 5700/6000 revs to 12,000 rpm. That is quite a lot of power . . . they never use it on the Targa, I tell you!'

During the first lap of the race Alfa Romeo lost Vic Elford's car with engine failure, and shortly after Merzario's pit stop (when he had already built a huge lead over local hero Vaccarella's Alfa) the Vaccarella car damaged its engine. The odds were coming down in what had looked like a hopeless duel in the strong Sicilian sunshine. As Cuoghi commented, the Targa always has 'something new from yesterday around every corner!'

The problems were not confined to Alfa though, Cuoghi recalled that sweaty first Ferrari stop 'Merzario came in and knock over a marshal! There was a car refuelling, not properly in lane, on the next pit to us. So Merzario was coming in sideways, a bit fast. So we 'ave difficulty to refuel and we had to change the tyres as well. Considering there were only three of us—Caliri in charge of myself and two mechanics—it was good to send Munari back out on the road at all!' Incidentally the only other Ferrari personnel on the island were a truck driver and a couple of mechanics looking after the refuelling up in the hills at Bivio Polizzi.

The Ferrari led all but two laps; even when Munari came in a lap early Merzario was up to the occasion and in Cuoghi's words 'he performed magnificently . . . and so did Sandro.' In fact Helmut Marko in the Alfa, earlier spun by Nanni Galli, set a succession of fastest laps in the closing stages trying to catch little Art, failing by just 16.9 seconds. Even then the gallant Austrian failed to crack Leo Kinnunen's 1970 record, which was some five seconds quicker: shame Porsche were not there that year. . . .

LAP 114 *of the Monza 1000 km in 1973 and Carlos Reutemann is ready to go while fuel and oil are added via quick-filling arrangements either side of the Ferrari 312P cockpit. Cuoghi is in front of helmeted co-driver Tim Schenken, this overheating car finishing second to the winning Ickx/Redman Ferrari. It was a bright spot in a tough year for Maranello*

Cuoghi outlined Merzario's appearance for the last corner, last lap. 'He came around in the lead, through the corner just before the pit with one hand on the steering wheel. The crowd were cheering like 'ell, Merzario was waving to them with the other hand ... and all the way sideways!' In that, the 56th Targa Florio, the greatest traditions of motor sporting history had been given another legend to weave within an already fascinating tale of this tough cross between a race and a rally. Street competition through the villages and foothills, endless bends, intense heat and fanatical spectators, all were part of a great individual event within a sports car championship, a series that meant something in the early seventies and nothing by the close of the decade.

For Ferrari the Targa also marked the ownership of the 1972 Championship title with seven straight wins. For Cuoghi there had been every justification for leaving JW at just the right time, a decision endorsed by British driver Derek Bell, who told me, 'JW, Ferrari sports cars, then Ferrari when Niki came. There are a lot of good mechanics around, but not all of them have picked such good teams as Ermanno. He is an exceptional mechanic with a tremendous sense of humour, a talent for bending metal, and sorting out stuffed bodywork.' Bell spent 1972 in the opposing JW/Gulf Mirage-DFV camp without Cuoghi, of course, and there were no wins to be had for the Anglo-American team that year, despite some notable performances from Bell at the Nürburgring and Spa.

Cuoghi and company's body-changing speed was fully tested at the Monza, the fifth round of the 1972 series. Peterson went off at Parabolica in the heavy rain that was to characterize the event. 'We put a new nose on, clean all the mud Ronnie has found off all the parts, while the organizers hold the race for us. In the race Ronnie has gone off again—this time at a different place, so he is learning something! So we put another nose on, some new tyres and he (with Schenken) gives us a third place.'

The final Championship round, Watkins Glen, gave the Gulf-Mirage for Bell and Carlos Pace their best finishing position, a third place behind a Ferrari 1–2 that was not all it seemed. Cuoghi explained: 'Andretti has a problem with the engine: when the throttle is off the engine is on full rich mixture. So Mario is losing time to Peterson. Then Ickx takes over the car and fights with Ronnie, no team orders, everyone sideways and wheels off the road!' Just ten minutes from the end of the race Ickx got the better of Peterson for good. Ronnie was

apparently bothered by inefficient brakes, though Cuoghi said, 'in a sports car Jacky was number 1. In a Formula 1 car at his best, maybe three or fourth best ... but in a sports car, untouchable.'

The 1973 season was not a happy one for Ferrari, or their workers. The year passed without a single grand prix win and the sports car attack met with stiff and successful opposition from France.

At the conclusion of their successful 1972 Championship hunt in the sports car arena, Peter Schetty left to rejoin the family textile business. Ing. Giacomo Caliri took over the sports car job with Forghieri becoming more evident at the race tracks once more: Schetty was even back to analyse the problems on occasion.

What could turn such a dominant force into an

outfit that took only two race wins out of ten the following season? The main snag to 1973 were the winners of Le Mans 1972—Matra—and their driving team, which included François Cevert, the Tyrrell Grand Prix team-mate to Jackie Stewart. François secured six sports car championship pole position times that season. He also acted as a very hard to catch 'hare'!

The year started mildly enough with neither Ferrari nor Matra venturing to Daytona's 24-hour annual (it had been of six hours' duration the previous year). Sebring was cancelled, a fate also thrown on to the BOAC 500 in Britain.

At Vallelunga, 25 March, Matra met Ferrari for the first time in a couple of years. The tight track on the outskirts of Rome was bound to cause someone tyre trouble and Ferrari suffered . . . but that

'LITTLE ART' *Merzario in the Targa Florio-winning 312P he shared with Lancia rally ace Sandro Munari. Cuoghi felt this was one of the outstanding Ferrari performances in 1972, for the car was sent with only a small supervisory team and stood up well to rougher roads than it was originally intended for*

was not the real point. Cevert qualified faster than Redman could manage in the best Ferrari and in a close race Matra won.

The Ferraris had been developed a little during the winter: at Vallelunga they had new noses, a longer wheelbase and engines that offered more power than in 1972. Cuoghi commented: 'The car has been developed, it was *modified*, but maybe there were too many mods? The track was wider on the front as well, but it was quicker in testing.

I think it was not that much better to face the increased opposition.

'We have a lot of problems with the tyres, Firestone has pulled back and we are on Goodyear for the first season.'

Before the season started Ferrari had said that they were not going to defend the title, but six chassis were retained and two or three 312Ps entered at each round. Team leaders were Ickx and Redman; the second car went to Merzario with Pace and the third car, when entered, was for Reutemann and Schenken. The French team fielded two cars at all rounds, save Le Mans, and used Cevert with brother-in-law Jean-Pierre Beltoise. Henri Pescarolo/Gerard Larrousse set a steadier pace and won five championship races, the first Vallelunga one with Cevert along to help as well.

Ferrari driver morale was not very good during the year for reasons other than just a comparative lack of success compared with previous years. Ickx was at loggerheads with Mr Ferrari over their lack of progress in Formula 1 and Merzario's unruly character rubbed up the courteous Pace the wrong way: the team had to argue pretty forcibly with 'Little Art' to get him out of the car at Nürburgring when he had overtaken team leader Ickx!

At Vallelunga at least they finished their 312Ps 2–3–4, emphasizing their reliability, but at Dijon second and fourth showed they were struggling. Pace had been faster than Ickx in practice, but the race result was the other way about, even though Ickx stopped for a new nose section giving less

downforce than the original. Throughout the year confusion seemed to reign on the body, for Ferrari with many different configurations tried, reshaped tails, higher downforce fronts and a number of air boxes for the flat-twelve engine, including a central large single one, and dual inlet scoops left and right.

Incidentally it would be wrong to think that only Ferrari suffered on the tyre side. Matra were also on Goodyear and had their share of problems. Looking at the confrontation six years afterwards, having seen what some former Matra people have achieved in the chassis design of the ground effect Ligier, and remembering that Jackie Stewart was always very complimentary about Matra chassis (he just stuck to using a Cosworth Ford-engined one!), it seems quite possible that Ferrari were at a distinct disadvantage on the chassis. Aerodynamics? Matra were involved to the highest aerospace levels and seemed unlikely to have anything but an advantage on that front either. In Grand Prix success terms the Matra engine was never convincing, whilst the 3-litre Ferrari flat-twelve has often provided a power edge over the opposition, as well as being magnificently reliable since its first full season in 1970.

At Monza, the third round of the 1973 series, Ickx and Redman made sure the pressure stayed on the leading Matra, and the French team eventually hit major problems with both stub axle failures and transmission troubles. Matra finished, but the Monza crowd gave their own special brand of welcome—rather fiercer than the reception one

THE 1973 *World Sports Car Championship fight was on from the first Vallelunga confrontation between Matra and Ferrari. Here Brian Redman in the Ferrari he shared with Ickx fends off the winning Matra 670 of Henri Pescarolo/Gerard Larrousse.*

imagines the Christians would have tolerated when being thrown to the lions—as Ferrari finished first and second in the order Ickx/Redman, Schenken/Reutemann.

That cheered them up a bit, but Spa had some bad news for Ferrari as Cuoghi told me. 'The oil coolers were cracking. We started losing all the oil through the gearbox oil cooler, it was a new type for this race, which has not had any real testing. It looked the same but had a weaker neck compared with the others.' Ickx was stranded out on the circuit with one such failure while Pace managed to nurse the second car home with no fourth and fifth, another cooler hastily jury-rigged up for the gearbox after a similar failure. While the job was being done 'one of our boys is knocked out, a clean KO, when the tail of the car falls on him . . . must be too 'eavy that body,' Cuoghi joked.

Cuoghi's third visit to the Targa Florio brought the team no luck, though they took two cars. The first for Vaccarella/Merzario and the other for Jacky Ickx, his first appearance in the event, and Redman. There were no Matras, but Alfa Romeo reappeared and David Yorke brought along his two Martini Porsche RSRs, production-based models being quietly developed after Porsche's previous prototype performances.

Merzario did a good job in practice, lapping only two seconds away from that elusive Kinnunen record, but in the race he touched the scenery, possibly because he had a puncture. Either way the Ferrari was soon eliminated with transmission trouble after that incident. Cuoghi commented of Ickx's retirement, 'He finds a stone, a boulder nearly, where there was not one before and damages all the suspension.' Always a mistake to go back!

Ferrari were back in business with another 1–2 at the Nürburgring 1000 km after both Matras had engine failure. Ickx and Redman were the winners, but the more interesting Ferrari was the second place car for Merzario/Pace as this had the single airbox rear body with a lower and smoother body line delivering air more cleanly to the full-width rear wing. The body could only be lowered in this way because the engine oil radiator was moved in below one of the water radiators, instead of sitting above the clutch housing. That car also had different rear suspension mounting points and hubs.

Le Mans brought the ultimate challenge between three Ferraris for the regular team members and four Matras. Cuoghi thinks the worst problem was 'the cars were pretty well prepared with longer tails for high speed and so forth. However, we have a smaller collector tank for the petrol system that was a bit too big for the vibration we encounter on the long, high-speed, straight like the Mulsanne. We never had the chance to reproduce twenty-four hours' racing at Fiorano at that speed, so it really was not proved. These pots started splitting and we were replacing them a lot of times. It was the collector made in aluminium between the main tank and the mechanical pump for the Lucas fuel injection.'

This happened first to the front-running Merzario/Pace car after just two hours' racing, Pace leaping out of the car with overalls drenched in petrol. Still, at midnight, after the traditional 4 pm start, Ferrari were first and second with Matra third and fourth, ahead of the delayed Merzario/Pace Ferrari.

Just after 2.30 in the morning must be accounted a low point in most human life: for Ferrari on Sunday, 11 June, 1973, this sinking feeling was emphasized by Mr Reutemann coasting gently to rest in the pits with a ventilated engine block. Since they had all been set a 10,500 limit and the engines were in endurance racing trim this was something of a surprise, though one must remember Enzo had originally decided to stick to six-hour races. Unfortunately he could not afford to let Matra run away with valuable points unopposed that season.

Daylight brought the kind of swings and roundabouts gains and losses for Ferrari and Matra that hold the unpredictable interest in long-distance racing. Ferrari had the special long exhaust system of the leading Ickx/Redman car give way, together with the hinges on the rear deck. Matra took the lead for the first time since before midnight.

When Ickx took over the collector tank split, as on the Pace car, and it looked all over.

Then the leading Matra had the starter motor jam. The race was on again. . . . With two hours to go Matra led Ferrari by just over a lap, and Pace in the second surviving Ferrari was third, four laps down. The Ferrari closed on to the same lap as the Matra, but the engine was audibly rougher—perhaps there was something more fundamental than an exhaust failure? There was, though it could have been that the exhaust contributed to the failure which was attributed to the valves. Ickx stepped out finally with under one and a half hours left. Matra had earned their victory, six laps ahead of the sole Ferrari 312P finisher, that of Pace/Merzario.

Cuoghi summed up the feeling inside the factory when it was known that Ferrari would give up sports car racing completely and concentrate on Formula 1—'it was a great shame after so many years. They had put so much effort in, and for a long time they were selling the cars they raced too. A pity,' Cuoghi shrugged sadly.

'Ing. Caliri is being blamed somehow, but it was not his fault—just a question of driver collaboration. Forghieri and Schetty came to some races, and most of those modifications you have written about were because of Forghieri's visits.

'Forghieri was out of the race programme for a while. When he came back in 1973 and start putting everything right again, there was some good co-operation between Forghieri and Caliri with the drivers. Very good.

'From those two years of sports Ferraris I enjoyed the Targa in 1972 the most. That was the most impressive race for us in my memory—and it was nice with just a small group of us. We went in there with not much chance of winning and we did so well. The following year we go down with two cars and the best drivers from around the world, we were sure we would win, yet for different reasons like the rock in the road we have lost both cars. That is impressed more on my mind,' Cuoghi admitted cheerfully enough.

So far as can be seen as the nineteen-seventies close that 1973 confrontation between Ferrari and Matra was the last year of the great marques fighting each other for the sole glory of nationalistic manufacturers, rather than the reputation of individual drivers.

Today Formula 1 has become the ruling force in international races. There driver glory still comes out on top.

For Cuoghi, as they cleared away the sports cars in the summer of 1973, it was time to start thinking seriously about Formula 1 again.

For a young Austrian driving BMW saloons, and the BRM P160 in grand prix, it was time to think more seriously than ever of Formula 1. Particularly how to make a living from it, rather than using bank loans to finance it . . . a hard task when you have a broken arm as a legacy from sliding a quarter of a mile at 155 mph, using the solid scenery of the Nürburgring to arrest the velocity of self and said BRM.

JUST OVER 150 mph. That was the remarkable winning average over 4 hours and 1000 km of the 1973 Monza Ferrari 312P for Ickx/Redman. This time the Matra challenge, here led by Jean-Pierre Beltoise, suffered the mechanical failures

8

Back in Formula 1

LOOK UPWARD, *ever upward! Ferrari personalities with Cuoghi* (left to right) *are: Salvarani, the gearbox designer; Ghedini, soon to be Niki's assistant; Tomaini, deputy to Forghieri; Dr Gozzi, voice of Ferrari; designer Forghieri, and 'the Speedline wheels man'. In the other 1977 picture Lauda is interviewed by Chris Economaki*

IT HAD BEEN nearly ten years since Ermanno had worked in Formula 1 racing, ten of the most eventful years seen in grand prix. When Cuoghi was forced by the finances of Tony Settember's outfit to return to Italy, the subsequent truck-driving job with Carroll Shelby and the chance to watch and contribute more and more mechanically had seemed the highest prize.

Now Ermanno was working for Ferrari, the most emotive name in motoring racing. However, the Ferrari Cuoghi worked for in that summer of 1973 was not a happy place. When Cuoghi spent his year with Shelby, Ferrari and John Surtees were able to take the World Championship from Britain's Graham Hill in a BRM and Jim Clark's Lotus-Climax. That was 1964. The following year saw the last 1.5-litre formula season and an all-British top three in the Championship points at the close of play: Clark in the Lotus defeating the BRMs of Hill and Jackie Stewart.

The 1966 season was the first for the 3-litre cars, but it was not Ferrari's name that figured in the final points tallies. Jack Brabham took the simple, overhead camshaft V8 from Repco (out of Holden in Australia) to beat the *other* Modenese, Maserati,

whose V12 engines were mounted in the back of Coopers.

The balance of power stayed with Repco in 1967 when Hulme and Brabham defeated Clark . . . but the new Cosworth-Ford DFV engine had emerged. That power unit was to power the winners of the next *seven* years in championship titles! The chassis were different, coming from Lotus, Matra, Tyrrell (twice each in this period) and McLaren, but what mattered was that Ferrari were having a very tough job getting in the results after a 1970 season that saw Ickx and Regazzoni chase Rindt home in the series battle. Rindt's awful death at Monza, before the season's end, underlined the superiority Lotus-Ford enjoyed, as the Austrian was posthumously awarded the title.

By the summer of 1973 Ferrari were as low as they could go. Matra had wiped out the memories of a supremely victorious 1972, and that Cosworth V8, financed by Ford, was still the driving force behind Tyrrell and Lotus, who were battling for the title again.

At Barcelona's Monjuich Park street circuit on 29 April, 1973, Ferrari raced their solution to the problem. At long last they decided to go for what the company then described as 'a British-type monocoque construction'. This meant they abandoned the mixture of spaceframe tubes and riveted sheets of alloy that had characterized Ferrari sports and grand prix racing machinery for many seasons, including the 312Ps that Cuoghi had previously worked on.

The model was the Ferrari B3 and continued to use the flat-twelve cylinder engine that Ermanno had become familiar with, as well as the conventional rear-mounted gearbox. Whereas previous Ferraris featured an engine installation that bolted on to a beam location, this engine was fully stressed in the same way that the Cosworth DFV V8 has appeared in the back of a 1967 Lotus 49.

Mauro Forghieri was closely involved with this project to put Ferrari back on top, but *Ingegneri* Colombo was looking after the car's engineering needs at meetings on many occasions that season.

The monocoques, two numbered 010 and 011, were designed at Ferrari by Forghieri's team, but manufactured by TC Prototypes in Northampton (home also of Cosworth!) Only the bare monocoque was made in Britain, Ferrari assembling the rather large, boxy ensemble themselves.

Unusual features included a large number of magnesium alloy castings in the suspension, the product of Ferrari's own foundry, the front featuring the inboard location of the coil spring/damper unit with a large fabricated top arm along the same principles as have found wide acceptance in Formula 1 in the late seventies, though few used the box-section single top arm adopted by Ferrari.

Ickx qualified on the third row at the car's debut, but it was not an omen of further success. True, Ickx did finish in the points on occasion, but by the time the Italian Grand Prix at Monza came around in September, Ferrari morale had taken a bit of a beating, with Merzario sometimes appearing and Ickx employed as an outside freelance driver (he appeared in a McLaren at that year's German Grand Prix), while Forghieri and the other engineers attempted to get to grips with Formula 1 again.

Cuoghi took up the story: 'After the sports car racing season finished in July, *Ingegneri* Colombo made a Formula 1 prototype which we called *Rospa* because it looked like a snow plough from the nose, based on work by Forghieri on the B3. During that period there was nothing to do on the sports cars, so I have started working on this *Rospa* machine.

'We prepared the car, it was already two-thirds built, and make it ready for testing at Fiorano. I make a few things, put it together and take it down to Fiorano, see how it is behaving. Ickx and Merzario were doing the driving, Arturo doing quite a lot actually because he was living in Modena at that time. So we did some running and testing in that car: they decide to prepare for Monza and take three cars there.' Ferrari had missed the Dutch Grand Prix and the German round at Nürburgring, so there was quite a bit of interest when they came back in force.

Merzario and Forghieri had attended the Austrian round in August with a revised chassis that formed the basis of what Cuoghi had been testing. The big change was the use of side-mounted radiators (they had been tried before without success), but slimline and mounted at a shallow angle on either side of the cockpit. The oil tank and radiator were also remounted closer to the centre of the car, again features that had been tried with success as Forghieri fought to stem the Matra tide on the sports car front. Visually the biggest changes were in the full-width front aerofoil—a feature that was to become a Ferrari hallmark in Formula 1—and the use of a single high airbox with two internal ducts to feed the banks of the boxer engine: previously the Ferrari had scoops let into the rear body. The aerofoil attached above the gearbox and the suspension was tuned to suit the extensively revised aerodynamics and weight distribution. Merzario was seventh in that Austrian Grand Prix.

'We had a few problems of sorting out the car at Monza. The front suspension had a very large overhang, so the drivers would touch a kerb and the top suspension arm was bending. So strengthen that all up: in the race Ickxy has kept away from the kerbs, but Merzario touched again and bent the top link again,' Cuoghi recalled. It was all too easy to clip a chicane at the revised Monza track and 'Little Art' had done just that on the second lap of the race, having practised 0.62 seconds faster than a rather uninspired Ickx.

Cuoghi said, 'Jacky was going round OK in the race, but we lose some of the lower bodywork at the side which feeds air into the radiator and it starts overheating. He managed to finish eighth anyway, so it was not *too* bad. In fact the car was not bad either because, with a lot of minor mods, that was the car we used to win in 1974. After that I did not go to America, and Ickx did not go either, but Merzario took a car over there. Just before Monza they had said to me that I would be working on Formula 1 in the future: no more sports cars from Ferrari for racing!

The plan was to organize the sports car people inside Ferrari and turn them into Formula 1 mechanics, plus the existing Formula 1 mechanics, for a much bigger effort on this side. That was the result of a policy decision by the Fiat sporting committee that controlled the direction taken by Ferrari, Fiat and Lancia in motor sport. In fact nobody really tells Mr Ferrari what to do, but it was obvious that something needed to be done to restore Ferrari's prestige in Formula 1, and the only effective way of doing that was to turn all the company's financial and engineering resources towards that one aim. Making sure that the money was not misdirected, reporting directly back to the **Agnelli** Fiat hierarchy, was qualified lawyer and member of the Italian aristocracy Luca di Montezemolo.

It was Luca who contacted Lauda, for Ferrari had heard favourable reports of the Austrian's performance in the BRM at Monaco (generally adjudged a driver's circuit, though overtaking has always been especially difficult) when he got the generally outclassed British V12 up to third overall. In August Lauda met Montezemolo in London and later that month, after trying unsuccessfully to race in Austria with his arm still painful after the Nürburgring fracture, Niki was down in Maranello talking terms.

Lauda said of the Ferrari set-up at the time, 'Okay, Ferrari had no success for years, but it was obvious to me that their potential was unequalled.' Lauda started at Ferrari as winter began to draw in, but the slightly later starts to the continuous testing schedule to avoid the worst of the frost were no deterrent to a Lauda fired with ambition. He had demanded a million Austrian Schillings a year, but earning money seemed to be of interest only in discharging the debts built up through the BRM period. Winning, or at least finishing some races for a change, was a strong motivation.

Cuoghi saw little different in his life about making the change from sports cars to grand prix work. 'It's the same thing,' he told me, 'but the Ferrari F1 team was not organized in the same way as that for sport car. The F1 team has engine men, gearbox men, a few mechanics jumping between jobs. Only one man is staying on each car all the time. That was not a very good idea. When 1973 ends they change over to the sport car system. That means we have three mechanics with one supervisor and that gives more results and a better quality of work.'

Ferrari had two 'new' drivers that season, both from BRM—Lauda and Clay Regazzoni—the latter described succinctly by Cuoghi as 'an old driver for Ferrari!' He laughed quietly.

'The only really new person was Niki Lauda. I was made the supervisor on his car because the old head mechanic [Giulio Borsari] has worked with Clay Regazzoni before. So he has chosen Clay himself, rather than work with a new driver, plus there was the language barrier as well because Niki could not speak much Italian at that time; but I know a bit of the English, so I was a suitable person.'

Cuoghi first met Lauda at Maranello in the factory. 'I knew there was something going along because I saw Montezemolo in September, during the Monza Grand Prix, talking with this pale-faced fella: this schoolchild!

'I knew of this Lauda before. When we did sports cars in Spa there was a saloon car race and he is fighting with his BMW against Jochen Mass in the Ford. A fantastic race, together all the time, and then a wheel and stub axle came off the Ford. . . . Niki won twice in saloon cars that day. His crash helmet was that funny red and I looked to see what he was like in the paddock. Then I saw him in September talking with Montezemolo and thought "fair enough", one driver is much like another,' he laughed happily at this sally on a future champion.

Cuoghi continued: 'When Lauda first came they said Ickxy will come to see the car and I was preparing to make one car for him. Lauda came in with Marko (Dr Helmut, the Austrian who drove for BRM before an eye injury forced him out of the sport) and the pale-face was introduced to me. We

put him in the car and make sure everything is right for him.

'He says everything is OK, but when he first went to Fiorano, nothing was right any longer!' Cuoghi laughed and remembered Lauda saying, 'Jesus Christ, what have I done: the car is terrible!'

'It was a sunny day and we put him in the car with a few of the normal adjustments of belts and things that you need for any driver. He did a couple of laps, came in, had the seat adjusted and start lapping a little harder.

'I tell myself, "you got to give this guy a chance". It's a new car, new driver, but you could see on his face that he was not happy. When we are getting to the end of those first tests I can see he is really unhappy, asking himself what he has done? He could *not* make the car work for him. The car was one of the latest specification ones, but neither Ickx or Merzario were good test drivers. Merzario had a nervous style of his own and Jacky just was not very interested in development, especially after so much trouble during the year.

'We were not satisfied, Niki was not satisfied. Then they start to work together, Lauda and Forghieri: try this, try the other, make a good collaboration. Niki has started to *know* the car—and Forghieri knew it more than anyone else—so they start to make progress together at Fiorano during that winter. They did a good job!

'We made a lot of alterations suspension-wise, including antidive. Niki has the car set up in the same way as he uses today. He likes a neutral car: actually what he likes is a little bit of understeer on the entry to the corner to give him a limit of entry, quite neutral after that. He doesn't like any real under- or oversteer around the corner itself, just neutral. So it was difficult to find a castor for him because the castor angle is $4\frac{1}{2}$–5 degrees on a Ferrari, and it is a bit too much for him, so Lauda keeps on reducing it to a point where it was OK for him to drive without losing the initial point of turning in. Ferrari has always been good on that anyway, it points into turns well.

'Aerodynamically we did quite a lot of changes, mainly on the top of the body. We round off the cockpit surround, make a narrow nose and a tall, slimline airbox. The wings were changed a coupla times too: all the car was made smaller ... slimmer to look at.

'We did so many things to the rear wings! And there was a big job to reduce weight by using different materials: all the brackets were steel, so we went to titanium, things like that. The exhaust system was in titanium too, all fabricated by Ferrari, but afterwards they went back to steel exhaust on Ferrari because—as soon as they touch a bit of water—they were cracking.

'We did so much work on that car, testing, testing

Opposite, top: THE START *of the 1974 season in South America and Niki Lauda has made the jump from BRM and obscurity to a Ferrari team set on single seater success. Though rather square-rigged, the B3 did a better job than expected from its 1973 performances*

THE 1974 *Ferrari B3 is readied for the Argentinian opening round of the World Championship. Regazzoni's sister car sits beside the YPF petrol pumps*

all the time! We saved one hell of a lot of weight I tell you. Everything, *every*thing was looked at by the drawing office, looking at nuts and bolts, even the number of ball joints: the B3 had been a heavy car.

'The engine? Well, there is development every day on this at Ferrari! Sure they got some better consumption, more power and keep on like everyone has to, but there was nothing radical on that or the whole car. They just go on developing it all, but we start to make the chassis all ourselves, all the time now: remember the first ones were made in England. We did not just copy what was done in England though, it was modified and really it was a *Ferrari* chassis in 1974.' The chassis numbers 010 and 011 appeared again in 1974, despite this.

Cuoghi added, 'I had a pretty busy winter, learning a lot of things, which is what I always like. Bad teacher, good pupil, that is me! Most of the time I am working with *Ingegneri* Caliri and a foreman; Caliri was in charge of the sports cars, but sometimes we have Forghieri too. Lauda seems always to be there!

'In the winter we cannot start testing early because of the frost, but by 11 o'clock we are out and spend all the daylight we can just running the car. Sometimes we 'ave run in the fog as well! Niki and Clay were doing the testing, one doing one stage while the other worked at something else: then they would change over to make sure of the work.

'Lauda had no testing reputation at all, but in Fiorano you have the speed traps, TV, plus information of the driver which you can check with the electronic equipment. You can read out the total time for a corner, and on the way in, and out.

'It is good for something like a new airbox. The driver can feel it makes a difference and look at the time, but at Fiorano you can see where it is quicker: on the straight, on the exit of a corner and so on.

'We did not use as many cars as you would think doing all this testing. The cars were so *strong* it was unbelievable: we did thousands of miles instead of hundreds.'

The car that emerged, the smoother B3 with its

angular side panels forming a visual link with the previous season as well as the broad nose beneath the transverse wing (developed in conjunction with an enthusiast metalworker who helped at Ferrari for the pleasure of being involved!) looked as though it might bring a reversal in Ferrari fortunes. A triumph of hard work and detail engineering, this was the tool for the restructured Ferrari to forget the humiliations of 1973 and concentrate upon one thing: World Championship Formula 1 victories.

'The first race, we were competitive straight away. I don't know if the management knew this before we went to South America, I certainly did not. It was nice to see, we came second, but our Ferraris were not second fastest on the road in the race. In practice Clay had been second quickest, but in the race they finished with Niki second and Clay third,' Cuoghi summed up the 13 January opening Championship round in Argentina.

The 1974 season did have all fifteen Championship rounds, despite the gloom at the beginning of the year arising from the fuel situation in the aftermath of the Arab-Israeli war. From a motor-racing standpoint it was the year virtually all the top drivers moved around in the wake of Jackie Stewart's retirement.

Ferrari's stalwart Grand Prix driver Jacky Ickx wound up at Lotus alongside Ronnie Peterson; Emerson Fittipaldi arrived at McLaren from Lotus, while Ken Tyrrell had to recruit Jody Scheckter from McLaren to fill the J.Y.S. vacancy and Patrick Depailler to replace François Cevert, who had been killed at Watkins Glen in October 1973. Emerging as Championship threats were both James Hunt (Hesketh-Cosworth Ford) and Carlos Reutemann (Brabham-Cosworth Ford), whose team-mate Carlos Pace was also an ex-

tremely effective Brabham driver.

The Ferraris had shown qualifying speed and race reliability; could we be set for a renaissance season for the Italian cars?

The second Brazilian round was inconclusive. Lauda qualified third fastest behind Fittipaldi and Reutemann, while Regazzoni was on the fourth row, his car being worked on for a suspected transmission vibration during the vital period of practice.

Cuoghi explained why Lauda came to the line with 'two Ferrari mechanics still working furiously to secure Lauda's airbox as the cars started to move,' in *Motor Sport*'s words: 'We had a bit of a problem there: we had to change an engine between warm-up and the race!' Cuoghi laughed cheerfully and grimaced, 'I cannot remember what the trouble was with the engine in the warm-up: only that it had to be changed very fast! At that time it took us just over two hours to replace the engine with another.' It was fortunate that the B3 had rather easier engine access than the previous models, but even so Cuoghi recalled that the oil tank had to be removed along with many other ancillaries before the job could be completed.

What happened in the race? 'When Niki is trying to start it as the cars move off it fires suddenly and he moves off *very quick*. Marelli didn't have time to disconnect the battery completely . . . oh, their man 'as a bit of a fright! Soon as Niki went the Marelli man is saying "Lauda is *mad*, I tell you

CHAMPION! LAUDA'S *raised hand acknowledges the hard work and constant testing that was behind Ferrari's World Championship form in 1975. The 312T* (with transverse gearbox) *took nine pole positions and five wins, this one the last at Watkins Glen*

mad!'" The Ferrari stuttered round for four laps before Niki retired. Regazzoni managed second place, fastest lap and the Swiss led the driver's points, the first time a Ferrari driver had managed this title lead since early 1971.

South Africa in March promised much, Lauda earning his first pole position and fighting for the lead with eventual winner Reutemann. Then, a really cruel streak of fortune: he lost his second place with three laps to go when the engine oil pressure dived in exactly the same way as Regazzoni's had earlier in the race. It was a lapse in Ferrari engine reliability that gave the opposition hope, but whatever the problem was Ferrari's engine department soon solved it, though Cuoghi was not told the results of their research into the South African engine failures.

Spain was the fourth round—this time held on the tight Jarama artificial autodromo near Madrid—and Lauda used the Ferrari's torque and even twelve-cylinder power delivery beautifully to steal a second successive pole position. However, it was to pit team work, Cuoghi and the sports car racing background of Ferrari in general that Ferrari owed their stunning 1–2 result, though neither Cuoghi nor his colleagues would ever claim that for themselves. The constant practice at changing wheels had been continued in the Formula 1 world 'so that we always get used to working at emergency speed, even if there is no need,' as Cuoghi explained.

In Spain they managed to change from wet tyres to dry in thirty-five seconds, Lauda springing into a lead that Ronnie Peterson had held while the track was wet. Lotus were in one of their chaotic moods that day and Ickx in particular must have missed that old sports car world of pit stops by JW and Ferrari sorely!

Belgium was notable for a fine track fight between Fittipaldi and Lauda, Scheckter and Regazzoni, the Ferraris finishing second and fourth. Regazzoni had been officially on pole, but despite protesting to the organizers that the time was not his (it belonged to Scheckter), Regga had to start from that position.

Cuoghi found plenty to keep him busy at Monaco, Lauda crashing his car and using the spare to take his third pole position of the year. 'It was not a hard job to repair his race car, you do not go off very fast at Monaco, but he drove very well to take fastest time in the older car. He had bent the wishbones a bit on the race car, but the chassis was unhurt. Funny enough, in the race it was Regga and Niki fighting for the lead. Then they came under pressure from behind and Niki was "pumping up" the distance between himself and Clay, sometimes very close, then falling back. Then Clay spun it under Niki's pressure! Lauda led for quite a while and then it stopped all of a sudden. Niki was walking in and I was running towards him, asking what was wrong. "Some kind of electrical problem," he says. In Argentina practice we had a similar thing, so I went up to the car, ask the marshall on the right-hand side of Rascasse if I could go in and try to start the car? I went in and it started straight away! So I drove the car back to the pit ... it was the magnetic spark box, we 'ave lost the race for that bloody thing. Goes for a long time, stop. Five minutes later you can start the car again,' Cuoghi informed me.

Cuoghi enjoyed the pre-race testing at the seventh round, Anderstorp in Sweden, with Ing. Caliri 'and a couple of mechanics. For what we had it was a very profitable test, but the car was no good there, like a lot of others!' There were no points for Ferrari in Sweden, but in Holland the long curves of 'Zandvoort-by-the-Sea' resulted in Ferrari lining up first and second on the grid ... and in the race result, Cuoghi's man first. 'The preparation was not so hard as usual.' Cuoghi confirmed his affection for Zandvoort, adding, 'the town is close by the race track so you 'ave all the home comforts. A very nice place and an enjoyable weekend.

'When Niki first won in Spain he was very happy, but he never shows much anyway. We did not go out for big celebrations as in my JW sports car days: the work is changing and it is a different world. We won so much in the sports cars at Ferrari that when we start winning in Formula 1—even after that gap in 1973—it just seem the natural thing.'

At the French Grand Prix Lauda and Regazzoni were third and fourth, Lauda's lead lost when tyre vibration stepped in. 'I know he was telling the truth because I see the great big blisters on his hands,' Cuoghi said simply, 'and we still can have this problem today.'

The British Grand Prix in 1974 was a farce. Lauda and Peterson shared the front row with the same time, but in the race a spate of punctures meant that Lauda eventually had to go into the pits while leading. 'Niki came to Britain earlier on that year and we lost the Race of Champions at Brands Hatch when we had that shock absorber trouble on the rear. Ickx passed Lauda in the rain, on the outside, going into Paddock! Niki had been leading, no problem at all until the rear shock absorbers packed up *completely*. Every time he hit the bottom of Paddock Hill the car was grounding and he had to lift off the gas.

'So Brands Hatch was a not a good place for us that year, because in the Grand Prix Niki had to come in to change the back tyre. The pit it was all blocked up with people, but we couldn't see Niki was trapped in there not able to get out!' There had been only two laps left when Lauda came in, so it looked like no result until an FIA enquiry awarded him fifth two months later!

Unbelievably from round 11 onwards, the German Grand Prix, Lauda added not a single point to his tally in the rest of the season. In Germany the Nürburgring demands the ultimate from a driver and Lauda responded with his seventh pole position time of the season: just over 7 minutes, i.e. around 120 mph average for the track that represents a kind of grown-up rally special stage. Regga joined him on the front row, but it was the Swiss Ferrari ace's race as Lauda continued what he has described as a learning year for the Championship title by an opening lap shunt with Scheckter. Cuoghi remembered: 'On the corner behind the pits there is a left-hander going slightly up hill that leads them away from us. Niki tried to overtake Scheckter, because he knew that if he left it any longer Clay would have flown away! Lauda couldn't make it, and did the flying over the road and bye, bye! Niki admitted straight away that it was a *big* mistake.'

Effectively this was the end of Niki's championship lead that season and he strove nobly to support Clay Regazzoni to secure the title. A battle that went all the way to the last Watkins Glen round, when Fittipaldi and Regazzoni arrived with the same total.

In Austria Ermanno's memories are primarily of the poor Ferrari mechanic who injured his arm trying to change a rear wheel on Regga's Ferrari while the Swiss was in gear, letting the drive-shaft revolve! Niki went out with engine trouble there after earning his eighth pole time of the season. Worse was Monza, where both Ferraris had engine trouble in the race traced as Cuoghi recalled it 'to a bad batch of bearings at the factory'.

At Monza Niki had racked up his ninth pole position of the year, but he was destined to have only the two race wins that season, finishing fourth in the Championship. Regga was second after managing a second overall in Canada ('which Niki led until he made a mistake avoiding Watson's accident,' Cuoghi reminded me) and eleventh in the USA. 'In America the cars were not handling well. Both drivers had trouble and Clay never showed in the race. He did finish, but it was after coming into the pits and having new tyres and trying to make the car better. Niki didn't finish because he has an engine problem as well as the handling trouble.'

It was the close of a fine opening season for Lauda and Cuoghi though, as Ermanno said, 'Niki made two mistakes and I made plenty! The one I remember was in practice for Canada. We had too much time for relaxation there! Niki is going off down the pit road: gets half-way along, stops, and has to tighten the left rear wheel by hand before he can bring the car back to us. He was not very pleased about that: tells me not to do it again. It is always dangerous when you have too much time relaxing, you don't concentrate. When you are tense, specific jobs to do, things are better—but always it is possible to make mistakes. If you do nothing with your life you cannot make mistakes so . . .' Cuoghi shrugged his shoulders philosophically, hiding the vital concern that dominates every proper racing mechanic's life, that a driver should suffer through an error of preparation.

Regazzoni suffered a pretty depressing final outing of 1974 at Watkins Glen, for in pre-race testing he severely damaged his intended race car. That machine was flown back to Italy and the factory had to suddenly race prepare an older chassis to be used instead. That was significant because it disrupted the test work that was going on at home on the mount we would hear an awful lot about in 1974, the Ferrari 312T, the suffix standing for *trasversale*, the Italian way of spelling out transverse, designating another feature that was to become as much a Ferrari hallmark as the flat twelve engine and separate front wing: the transversely-mounted gearbox.

The normal five gears and reverse were offered, the advantages including a further concentration of the car's weight between the front and rear axle lines, plus a very light and strong gearbox construction, the casing made in magnesium and the best possible use made of titanium's light weight, allied to strength, within. The overall size of the gearbox was also kept to a minimum and was mounted in unit with the back of the engine, from whence it received input through bevel gears, passing on drive through spur gears to the final drive.

Over page: A FINE LAT study of the 1975 Championship combination, Lauda plus Ferrari, on its way to the fifth win of the year at Watkins Glen. Behind, the champion who lost his 1974 crown, Emerson Fittipaldi in the McLaren M23

'Ing. Forghieri and Franco Rocchi worked together on that idea; Rocchi was also very good on the engines and chassis. Ing. Giancarlo Bussi was in charge of the dynamometer developments and he works on this gearbox development too. Most of the ideas seemed to come from Forghieri at that time.

'What was the transverse gearbox like to work on? It is a bit more difficult than a normal gearbox, it takes longer to change the ratios, but it was a marvellous bit of machinery to work on, really nicely made inside. I would say that gearbox is a little jewel: everything is fantastic because it is compact and you have no overhanging weight at the back.

'It was still good in 1979, you know? Maybe you noticed that the wing at Monaco on the Ferrari T4 was mounted straight on top of the gearbox, so the downforce is going exactly in the right place. A very clever idea, but it had not been copied anywhere except in America, where the idea is used in an Indy car. Now I think it will come to Europe again, perhaps even on the Brabham, who knows!' Cuoghi did, but was not saying.

The 312T had more to offer than just the new gearbox layout though. The body, already cleaned up during the B3's 1973 season to include a far more rounded airbox, now had the narrower chisel nose supporting the transverse front wing and the distinctive contoured sections around the inside edge of the giant back magnesium wheels. At the time it was felt that the flat twelve engine offered an advantage not only in power—just 500 bhp was quoted by factory documentation at the close of the season, between 12,000 and 12,500 rpm—but also in feeding the air to the rear wing. By contrast the Cosworth V8s with their tall airboxes and engine lines were thought to disturb that rear end flow. Later the tables would be turned as Lotus developed the ground-effect side-pod and skirt concept, but by then Ferrari had Michelin rubber.

The rear wing had a distinctive vee effect on the trailing and leading edge. The Ferrari's side view was notable for the ducting leading to the rear oil radiators tucked away neatly just aft of the front wheels. The suspension continued to use the long box section top arms fabricated in steel at the front, operating a spring/damper hidden away towards the centre of an alloy casting, bolted to the front of the monocoque chassis. The rear wing upright looked smoothly moulded, but the small air inlet in its 'face' was for the gearbox oil radiator crafted carefully within. The front wheel ducting to the centre of the disc brakes was carried over from B3 development in 1974.

Few stickers adorn a Ferrari, not even one for Fiat in 1975, but Ferodo were there in the side panel ducting, supplying pads for the larger 1975 ventilated Lockheed AP disc brakes—mounted within the front wheels and inboard, either side of the final drive casing, at the back. One nice addition to the Ferrari decor for 1975 was that of the Italian national flag colours upon the airbox.

The year did not start very well in the South American continent, Lauda finishing sixth in the opening torrid Argentinian race and fifth in Brazil; Regazzoni was a place ahead on each occasion. As Cuoghi revealed in his assessment of Lauda-the-driver (Chapter 11), Niki was not at his ultimate in a car that was less than 100 per cent—and the team were still racing the B3 model, the transverse box 312T left at home for further testing. At the time some people thought this meant the 312T would be no good. . . .

Cuoghi recalled that the heat was melting the glue and tape that secures the wheel weights on the Goodyear covers, 'unfortunately this was happening quite often, and the driver had a hard time to hold on to the steering wheel!'

For the third round of the Championship, Cuoghi was back at Kyalami and Ferrari entered two new 312Ts and a spare B3. The event was in March and Lauda had spent most of February with Regga grinding round Fiorano looking for any weaknesses and honing both himself and the T into a really competitive state. Lauda started from the second row, less than half a second adrift of the Brabham twins' front row pace. What Cuoghi remembers on that occasion is a feeling that he had enjoyed quite a lot since working for competitive teams, the pride of racing a new car. 'This time though Niki has a problem when following Fittipaldi and getting a full splash of oil across the tyres in practice! He went spinning off into the barriers and banged the chassis about all over the place: my brand new car! Anyway, it's a big mess and there's a lot of work to do. Luckily some of the English mechanics decided they had done enough work with all the practice accidents they had that year and they cut some of practice down: I join their union OK—we have a little more time to beat Niki's car into shape!

'Normally I always enjoy presenting a new car. You reach the last few days of the preparation, it is an exciting thing because you know you have a lot of your personal effort in that car. That is enjoyable, but it is best when you present it and run: you are in there waiting to see how he goes. Better than the previous car? Then it is a marvellous atmosphere ... champagne out!'

Well, it was not quite time to bring on the bubbly ... yet. Lauda actually finished fifth after shadowing Regga to within a few laps of the end when the Swiss driver was put out by a deranged throttle linkage.

However, Niki made up for all that on 13 April in Britain. Running in the non-Championship Formula 1 race at Silverstone Lauda outlasted Hunt's Hesketh and out-drove Fittipaldi in the McLaren to take the 312T's first victory. Cuoghi's most vivid memory was of the Ferrari in practice, for it had settled on its springs when hurtling around all those long aerodrome right-handers and looked to be listing over 'ready to go down like a boat,' Cuoghi chuckled.

Although the Ferraris were on the front row together for the fourth round at Spain's picturesque Montjuich, it was a race that saw them both collide at the start! This was not all bad because this was the dreadful race in which Rolf Stommelen's Embassy-backed car scaled the armco and killed four people and the event was curtailed, but not fast enough. The outcry against safety standards over the weekend was enormous and the challenging track has not been used since for Grand Prix motor racing.

Cuoghi commented, 'I remember Fittipaldi and the other drivers were bolting up the crash barriers before practice could start at all. Then our new car is going really well with Niki and Clay on the front. Unfortunately Andretti was there at the start and, as he pushed through, our cars hit each other. It was very uncomfortable experience for us and a sad day for motor racing altogether.'

When they got to Monaco though Niki was in a class of his own in the 312T. Cuoghi recalled, 'Niki was playing that time. During qualifying he was going along, waiting until someone was getting closer to him and blowing them off. Then he would sit in the pits. Watch if anyone was close to him and then shoot out for a better time straight away! It was so good, we just couldn't believe our eyes.

'The race itself was wet at the start and then we had to change on to dry tyres. We made a good changeover, but Niki's was slightly slower than Clay's. Niki is leading toward the end comfortably and the journalists say he has slowed down because of his oil pressure, but he is never in danger from Fittipaldi. The oil was OK actually, and I think it could have been the gauge that time: the engine was perfect.

'Maybe he was less than three seconds in front at the flag, but at Monaco the drivers know it is very hard to overtake, so they all close down the throttle a little for the finish, it happens a lot of years. The spectators, they go berserk and the journalists start talking ... for nothing.'

From Monaco onward it began to look as though nothing was going to stop Ferrari and Lauda either. The next two Grand Prix, the Belgian at Zolder and Anderstorp's Swedish event, brought wins, though it was Lauda's choice of a tougher tyre compound than leader Reutemann that actually brought Ferrari into contention, as the Ferraris, like many other normal front-runners, were not so competitive in Sweden: a fact usually attributed to the long, constant-radius corners. 'In the beginning the car was quite difficult to drive, but everyone else slow down towards the end with tyre problems. It was only ten laps from the end that Niki could get by Carlos,' said Cuoghi.

Lauda and Regazzoni monopolized the front row at the eighth Championship round, Zandvoort in Holland, and Lauda looked set for a fourth win. 'For Ferrari Zandvoort has always been good (five wins for the marque up to that race), but this time we 'ave to do a lot of tyre changing from wet to dry again. The result is Niki is 'aving a fantastic race for forty laps with James Hunt. Sometimes he is alongside: once I think he even was ahead. What I remember is Montezemolo being knocked over by Peterson's car in the pits ... Luca 'as a broken leg!'

Hunt scored the first victory by an Englishman (as opposed to a Scotsman) since Gethin at Monza in 1971, hardly a second in front of Lauda after a really tough motor race. It was business as usual again in France, Lauda having an enormous lead on the first lap—'again everyone was getting excited towards the end when Niki slow down and James finishes about two seconds behind. But if you win, that is all that matters, I think!'

The British weather made a complete farce of the Silverstone round, but Niki did his bit too. He and Regga started from the second row. 'In the race Clay spins off when he is leading and it starts to rain. Then Niki comes in: we do our best to change the tyres really fast, but Niki is too impatient and roars away with one back wheel not done up!' They got plenty of practice in the Ferrari pit that day because Lauda made four stops, finishing an official eighth, though nobody saw how the results could be pronounced because, when the RAC decided the race had finished, the majority of the field were either grazing in the catch fences or engaged in pit work! Ferrari protested the result, but to no avail.

'For Nürburgring Niki was just fantastic, the first man to practice under seven minutes, but in the race he has a puncture while leading the race. We replace the left front, but he had done a lot of miles on it: we were despairing while we waited for him to come around: he lost a lot of places. The loudspeakers say that he is crawling around. It was not very good for the car, but we give it a check and he goes out again and passes a lot of people again to make third. It was a brave drive.'

Lauda went to his home country with a seventeen-point Championship lead, took pole position and led the initial wet weather nightmare on the super-fast curves of the Oesterreichring. 'They were kamikaze conditions that day,' Cuoghi felt, 'the only time Brambilla could take his hand off the wheel, to celebrate his race win, he spun going past the flag! There was a lot of luck needed with everyone stopping on the grass and spinning off everywhere, losing control on the puddles.' Lauda stayed on and finished sixth, but he got only half a point for his troubles as the race was prematurely stopped owing to the conditions.

As the cars assembled for the final European Championship round that year, at Monza in September, Lauda and Ferrari were practically assured of the title, for Lauda was $17\frac{1}{2}$ points ahead of Reutemann's Brabham–Cosworth Ford V8, and Lauda took his eighth pole position of the season, a good half a second in front of Clay's 312T. Regazzoni ran away with the race, Lauda content to finish third after 1974 Champion Emerson Fittipaldi had put in a fine drive to finish second. That third place was all Lauda needed and it ensured the title, before the series went to the final World Championship round of the year in America, Canada's Grand Prix being cancelled that year.

It was Ferrari's first title since 1964 and Niki was nearly as young as the previous youthful title holder (Fittipaldi was twenty-six when he first won the title in 1972), but what we had underestimated most of all, perhaps, was the supreme mechanical reliability of the Ferraris in 1975. They started twenty-eight races and finished twenty-two, gathering in two non-Championship wins, five Grand Prix wins for Lauda and one for Regazzoni. The 312T may have sounded complicated, but it all worked faster and rather more reliably than the opposition, thanks to the efforts of the whole Ferrari factory, who truly made the most of their car from gearbox to front aerofoil.

Cuoghi remembered only the aftermath of Monza. 'The crowd were terrible. To keep them away there were police with horses: I was crushed between a saloon car and the people before I could get back to the transporter. I forget it's not my car and go walking over it, making dents on the roof! I was really scared, all those people shouting and screaming, they can get in anywhere I tell you. The people always trap you in the transporter: there was a fight that year between our mechanics and the crowd as we tried to keep them away from the transporter. You have to lock everything up, not so much because they will steal things, but because they will never go away, touching everything and always crowding in toward you. Monza is a terrible place . . . the crowd is always getting overexcited.

'I didn't need to tell Niki at the end that he was Champion, he was making his little calculations all the time he is driving! In Monza, when Niki comes in, I try and go with him straight away to the *Parc Fermé*, so there is no people in there. I stay there for an hour until they move away. That year the crowd did not go away, even when we took the car out of *Parc Fermé*. Pushing the car to the transporter was a nightmare.

'To celebrate in the evening there is a place that is very special to Ferrari in Monza . . . and it was even for Surtees in the times of Gilera motorcycles: the St Eustorggio, a very nice hotel with marvellous food in the restaurant. You enjoy it there if you win or lose! That evening the owner brought out the champagne quite a few times. . . . A great occasion, but of course Mr Ferrari is not there. He has not been coming to the races for some years, but he has direct line TV, so there is no worry that he does not know what is going on: he is super-informed.

'We finish the year going to the USA and Lauda wins all the money, takes pole position, wins easily from Fittipaldi. Thank God there was no Canada that year. . . .'

1975

Lauda was worried, despite the last success of 1975, for he felt that Ferrari had given up on development and were getting complacent. The new Austrian champion was also a realist about the politics within Ferrari and knew he could not race effectively without the kind of pressure Luca di Monte-

Opposite: ON THE *way into Monza chicane 1976. This was Lauda's comeback drive after the Nurburgring accident. Cuoghi felt it took even more courage to face the press and the photographers than to drive the car to a fine fourth place*

ON THE *way out of the chicane at Monza in his courageous return to GP racing in 1976. This unusual shot shows how much the lines of the GP Ferraris were cleaned up over the years (compare with that first picture of the B3) and how little mechanical rear overhang there is with a transverse gearbox*

zemolo exerted in the inner circle at Ferrari. . . . Now Montezemolo was going, back into the Fiat hierarchy where he would zoom up the Public Relations organization, part of his grooming for what everyone at Fiat tells you will be a golden future.

Former Lancia rally co-driver Daniele Audetto would be the new man for a season that put more pressure on Lauda than any racing driver has successfully borne before. By the end he would be badly scarred and an ex-champion, but he gave a new meaning to the cliché of sporting comebacks. . . .

Mechanically speaking Ferrari did not seem to be resting on their World Championship laurels. Cuoghi and the equivalent chief mechanic on Regga's car, Giulio Borsari, were on hand in November for the presentation of a distinctive twist to the 312T theme. Shown complete with vestigial front mudguards the 1976 bodywork (without the tall airbox, a duct on either side of the cockpit front surround taking engine air in) and a de Dion rear end, the 312T2 really set the press talking.

Lauda and Regazzoni put a lot of test miles into the de Dion Ferrari during 1975 and early 1976, but neither that concept nor the front mudguards were to appear in public more than briefly. The de Dion rear end was swopped on and off Lauda's 312T in pre-race testing for the South African Grand Prix in February 1976, 'but it was a second slower,' Cuoghi recalled, 'and we never did get to the point of racing it. There was no advantage. In theory, yes, it should have kept the big tyres nice and flat, but at the races, no! In the end we could change over the rear end of the *trasversale* from the normal suspension to de Dion, but in South Africa it took nearly all night one time because it did not fit properly. Jesus! What a way to spend a night.'

The front mudguards were ruled illegal when they appeared on the car for practice at that year's French Grand Prix because they moved with the wheels and the aerodynamic function: they were also part of the traditional Ferrari front brake scoop. In France the de Dion layout was tried again in practice on the spare car—as it was at many meetings—but even on the smooth Ricard track no advantage in lap times could be found.

The bodywork worked well though! From 1 May it was illegal to run the high airbox scoops to the engine that had become the height of fashion in F1 in much the same way as wings and side pods had been. Ferrari were ready for this the previous winter and we saw the results in the non-Championship Race of Champions at Brands Hatch in March 1976. Lauda drove the 312T2 in its conventional lighter weight trim without the de Dion rear end and with the cockpit ducting instead of the airbox: unfortunately the car had to be retired with a brake pipe failure in the race. Ferrari continued to run their distinctive tall white airboxes with the Italian national colours until the Spanish Grand Prix, when everyone had to swop over to this system and bring their rear wings closer to the main bodywork as the rear-end overhang on some of the cars was ridiculous. Italy's colours were then striped around the cockpit.

So the Ferrari 312T2 that Cuoghi worked on through most of the season was not the radical car that had been expected at the beginning of the year, but it was still a very effective car in the hands of Lauda or Regazzoni. Unfortunately the year turned into a sour confrontation between Ferrari and McLaren with the rule book waved on every possible occasion as the struggle grew more tense. James Hunt's McLaren was disqualified from winning the Spanish Grand Prix for being fractionally too wide, then it was reinstated. The Ferrari team were then incensed by the British Grand Prix again. The British Grand Prix has been the most controversial of World Championship qualifying rounds on the organizational side through most of the seventies. In 1974 the question of using spare cars after a startline accident involving Lauda and Regazzoni with Hunt skimming overhead was the thorny topic.

It was a thoroughly nasty season in that sportsmanship was shown to be an unknown factor at the front of the F1 field, but there was some great racing. Lauda was to owe his life to some fellow drivers at the back end of the field by the end of the season.

By the time the teams assembled for the eighth round of the 1976 series at Paul Ricard for the French Grand Prix, the battle between Ferrari and McLaren was white hot. Lauda had won in Brazil, South Africa, Belgium and Monaco, but Hunt was providing consistent opposition. James had beaten Niki in Spain—'but there we 'ave to lift Lauda in and out of the car because he has damaged his ribs in that tractor accident', Cuoghi sadly said. 'Niki still finished second there, as he had in Long Beach when Clay won, so we were winning a lot that year, looking good for a second championship.'

It didn't look so bright after the French Grand Prix though. Hunt won while both Ferraris went out with engine failures. It was to prove an isolated case, as Cuoghi explained: 'It was not the crankshaft itself that is the cause. At the end of the crankshaft there is a flange pressed on: when this unit is put on it has made some tiny fractures that we cannot see. No crack detecting machine was showing it, but that is what caused the breakage of the crankshafts at the French Grand Prix. That long straight at Le Castellet allowed the engine to get into a critical vibration spell, which helped break it too.' For Lauda it was an unpleasant surprise, as he was leading and travelling at over 12,000 rpm in top, towards 180 mph, when the unit came to an abrupt halt internally, locking the back wheels!

The British Grand Prix was the usual confused affair after that Lauda versus Regazzoni first corner fracas at Paddock. To Cuoghi, to this day, Hunt should not have been allowed to start in the second running of the race, but on the day the crowd were *not* prepared to accept the officials restarting the British Grand Prix without Hunt. There were nearly 80,000 spectators there that sunny day and, when the commentators told them that James was not going to take the second start, the grandstand opposite the pits threatened to erupt as the stiff upper lip mentality was substituted for the ugly mood of a bad referee's decision on the football terraces. You would have thought you were at Monza and that Brambilla or Regazzoni had been disqualified.

Anyway they did start the second time with Hunt in the field and it was James pursuing Niki's Ferrari. Then they hit the mid-field runners to lap them for the first time. Cuoghi took up the story: 'He had been leading the race comfortably, it was such a shame! Then he has a big problem with the gearshift: a little bush between the shift and the arm has seized up because it has the wrong clearance. He had to slow down, just couldn't change gear properly.' However, the FIA later ruled that Niki had won that race. It was *that* kind of year, this time it was Hunt who was disqualified!

That brought them to the tenth round of the Championship to be held on the Nürburgring (for the last time on the full circuit?). Just the week before the event a brilliant interview from Pete Lyons, the American writer whose work appeared in *Autosport* in Britain regularly at that time, exposed how Lauda felt about the circuit. Despite his safety reservations, the Austrian pushed his Ferrari round to second fastest time to Hunt: less than a second separated them, but both were over seven minutes in imperfect conditions.

The race started on a wet track and Lauda was lying ninth when he decided to pull in for dry tyres and rejoined amongst the back of the field. He got only as far as *Bergwerk*, subsequently taking a left after 10.6 km of the lap. At something over 120 mph the Ferrari slid normally on opposite lock then flicked savagely right. It hit catchfencing and sheared through, bouncing from the banking back on to the track. The scarlet Ferrari number 1 was enveloped in orange flames. It was struck by Brett Lunger's Surtees and Harald Ertl's Hesketh. Lunger, Ertl and Guy Edwards helped haul Lauda from the car, but ironically (because he loathes Lauda) Merzario made it possible by undoing the seat belts within the inferno.

For Cuoghi the ultimate nightmare was reality that grim afternoon standing within the drab concrete pits. 'There were so many different reports of what was happening: Niki is not hurt; he is badly burned; there are no breakages; it was not until later on that I knew what had happened. Meantime, they have said that a wheel has come off, that was the first report over the loudspeakers. "Niki Lauda 'as lost a wheel and crashed the car," they say. Before the second start, they have brought the car back to us in the paddock. Soon as I find out it is on the way I went down to see what is the situation with the car: the second race has already started when I am on my way. I saw the car as it came in. All four wheels were there: one wheel was off, but with the full suspension corner, wishbones, hub nuts tight. The first thing I did was to talk to Franco Lini, the Italian journalist, and say that, considering what they were saying over the loudspeakers, would he take some photographs, proving all the wheels were attached? If they are off the car, they have been ripped away on the impact. I go upstairs then and assure the boys that the wheels were on tight. Whatever had happened has happened, but there is no blame for the mechanics. There was *no* mechanical failure whatsoever: I checked the suspension links, everything.

'I had to tell the boys. For the mechanics, when a driver is hurt, this is the most important thing ... a bad feeling.

'After that, as soon as they finish the race, team manager Audetto took a car, come out through a small back way of the 'Ring and down to Mannheim because Niki was taken there after they first put him in Adenau. Went to the clinic in Mannheim and they said he was not there. A nurse told us that he had been moved to Ludwigshafen because Mannheim was not right for him. Niki's Missus was already at Ludwigshafen when we got there and the doctor from the Formula 1 series is telling me that Niki has been put in a sterilized room: nobody can see him. The doctors were worried about his lungs, not the wounds from the accident. His wife was able to see him for a while and then his relatives. It was the first time I had met Lauda's parents, for we stay in the same hotel for the night in Ludwigshafen. The morning we try and get some more news, but we still could not see him, so in the afternoon we flew back to Modena, hoping for Niki all the time.'

Ermanno was told that if Niki pulled through the first three days, he would have a good chance. 'Luckily he was pulling through, but when he first came back to Modena because he wanted to drive again, nobody could believe he had recovered so fast. That was about a week before Monza in September!

'He had been telephoning us, the mechanics, for some time telling us what he wanted done with the car! "I want my car right": Jesus Christ, we just would not believe it ... but he came, and when he came it was very, very sad to see his head. It was bald completely with a dark wound across it. He was not damaged at all in the accident apart from the burns—at least that was what we thought at the time, but it turns out his rib injury in Spain, 1977, probably went back to that Nürburgring. The cockpit of the car had stayed together, it was really quite remarkable how it had come through it all, and how Niki was saved from fractures.'

Softly and sadly Cuoghi recalled their only problem at that first test session after the accident was, 'to make a crash helmet that was suiting him without hurting his wounds. He had a doctor with him, making sure that his head was protected, and there was the AGV man from the helmet manufacturers. They made sure that the helmet could not touch any open wounds which had happened when his helmet moved in the accident.

'He got into the car, did two or three laps, the crash helmet was hurting him. It was made better, Lauda went out again did a good time and said, "the car is OK, bye, bye!" You should have seen the crowds outside Fiorano . . . they could not keep them back. For myself I had seen him in the office from the lorry on the way in and prepared myself for how he looked before we met.'

For Ferrari themselves Lauda's lightning comeback was slightly embarrassing. They had Carlos Reutemann on hand to replace Niki, the Argentinian having bought his way out of his Martini contract at Brabham. Regazzoni was still there, and Lauda insisted on racing at Monza, just six weeks after Nurburgring and having the Last Rites read.

In Lauda's recovery time Cuoghi 'stayed at home. I didn't go and work on Clay's car in the two races Niki missed. I made sure Niki's car was ready, had a coupla weeks' holiday, talked to Niki on the phone or to Marlene asking if Niki's head is getting smaller now in a joking way!

'That Monza took Niki a lot of nerves, a lot of courage. Not to get in the Ferrari, but to tackle all the journalists, all the photographers, all waiting there and ready for when he was taking his balaclava off. They just wanted to photograph his scars. Even now he wears his balaclava on top of his head: it saves him putting another hat on! It was a very upsetting thing to see the photo-reporters waiting for him.

'So far as the driving went he came fourth and I don't think he could have done any better. He was not even tired at the end and lifted himself out like always. The crowds at Monza that year were good though, they did not crowd in so much as usual, Niki had more respect for doing such a job: everyone cheering him, that was marvellous.

'I think that having Carlos Reutemann in the team at Monza upset Niki a bit . . . and he went out and proved that it was unnecessary to have Reutemann.'

Cuoghi confirmed that little testing had been going on while Lauda was recovering. 'Up to that point it was a super-competitive car. When Niki came back there was a lack of progress and the cars were not so competitive in North America.'

The Canadian Grand Prix at Mosport's bumpy circuit was pretty disastrous, for Lauda suffered a suspension link failure and slipped out of the top six-point-earning finishers. In the USA Grand Prix at Watkins Glen things were a little better as he qualified the car on the third row and finished third . . . but in both cases Hunt won and that meant the two would go to the final Japanese round on even points, Hunt having a slight advantage as he had won six races to Niki's five.

For the mechanics and Cuoghi the North American races had been worrying with the loss of the Ferrari's competitive edge, but also slightly annoying as they had to move the gearbox cooler out of its neat home in the tail and site it on top of the gearbox casting itself as the CSI said it had been too far back. It really was a lawyers' season....

Back in Italy they tested furiously, working hard to get the suspension system back to giving the handling advantage which Lauda has always maintained was the car's true strength, rather than the sheer power of that magnificent engine.

Conditions were diabolical for the Fuiji race. Lauda retired after two laps, handing the title to James Hunt. Cuoghi commented, 'Niki just said it was impossible to drive, you could see nothing, just really big clouds of spray. All the drivers, before the start, they had agreed they would stop—even Clay—and Niki has stuck to his word. In my opinion it really was too bad to race.

'In that year Lauda had to lose the Championship. Because everything was going wrong from Nürburgring on. All the circumstances were wrong: even if he had gone on in that race he might have crashed or something would have broken. You are predestined in these things. Sure, if he *had* been able to stay on the track he would have won the championship....'

I asked Cuoghi how the relationship between Audetto and Lauda had fared during the year and Cuoghi told me, 'Niki was so used to having Montezemolo around. It takes time to adjust to a new personality, I think it could have worked in time. To us it made little difference, we had respect for him. I think he was trying his best . . . I thought he was perfectly OK, in fact he did a good job.

'All the same he was out at the end of the year

and we had *Ingegneri* Nosetto, a man who had worked for Ferrari for twenty years. We worked hard in 1977 and it was a much better year.'

Looking back at the failure of the de Dion rear end Cuoghi said that its performance was unpredictable. 'Sometimes the results were quite good, but it varied a lot from track to track. At one stage it was faster at Fiorano, but it was so hard to tell anything at all because Goodyear were playing about with the tyres so much that year. Unfortunately Goodyear could not make Ferrari favourites: we had always to suit the suspension to the tyres. Never suit the tyre to our suspension! That was worse when you have something technically different like the de Dion, for you 'ave tyres that are intended for normal cars, most with Cosworth V8 engines,' Cuoghi concluded thoughtfully.

For 1977 Ferrari dispensed with Regazzoni's services and brought Reutemann in full time, returning to a two-car team on a regular basis. For Cuoghi the year was split between the racing activities with the T2—which suffered a lack of development at the beginning of the season inherited from Lauda's 1976 accident—and the beginning of an exciting new era on Michelin tyres with a new chassis to go with them, the 312T3.

Lauda, and therefore to a degree Cuoghi, seemed to be under some psychological pressure to accept Reutemann as the number 1 following Niki's pull-out from the Japanese Grand Prix and McLaren's win of the title at the eleventh hour. It suddenly became tougher for Niki to get test miles in and he was not originally asked to take part in the winter Paul Ricard trials that saw the Ferrari trying out various body changes. When they went to Argentina and Brazil for the opening championship rounds the pressure still seemed to be heavy on Lauda to prove his worth. He was faster than Reutemann in practice for the Argentinian's home event, and the opening round of the 1977 series, but twenty-one laps of the race saw them out with a rare fault in the metering unit for the Ferrari's Lucas fuel injection: Reutemann was third.

It had been the first time Ferrari carried the name Fiat upon the scarlet body.

In Brazil Lauda had a troubled practice, culminating in a fuel leak right at the time he was to try and improve his position, while Reutemann got a new rear wing layout that Forghieri had developed. There was no duplicate for Lauda! Only the drivers concerned could tell if that made a real difference—it was perhaps a sign of Ferrari feelings at the time that they did not seem to know where the improvement was needed in the car either. However, Reutemann won and Niki was third.

That fired the Austrian up all right! He made sure that he, Lauda, would be doing the test development for the third round in South Africa. Cuoghi commented of the situation: 'There was some reluctance to ask Niki's opinion about small things like the performance of a wing. They fired Clay because they thought Reutemann would be better, but Niki and Clay were good together and had a good understanding of our preparation. With a new person you have to start all over again. I found Carlos an uncertain person and it was possible to get the wrong impression of what was wanted. Niki and Carlos would 'ave to work together in the year, but it was not done willingly.

'Borsari retired as head mechanic on the other team car, but I never thought of working with Reutemann. Anyway they now had Bellentani to take over....'

By the time it was race day in South Africa the Ferraris featured revised front suspension geometry and had new mounting points for the rear suspension; the battery and oil catch tank had been moved forward. Subtle aerodynamic tuning continued to make full use of the narrower nose and rear panels that provided a better flow for the latest rear wing. 'Niki wins there all right, starts from the second row, follows Hunt for a couple of laps and then he is ahead for good. It's the first time he is leading a race since his accident, but it was a close thing to the end because there is damage on both bottom wishbones, the radiator has a hole in one side, and he has little oil or water left at the end. All because he has picked up some of the wreckage from the Tom Pryce accident and carried it around with him to the end.

'Niki found out what had happened on the prize-giving podium and he was pretty upset, for they had been friends. Of that accident I think people never learn: today we have people walking all over the track in the races, just the same. Tom was a quiet boy, nice to see driving and it was a very bad thing that Pryce should 'ave been killed by somebody running across the track.'

Lauda's next win of 1977 did not come until July, but he was steadily amassing points with second places in the US Grand Prix (West) at Long Beach, Monaco, Belgium and Britain, and a fifth in France. Cuoghi remembered the irony of that second 1977 win was that it was the German Grand Prix, but this time held in the concrete basin that is Hockenheimring. 'The car is going really well that week, but it was very hard to win that year in

THE RACING miles as Lauda fought Hunt in World Championship events were something to remember. This is Niki and James in 1978. The following year Hunt retired, while Lauda waited until the end-of-season Canadian GP to walk out on Brabham

Opposite: LET'S GO! *Cuoghi waits alongside a Lauda waiting to get on with the job in the 1977 US GP at Watkins Glen. The race went to James Hunt's McLaren M26 but the title, and three GP wins went to Lauda*

Formula 1 for us. Hockenheim is a very fast track in the back, so we reduce the wing until it has no effect on the car through the slow infield in the stadium, where there are a lot of camber changes. Niki says you can gain most time between the first chicane, the *Ostkurve*, that is the really quick right at the back, and the next chicane. The Ferrari had enough wing to help through this section and give the good balance in the car at that point.

'Niki had been pressing Scheckter in the race and when he got through to lead again, we were so pleased. There were two or three of us watching for him on the infield, jumping up and down with the excitement to see him win *that* race and forget all that terrible business a year before.'

A month later Lauda won the Dutch Grand Prix, taking his third win and fastest lap of that year. A second in the Italian Grand Prix and a fourth in America's Watkins Glen were enough to secure that year's title with two rounds left to go.

There was a tremendous amount of trouble brewing in the team. Lauda, really resentful about the way Ferrari had treated him after the rigours of 1976, and bolstered by a second World Championship, was getting ready to quit.

Cuoghi was very much aware of the situation between the management and Niki, of course, and was becoming involved in it as we shall hear, but for Cuoghi there was the interest of development work on the T3 to take some of the sting from the biting enquiries as to his position in Lauda's future. 'The T3 had a completely different chassis, all the frame and inner panels, all were changed. With Ferrari there is always a basic car to start from though: all their cars are stage developments over the one before, not like the brand-new car designs we had at Brabham quite often. Even when Ferrari did the T4 wing car there was an adapted old car developing the wing section before it appears on the T4.

'For the T3 we had the weight distribution moved, and the suspension had round wishbones, instead of box frames at the front, and we used more castings for the front suspension as well. Though some of it did not look very different there was practically nothing on the hubs or any other place that would fit the T2 from the T3, even the radiators were in a different place and now you could see the front shock absorber mountings sticking up through the body—and that body was changed too with big "flick-ups" in front of the rear wheels and fences around the edge, almost like a sports car! Of course the big changes were all needed because they would run Michelin in the next season.

'I remember going testing with the Ferrari on Michelin tyres at Monza and it was *two seconds* a lap faster than before. That is one 'elluva lot in grand prix racing and it made me realize how fast Ferrari were going to be . . . but Niki had already made up his mind,' Cuoghi said slightly wistfully.

Looking back on 1977 and Lauda's Championship win with three wins, six seconds and a third, Cuoghi felt 'Niki was much more human. He was aggressive in his races until he realized the car was 99 per cent, not 101 per cent, and then he slows down toward the end and make sure of his position.' Remembering that Reutemann won once, took a pair of seconds and three thirds, plus other points-earning positions during the year, emphasized Cuoghi's next point: 'The other teams don't realize how *reliable* the Ferraris are. Always they have been testing, even when it was at Modena and not Fiorano. They are building up experience all the time, perhaps in the sports car racing as well. Learning all about that engine from 1970 onward,

that's a lot of knowledge. Today they have that engine and the transverse gearbox, everything else has changed quite gradually. I did not see revolutionary things at Ferrari, but most of the things they tested they could use in races, just little developments, step-by-step. The de Dion rear end was the most sudden thing, but they did not have to commit the whole year of cars to that: always they are experimenting and working, you can be sure of that!'

The team went to Watkins Glen 1977 in early October. There were three more Championship rounds scheduled to complete the year.

Cuoghi would not finish the season.

9

Leaving... Cuoghi's full account

'NIKI STARTED to think of moving away from Ferrari in the middle of the season, around July. He was talking about that and saying that he did not like the management or the politics. He was not happy and he asked me if I was going with him?' Cuoghi began the account of the hardest months in his life as an international mechanic to the best, but it was not his talent that was to be tested.

It was his loyalty. To Italy and Ferrari and home life. Or to leave and possibly work in England again without his family? Britain was the home of so many top teams that were interested in Niki Lauda: Lotus, McLaren, Wolf and Brabham. All were possibilities.

'So he had asked me at that time, I knew from the beginning that he wanted to go. We normally speak together in English—only when we speak of secrets do we speak in Italian!' Cuoghi chuckled and continued, 'I was very happy at Ferrari. It is a wonderful place to work, especially for a man from Modena.

'But you must push yourself. I am not a pushing person at all. There are politics even for me. At Ferrari there are politics for everyone: for a mechanic, for a driver, for *everyone*. You have to have influence, talk in the right places. I was happy in my job, happy with the mechanics, glad to be with Ferrari people. The surroundings to the mechanics I worked with were not so easy....

'I worked with most of the same people all the time I was there. Perhaps there were a few new boys from other parts of Ferrari, from the production line and so on, because they had the right attitude, but generally it was the same six that I looked after, plus there were two floating guys: the other head mechanic has eight as well. There was a permanent staff of another nine doing things like the glass-fibre, the panel beating, things like that.

'For total racing staff there is a lot more of course with the engine department, gearbox, Fiorano, the research engineers: all have something to put in the racing programme.

'I did not feel free working inside Ferrari, but I enjoyed the work itself. When Niki was talking about leaving, the decision for me was personally of not much matter . . . but the involvement of my family, my son, parents, the house, the way of living. To settle all these domestic details was hard, very hard!

'My wife was not very pleased in the beginning. Afterwards, she understood. I would be happier making that move, and so she has agreed.'

The strength of the relationship between Lauda and Cuoghi can be judged from the fact that Ermanno was prepared to take such a step, for by this time he knew it must mean moving to England.

Cuoghi elaborated, 'Niki did not know straight away it would be Brabham, but for my involvement it was only Brabham; I was not involved in Niki's discussions with any other team. Just before the Italian Grand Prix Niki told me it was going to be Brabham. Lauda came in Italy especially to talk with Mr Ferrari, and after he has talked with Ferrari, Niki sees me on my own and tells me what he has said and what he has done. Niki did not tell Ferrari that he would be taking me, and I did not say anything either. There was a rumour that I was going to leave with Niki, and Mr Ferrari 'as found this out. He asked me my intentions? His son, Piero Lardi, is the one who is asking me. I told them there was nothing in it, I would not move from Ferrari.

'If I had told them the truth, they would have put me out in September. I lied to them up to Watkins Glen. The rumour came out again at Watkins Glen because they 'ave seen me talking with the Alfa Romeo people. Then they 'ave put me against the wall and asked me what I was going to do again. I could not lie to them then.

'I told them "look, I have not decided anything . . . yet." I also informed them, because I knew I must tell them what I was doing as soon as possible, that I would ask my wife about the next move. This 'appened on the Saturday afternoon of practice for Sunday's Watkins Glen race.

'It was six o'clock. Too late to phone home. I telephoned my wife on Sunday morning and asked her what she thought?' Cuoghi reflected on that decisive transatlantic call and told me the reply—'"do whatever you think is best," she said. So I

FUNNY HAT *from America for Cuoghi lightens the mood as Lauda waits the start of his home GP at Oesterreichring in 1974. Note the smoother airbox line and distinctive separate front wing that, in one form or another, has become a Ferrari trademark.* Below: ANOTHER STUDY *of Cuoghi at work at the same meeting*

went to the Ferrari race management on Sunday morning and said to them I would leave Ferrari at the end of the season.

'Apparently Ferrari had asked Mr Nosetto, the engineer who was the team manager at that time, to find out my intentions. Nosetto never talked to me. He has talked to one of the technical engineers (Mieni) to tell me the old man's enquiry... Nosetto did not have the courage to ask me himself! They told me straight away that, because I was going to leave Ferrari, they would have to keep me away from the team. They would not even let me near Niki's car on Sunday. After that they said I could not wear the uniform... couldn't wear a Ferrari jacket! It was the only rally jacket I had—then I found I had nothing else to wear so I put the jacket on inside out! I went to the race and watched it like that with my jacket all turned around.... For the race I was between Ferrari and Shadow pits, but Niki needs only a single point to be World Champion again. He is fourth, it is enough. I had been with Niki on the starting grid as a spectator...!

'When the race has finished Niki has asked me to go on the top of the car with him. He goes to the prize-giving and dedicates that race to me, *his* mechanic. That was touching my heart: I was finished with Ferrari.

'The funny thing was that my ticket from Ferrari was for Watkins Glen and Canada, my ticket was not valid until after the Canadian Grand Prix. I had the ticket, but it was no good! I must stay a few days longer and fly back from Canada. I could not stay there, I did not feel like 'aving a holiday in that country, in that condition. All I wanted to do was go home straight away. I asked Nosetto to provide me with a ticket to go home. "You got the ticket, take a flight and go home." I can try to do that, fair enough. Fly from New York instead of Toronto, but how can I go from Watkins Glen to New York?'

The Ferrari team manager had no doubts on that: 'Find your own way,' he told Cuoghi. 'I was upset with Nosetto and told him there was something wrong with his head, you cannot treat people like that. I am still employed by Ferrari to give me food, sleep and travel, and *money*! Otherwise I go to the Italian law he finishes up in jail!

'Nosetto tells me they have a truck that Ferrari have rented in New York. If I want to, I can drive this truck back, to Avis, then go to the airport.' Cuoghi laughed unexpectedly at the memory and resumed, 'then tell Nosetto I need money for petrol. And for food. He gives me sixty dollars and the truck. We were staying the Lake View Hotel in Watkins Glen: Niki, Ronnie Peterson, a lot of people were staying at the Glen Motor Inn, about a quarter-mile down towards Watkins Glen. I drove the truck up to the Motor Inn and told Niki what has happened.

'Sante Ghedini is there too, the one who has been more of a personal manager to Niki, and has already been fired by Ferrari. Ghedini is having the job with Parmalat to stay with Lauda at Brabham. They asked Ghedini the same questions as me. He has not lied!

'Niki tells me not to worry, Ghedini has organized with Air Alitalia, booked me a flight, paid it himself, the first one available that afternoon. The best way was to drive down with somebody on that flight, and that was with Ronnie Peterson, his wife Barbro and a friend. They were driving down to New York and gave me a lift. I say thank you to Ronnie and away to Milano. Big Mafia job!' He laughed shortly, discharging the emotion built up in recounting the most humiliating weekend of his motor racing life.

The details of his move from Ferrari to Brabham were not all finalized at the time. The problem was that, under Italian labour laws, you do not go straight from one company to a competitor... and the intention was for Alfa Romeo to employ Ermanno Cuoghi. The Milanese car giant provided the flat-twelve cylinder engines of sports car descent that had powered the Brabham since Ecclestone switched the team over to Alfa power at the end of 1975.

'Niki has practically handled everything with *Ingegneri* Chiti at Autodelta, the competition people for Alfa Romeo. A few years before I had been in contact with them because, when I was going back to Italy, after JW, Alfa Romeo has asked if I would work for them then? I turned it down because it was better for me to work near Modena than Milano. I knew them from many sports car races, apart from anything else, but everything was arranged through Niki. I did not sign a contract, under Italian law you do three months' trial. After that you are automatically employed, so I was employed by Alfa Romeo from 14 November, 1977: Ferrari fired me on 2 October at Watkins Glen. At the time it was said I was joining Brabham, but now it is more widely known, that it was actually Alfa Romeo.'

Effectively Cuoghi's new job was working full time in Britain again for Bernard Ecclestone, proprietor of the Brabham team at Chessington in Surrey and leader of the Formula One Constructors Association (FOCA) for some years. Cuoghi's im-

LOOKING GLOOMY *before the start of the 1977 Monaco GP, but the Lauda, Cuoghi, Ferrari partnership were rewarded with second. That was achieved after a brilliant drive back through the field from Lauda*

pressions of his new boss, and a recollection from a Canadian Grand Prix before Cuoghi made the move to Brabham, showed he would work in a very different atmosphere and that Ecclestone is not quite the forbidding figure he appears....

'I knew of Mr Ecclestone of course. In Italy he is a very well-known personality in racing—some people don't like him of course. At first he gives the impression of another strong Mr Ferrari type of man. You can communicate a bit better with Mr Ecclestone though.

'I have seen him many times in motor racing, but without being introduced. Sometimes we play jokes on each other. I remember one very well. As Italians we always had difficulty getting enough passes for our friends and family, things like that. So, once we were in Canada a few year ago, and Mr Ecclestone was by his pit ... watching practice going on. I went quietly beside him, with a pair of side-cutters....' Cuoghi laughs at his stealthy approach to the man most regard as the most powerful in today's grand prix racing world, and I wondered what the hell he is going to tell me he did with the cutters! 'So, he has his pass on the belt and quietly, oh so quietly, I cut it off and take it away! But 'e 'as realize what I was doing when I was moving away. So he has grabbed me and we are jumped up and down like two gorillas! It was so funny to see, everyone was watching....'

I am sure they were, I cannot think of anyone who would have the nerve to do that apart from Ermanno; a piece of horseplay that tells you quite a bit about the cheerful Italian's unique brand of humour.

Talking more seriously of Ecclestone, Cuoghi added, 'he is coming in the workshop two or three times a day, asking us how it is going along? He is actually a very nice person to work with, very approachable. Sure, sometimes he comes in shouting his head off, but that's natural in racing. With the mechanics, if you have something, anything, bothering you, then you go straight to 'im, anytime he comes around. Talk with him and he *does* something. He really tries to help the mechanics every way he can.'

Life would be very different back in Britain once more, for the Brabham-Alfa Romeo alliance worked flat out producing new cars and engines in the next two seasons. The pace of work on both sides of the alliance was unbelievable, as Brabham sought to become regular winners in years dominated first by Lotus and then, as expected, by Ferrari. There was a whole new science to learn, that of ground effect aerodynamics, and Gordon Murray, with his drawing office staff, was to produce 1978's most controversial design.

Yes, 1978 would be different for Cuoghi!

10

Tough times at Brabham

THE BRABHAM team of that 1977/78 winter was a very changed enterprise over the original Brabham motor racing team. Formed by Australian World Champion Jack Brabham (now Sir Jack) in 1961, the Surrey-based equipe were not only manufacturers of successful Formula 1 cars, but also of a string of racing machinery for other formulae.

Brabhams for the lesser formulae acquired a reputation for offering the private owner the best deal in terms of a competitive car that could be comparatively easily maintained. Brabham himself and long-time team-mate Denny Hulme of New Zealand had spells of dominating both Formula 2 (with Honda engines) and Formula 1, Brabham winning the World Championship (his third... in 1959 and 1960 he won the title for Cooper) in 1966 and Hulme the following season, both with comparatively simple Repco V8 engines and straightforward chassis design.

Brabham had been the first man to win the World Championship title in a car bearing his own name. Retiring in 1970 at the age of forty-four, Brabham proved as competitive in his late seasons as he had in his characteristically dogged earlier years.

The Brabham operation remained in the care of Jack's old friend and chief designer Ron Tauranac for a while. It was sold to present-day Formula 1 Constructors Association (FOCA) supremo Bernard Ecclestone—a former 500 cc racer and motor trader—in late 1971.

Ecclestone enjoyed quite a bit of success with the Gordon Murray BT44 design. Powered by the ubiquitous Ford–Cosworth V8 engine Carlos Reutemann took three victories for the team in 1974, Pace and Reutemann had a win apiece in 1975.

That was not quite up to the expectations of the team and Ecclestone began the hunt for a fresh power unit, reportedly feeling that an alternative was needed to the Cosworth V8.

Thus, in the 1975/76 winter Murray was penning a brand new design, the BT45 with a flat twelve Alfa Romeo power unit. Drivers of that car and its derivatives included Carlos Pace and Carlos Reutemann. Pace's death promoted John Watson to number 1 driver for 1977, Reutemann having left during 1976—as we have heard—to drive for Ferrari.

In 1977 Watson was joined by the erratic, but often very quick, German Hans Stuck, but 'Wattie's' luck was diabolical and last lap dramas with petrol and its flow to the engine cost him several certain victories.

When Niki was definitely signing they dispensed with Hans Stuck and made Niki number 1 with John as the experienced number 2. With Niki came one of the biggest sponsors, Parmalat, to support the economics of hiring the current World Champion.

Just what a high-pressure season Brabham was to provide from the mechanic's viewpoint can be judged from the fact that Cuoghi worked on three very different versions of the flat-twelve engined Alfa Romeo in 1978. First there was the development of the original Brabham–Alfa (BT45C), then what was intended to be the revolutionary surface-cooling model (BT46), which was only raced with conventional water radiators and, for just one race, which it won, the BT46B fan car.

Now you can see just how hard Gordon Murray tried to provide the newly arrived champion with a winning car. From Cuoghi's viewpoint there were other, more immediate problems to solve shortly after he started work again in England on 17 December, 1977. 'I met up with another guy (Richard Taylor) who had nowhere to stay either, so we went and lived in the same hotel in Epsom. Spent a month and a half there, and then we find this two-bedroom place in Sutton.' That home was to last Cuoghi for the 1978 season, high up on the ninth floor of a modern tower block, overlooking the sprawling mixture of surburbia, office blocks and countryside that characterizes the outer fringes of South London.

Cuoghi noted that the British weather forecasting system was still as accurate as ever: 'always it is telling you it is raining... always, it is right!'

THE DEVELOPED *Brabham BT45C with complex nose at the start of the 1978 season in Argentina. Gordon Murray, designer, listens to Lauda's comments on the big flat-12 cylinder car while Cuoghi listens in, supported by Goodyear. The Brabham scored a debut second place for Lauda*

Tough times at Brabham

Cuoghi had spent less than a month in Italy after flying back from the US Grand Prix from the Ferrari fracas, because there was a test week for Brabham at Vallelunga, near Rome. 'So I went down with the Alfa Romeo people of the team and start work from the beginning of November, *before* I came to England. That was the first time Niki and I worked together on the Brabhams.

'That was the 45B model, with the engine lower in the body and, for that weekend they try a different crankshaft to lower the roll centre, but it was just overheating so they give up the idea. Later on they use that engine with a different scavenge pump, so it was a useful week.

'Coming straight from Ferrari, I had never seen the Brabham set-up before. When they show me the factory in Chessington I was impressed. A very nice place to work, tidy and clean with white walls and three bays for the cars—two racing, one T-car. An experimental bay too, good workshop—the fabrication side is a very well-equipped area too. They make their own chassis, doing all the work on the welding and so on.

'I was surprised, because the English teams I had seen before—except for JW—were in small huts all over the place!

'So I was pretty confident about my new team. We knew that after the first races in South America we would have a new car (BT46) and that was the one with the surface-cooling radiators. I never worked on the car in that form, that was for the experimental team only... but it was a very beautiful car to look at, so nicely presented.

'The 45C was an old design, and old car for Formula 1 standards, but in 1977 that car, he was a winning car. For different reasons he could not manage to win a race. Driver mistakes and lot of other things happened, some engine troubles too, but the car *itself* was a winning car: nothing wrong with it.

'I was very interested in the gearbox as well as the engine because it had some Alfa parts and some Hewland to make it suitable for that engine. The bellhousing, the starter system (we have an air starter), the crown wheel and pinion had always been the weak part of it because of the power of the engine. There is a helluva lot more torque than a Cosworth! The gears were standard Hewland, but they had to be prepared very accurately otherwise there is trouble. The crown wheel and pinion are made by Alfa Romeo at that time, stronger: today it can last two races, but nothing more than that.

'It was a slightly weaker area, but with its own cooling radiator and lubrication system, plus the

other changes, they have made the best of it.'

The Alfa Romeo flat 12-engine was originally developed for sports car racing, and has often been charged with merely being a heavyweight copy of Ferrari's fabulous twelve. This does not seem a fair charge, at least based on figures supplied to the annual *Autocourse*. Here the Alfa 115–12 type engine is quoted at 520 bhp at 12,000 rpm for an engine weight of 375 lb. By comparison the same source quotes the Ferrari with 510 bhp at 12,400 rpm for a weight of just 5 lb less. The 475 bhp Cosworth V8, a far simpler engine altogether with four less cylinders to complicate matters, is quoted at 365 lb—just 10 lb less than the 'heavyweight Alfa'. Even with a single turbo the Renault V6, which was to prove the revelation of the 1979 season, was quoted as weighing 397 lb, so the Alfa Romeo designers certainly seemed to have done their job in power-to-weight terms.

Incidentally the Alfa twelve and the Ferrari twelve did not share common bore/stroke ratios either, though both naturally enough had adaptations of Lucas fuel injection and Marelli Dinoplex ignition.

Coming back to the gearbox Cuoghi was happy to find a distinct bonus compared to Ferrari: 'the Brabham was much better to work on than the Ferrari, because of the Ferrari's transverse design. Just to change the Ferrari gears you have to get out flanges, the gearbox, drive shafts, a big job. On the Ferrari it takes about an hour and quarter, an hour and twenty minutes just to change ratios for Ferrari. On the Brabham you can do it in fifteen to twenty minutes!'

Cuoghi then thought about the completely different approach to chassis-building in England and Italy, 'the Brabham is a simpler car to work on. For Ferrari you can change an engine in about an hour and a quarter, something like that. Same thing for Brabham, but the basic car is easier to work on in Britain.'

The season started well for the Parmalat Brabhams of Niki Lauda and John Watson at the Argentinian Grand Prix. Cuoghi recalls they had a slight problem balancing the car up, and that the left front tyre was getting 'too 'ot' but otherwise Lauda seemed to have carried his canny 1977 style over to the following year from Ferrari as he drove into second overall. This despite the fact that Niki started only fifth quickest after a fuel pump interrupted his quest for the best tyres, and the fact that Ferrari had 'Switched to Michelin'. Reutemann was on the front row.

Looking at the race result Lauda and Cuoghi could afford to grin, for Andretti's Lotus was the only car to beat them—and that was to be the

Left: MODIFIED NOSE *used by the Brabham BT45 in South America was the result of last minute handling problems, the design dating back to the previous year's BT45B. Starting from the fifth row, Lauda finished third*

FORMER FERRARI *man and now the boss of Autodelta, Alfa Romeo's Carlo Chiti . . . now he is Cuoghi's boss*

Championship combination of 1978—and Reutemann's fastest lap was only a hundredth faster than Lauda had managed. With the new car coming later, things looked good.

Things are never that simple in racing! Lauda had a fight to get on the fifth row of a grid lined up in searing sunshine upon the new *Rio Centro Autodromo* for the Brazilian second round to the series. Mr Ecclestone even lent Niki's car, which had the older nose, to Watson in an effort to improve the Ulsterman's starting position. They were in real trouble!

'The front tyres were really overheating, so we flew in very urgently from England, the old type nose from the B model, so we 'ave fit that very quickly and Niki is racing to third with that fitted. But he was very lucky to be alive! During the race a wheel balance weight from another car flew into Niki's Brabham, hit the screen and bury itself a coupla inches in the rear wing ... if that had been Niki's head....

'So we went backward for that race, but the 45 was only a preparation job. We were not looking to develop that car, just waiting around for the 46 to come. When Niki first drove the Brabham at Vallelunga he says that it is a very easy, predictable car to drive: much easier than the Ferrari. The Ferrari has always been a bit more nervous, so Niki was very pleased in the beginning with the handling. A driver must adapt to a Ferrari, it takes a bit of getting used to. Even Schecker had a problem at the beginning of 1979 for that reason and Villeneuve took time too, but now they have the Michelins and this is a big advantage.

THE BT46 *was a clean design marred by the fact that front radiators had to be adopted after initial testing with the surface cooling system intended for this model proved it inefficient*

Opposite: READY TO *race. Cuoghi and Lauda with the BT46 at the 1978 British GP at Brands Hatch. Lauda was outfumbled by Reutemann's Ferrari for victory*

Tough times at Brabham

'When we went testing before Monza in 1977 at Fiorano they were two seconds a lap faster than our Goodyears! This is a lot of reason for their speed, along with the engine because still [of the 1979 Ferrari T40] they do not 'ave a proper wing car.'

And now Niki and Cuoghi were at Brabham, knowing the kind of advantage Ferrari had for 1978. However Cuoghi felt 'Goodyear 'ave done a lot of work since then to try and cut the difference. So far as the two flat twelve engines go, from Ferrari and Alfa Romeo, Niki does not reckon there is any difference in power, but to me, to work on the engine, the Ferrari is more refined. If you look at the castings, beautifully made: it's a better *looking* engine.'

Cuoghi commented of the BT46 before its arrival in racing trim for the 4 March South African Grand Prix, 'the research team found that the surface cooling did not work. There was just not a big enough area to cool that engine. It simply needed a bigger surface than could be found on the car.' Other sources have commented that Murray was unintentionally misled by contacts in the aviation industry as to the altitude at which the idea would be effective. It has been jokingly said that the Brabham would have needed the surface area of a London bus to make the idea effective at racing circuit levels!

Cuoghi continued, 'Unfortunately this was to be the biggest trouble of the BT46 because we 'ave to put a front radiator and that put the car out of balance. It was not a happy car to drive after that. We did a 46C version with radiators vertically on the side, just behind the front wheels. We tried these in practice for the German Grand Prix in July, but we did not race the car like that.'

The BT46 started its career well. As at Ferrari on occasion, Lauda began the South African Grand Prix on pole position with a new car, even lapping faster than Andretti's Lotus. It was a proud moment for Lauda and everyone who had worked so hard on the new BT46 with its 'pyramid principle' bodywork.

The race was a different matter, Niki never holding higher than third place, from the close of the first lap onward, and suffering the first of many engine failures after fifty-two of seventy-eight scheduled laps.

There were thirteen more rounds in the 1978 Championship. Lauda won two of them, but in very unusual circumstances, as we shall see. In the other eleven races he had *eight* further retirements, four attributed to the engine, three to accidents and one to the ignition system of the engine.

In the remaining three unaccounted races Lauda took the BT46 to a brilliant second at Monaco, despite a pit stop; an unhappy second at the British Grand Prix—his usual UK luck demanded that Giacomelli's McLaren step in the way just at the crucial moment of his duel with Reutemann's Ferrari. Then there was a fine third in the Netherlands. There the Alfa–Brabham combination was 'the best of the rest' as the Lotus 79s of Andretti and Peterson led one of many race-long replays of follow-the-leader, Mario playing the leading role.

What about those wins? Cuoghi recalls the car and the the Swedish weekend of the first with the outrageous Brabham BT46B 'fan car'.

'We had the usual side skirts on the 46, but the only real ground-effect car we made that year was the fan car. It worked well, considering we built it up in a coupla weeks' time! Actually, they prepare themselves a little better than that, we even had time for a little test in Brands Hatch on the club circuit with very good results: it was much faster than anyone expected! Do you know that it was only a year later that we are able to beat the fan car's times with our wing car on that circuit. Jesus, that *is* progress!

'The fan car was a bit complex to work on bodywise. It involved moving the radiator from the front and on to the top of the engine, so the fan could suck air through the radiator at the back. That gave us the depression on top of the body, the car just sucked on to the road. We tried to avoid it sucking any air underneath, but some got in and that spoilt it a bit.

'The fan was a special one that was driven off the back of the gearbox and there were quite a few parts to make up, plus all the special skirts around the engine/gearbox area.'

Gordon Murray, apparently, first had the idea prompted by experiments in the South American races, when oil radiators were mounted on top of the engine at one stage, and use was also made of a small electric fan to drag air through from underneath these experimental radiators. When the layout of a large single radiator lying flat over the engine was finalized, testing commenced at Alfa

FAN REVEALED: *Ermanno works on the one-race wonder, Brabham's BT46B fan car, at the Swedish GP. In the background are Simon Taylor* (BBC) *and bearded Denis Jenkinson* (Motor Sport)

THE TIME *for chatting over, Lauda gets on with the job of pulverizing the rest of the field*

Tough times at Brabham

Romeo's private Balocco track, just about midway along, and very little distance from, the *Milano-Torino Autostrada*.

As a result of these experiments Murray maintained that the fan served toward a 70 per cent water-cooling function and 30 per cent sucking the car down, 'ground effect' style. That meant that the primary purpose of the fan was for cooling in the Brabham team's eyes and they presented the idea to the Madrid meeting of the CSI sporting commission just after 4 June's Spanish Grand Prix. By 15 June two converted Brabham BT46-Alfas were ready for practice in the 17 June Swedish Grand Prix, the CSI having said that the idea was all right in principle.

At first the opposition was tempted to laugh, the Brabham equipe covering their fans (literally) with dustbin lids! That prompted McLaren to simply tape a dustbin lid to the covered outline of their M26 with the simple legend 'sucker'.

As soon as Brabham had sorted out a few details like the skirt performance at Anderstorp and the right tyres for this unique circuit of long, constant-radius curves, the others stopped laughing. Watson and Lauda leapt from ninth and tenth places on the grid to second and third quickest behind the inevitable Andretti.

The protests and hot air filled the air from the opposition, but Bernie Ecclestone, holding an impromptu press conference in the pit lane, assured everyone that the cars would take their place on the grid the following day. And they did. . . .

Despite the other drivers' misgivings about the BT46B turning debris and dust into the equivalent of the Great Dust Tornado (or so you would think from their comments) it was quite a race, Lauda and Andretti duelling, Niki able to drive around the outside of the Lotus—something the Chapman cars had been doing to their opponents with regularity that season. However, he finally overtook Andretti on the inside when the Champion-elect made a mistake. The Lotus followed the Brabham for a few laps and then suffered engine failure, leaving Lauda a win by nearly half a minute and a new lap record equivalent to 106.288 mph.

Watson was not so fortunate, spinning off avoiding Riccardo Patrese, the young Italian who was the centre of as much controversy in 1978 as the fan car itself.

The BT46B never raced in a Grand Prix again. It was banned, even though Ecclestone's fellow constructors would have let it run a few more Championship rounds before meting out the same verdict.

For Gordon Murray it was a very sad affair. His original BT46 design was for a slim-nosed car of dart-like proportions with no radiators cluttering up the frontal lines. First the surface radiators malfunctioned and then, when he found the solution in this ingenious fan car, the result of his and the whole Brabham design team's labours—to say nothing of the effort of converting the cars so quickly—was arbitrarily thrown out. It is said Murray and company produced over 100 drawings for the fan car. Henceforth they would be fit only as a reminder of how they could have broken the opposition.

Cuoghi recalled, 'Niki said it was a fantastic car to drive with just slight understeer on the beginning of the corner, but then you could boot it round corners just flat out. No oversteer at all. He always like a car that handles like this, with very positive pointing in, understeer to give him a bit of a limit, then boot it on and go!

'The big loop corners of Sweden gave us and the other ground-effect cars a big advantage. All the other cars were always on and off on the throttle, because they slide away when the power is put on. With ground effect and the fan car, you just drive round. I tell you, we had no problems.

'We ran most of the time with full tanks to see that the car would stand the stress. We had harder springs and so on for the suspension, but the wishbones and things like that were the same, which shows how strong they were to take all that suction. Just toward the end of the race the fan came a little bit loose, we had realized it, but Niki didn't know it because the pitot tube was giving the same pressure reading underneath the car as before. At scrutineering we found there was a little bit of play on the fan, but no real big problem. It could have done the distance again.'

The second win of the year came at Monza when Villeneuve (Ferrari) and Andretti jumped the restart after the Peterson tragedy and were penalized a minute. That gave Lauda, running third on the road, the race. Lauda showed exactly what he thought of the whole day by not collecting his rewards and flying straight away from the circuit, and an event, that had injured his friend Peterson with what were to prove fatal results.

Opposite: A WORKING *relationship that did not produce the results expected, despite the frantically hard work put in by the Brabham team members. Lauda studies, while Bernard Ecclestone looks into the BT46 cockpit*

Tough times at Brabham

Cuoghi felt that the race win was real enough—'it counts in the record books'—but remembered that, as at Monaco, the Italian spectators still had not forgiven either he or Lauda for leaving Ferrari. 'They still call me all kinds of names,' Cuoghi shuddered at the memory of Monza in general and on that sad day in particular. The Italian attitude to motor sport has a fanaticism that only football fans seem to really come close to in Britain.

After nine retirements in sixteen World Championship rounds Lauda finished a remarkable fourth in the 1978 World Championship, beaten by Reutemann's Ferrari and the two Lotus drivers. Ground effect were the magic and obvious key words for 1979 and Alfa Romeo with Brabham's Gordon Murray began radical preparation along those lines around the time of that horrific 1978 Monza race.

According to Cuoghi, 'the people at home 'ave been working since the fan car was buried officially in July. The chassis is ready first, then the new V12 engine. In four months' working, or less, Brabham and Alfa Romeo have created a brand new car. It was a fantastic achievement for everyone I think, though I must say we did not start working on the car, on the racing side, until the end of the 1978 racing season because we still had to race the BT46.'

It really was a marvellous achievement. They had created the first all-new Formula 1 engine in ten years according to contemporary reports, though as Cuoghi says the 60-degree V12 actually shares quite a lot with its flat twelve forerunner. 'The rods and pistons are basically the same, the crankshaft has to be different of course, the cylinder heads started off the same, just modified version of the boxer motor, now they are completely different. Both cars had the titanium exhaust system, both are critical to make, but on the flat twelve you could not really see how hard it was.

'We had to have the vee engine to be narrow and to let the air past for a ground-effect car. In fact it is a very narrow engine so we can have plenty of space for the aerodynamic side pods either side of the car. The engine is a big and tall one, but it does not affect the roll centre of the car. Maybe Gordon had designed suspension to go underground!' Cuoghi quipped.

Looking at the BT48 chassis itself Cuoghi said, 'it is a very narrow monocoque with the petrol tank at the back of the driver, just one big tank. It is just as narrow as possible to have as much of the car devoted to ground effects as possible. The back is all cleaned up to let the air out too—shockers and springs have been moved inboard, brakes moved outboard, as everyone must do.

'The car was tested in South America without a proper back wing (together with the deletion of the front wing, the ultimate aim of designers in 1979 was the true wingless car, depending purely on the ground-effect adhesion). The first car we made was like the shape of the last Lotus. To be sure we can balance the car up we put a rear wing that we knew would work on it. We start off without nose fins for the first race in 1979, but after the warm-up Niki decides to put them back on, it was too much of an unknown quantity. Then, at Kyalami for the South African Grand Prix, we made real progress and found the car was better *without* the front fins.

'After two days' running we were practising with a very small amount of wing. All of a sudden, on the pit straight bump, the wings came off the front! Gordon says "OK, now we try the proper wingless nose, see what is the difference." A big improvement straight away, a second or so I think. The wings had been disturbing the flow to the side pods.

'In the beginning we were completely inexperienced with the side pod "wings" and the car was behaving badly. We go stiffer, stiffer, on the springs to tolerate the downthrust. It is just a question of getting the combination right between the chassis and the new aerodynamics. This is especially true of the centre of pressure in the side pods: it moves back and forward, but not the way you would expect from a wind tunnel! You don't know where you are, but for sure we are learning. . . . At the beginning of the season there was so much work to prepare the cars and the one-third scale models for wind tunnel testing that we were in South America while the model was testing in the tunnel!'

The Alfa V12 engine maintained the 78.5 mm by 51.5 mm bore and stroke of the flat twelve and the classic double overhead camshaft per cylinder bank layout with four valves per cylinder. No weight was quoted for the new power unit, but power was again claimed to be 520 bhp beyond 12,000 rpm.

The 48 looked and sounded superb, if rather long on its 108-inch wheelbase with a lengthy engine and its long side pods, and radiators, now firmly mounted out of sight within. The engine served as a stressed member—unlike the flat twelve in the 46—and there was exclusive use of carbon fibre and aluminium for the monocoque with no steel or titanium used in the chassis construction. Though Murray had made use of expensive titanium pretty widely before and now seemed happy to dispense with it (in the chassis, at least), Bernie Ecclestone was still reported as saying that the 48 was, 'possibly the most expensive Grand Prix car ever built.'

The Argentine Grand Prix opening round to the 1979 series saw Lauda and a brand new BT48 chassis struggling to make the starting grid at all, Niki even trying the flat twelve car allocated to new team-mate Nelson Piquet (Watson went to McLaren) in order to start the race from the back row! The first time Lauda had been subjected to such an indignity in Grand Prix racing since his rental drive days. In the race the V12's fuel pressure sagged and the Austrian was out after eight laps.

Things could only get better, and they did. For the second round Brazilian Grand Prix Niki stuck doggedly at the task of making the 48 work and qualifying eleventh on a twenty-four-car grid, only for the gear linkage to fail after six laps' racing!

By March and the South African Grand Prix, Ligier's South American dominance had been exchanged for the spectacle of a Renault taking its first pole position time and Lauda had bounced back to fourth quickest qualifier. In the race Cuoghi and company got a surprising chance to demonstrate their tyre-changing expertise as it rained, Gilles Villeneuve winning the tactical battle against new Ferrari team-mate Scheckter. Still, both the 48s finished, Lauda in the points for the

OUT ON *the bench the Alfa 60° V12 looks rather more compact than in the car. The engine was produced in a remarkably short time, using some essentials from the previous flat 12, for the 1979 season*

Below: THE INSTALLED *Alfa-Romeo V12 in the back of the 1979 BT48 with its complex titanium exhaust system.*

first time with the new car in sixth place and Piquet beginning to display the devastating 1979 form that came fully to light a little later on.

In the US Grand Prix (West) at Long Beach, Piquet and Lauda qualified side by side, little better than half-way up the grid. Cuoghi's 'man' was eliminated on the first lap when Tambay took a flying lesson over his helmet: Piquet was eighth.

In Spain things looked a little brighter, but Lauda was entering a long spell outside the finishing points and was soon to have the psychological pressure of Piquet turning faster practice times than the master. The young Brazilian first exhibited this kind of speed with a startling lap record performance at the non-Championship, postponed, Race of Champions at Brands Hatch in April.

So Spain brought no points, though Niki was running third before the water temperature went sky high. 13 May's Belgian Grand Prix left Lauda over a second slower than Piquet in practice and out of the race with engine failure after only twenty-four laps. The seventh round was Monaco and I asked Cuoghi to tell me a bit about the routine preparation that goes into this event, the one that represents motor racing as a glamorous sport in the public eye. Behind the scenes, ah, a different story....

Cuoghi began the story of the fourteen days between the Belgian Grand Prix and Monaco, 'we 'ave a very good truck driver at Brabham, Chris Robson. He gets our big Volvo rig to Chessington at six o'clock that Monday morning, three hours before he was scheduled! So when we went to work the truck was there with the cars unloaded.

'So we 'ave start putting the cars in our work bays. There are always problems with a racing car, so you start the strip down. As we take it down the suspension parts like the hubs are sent for crack testing, also the uprights, drive shafts, practically all the metal parts.

'The monocoque chassis is almost bare at the end. The instruments are still in, also the fuel tank, though we give that a check up every other race too.

'Then we start cleaning down and washing all the stuff. That's an 'ard job, I tell you. We can strip the car down in a day, perhaps a day and a bit. Incidentally the guy in charge of the truck is doing the job of having the Momo wheels crack tested. He takes *all* the wheels that have been used, take the balance weights out, check for damage and crack test. Meantime the three of us—our very tall New Zealander I call "Kiwi" and the other is ex-Hesketh and the brother of club racer Nick Whit-

ing, 'is name is Charley Whiting—are taking the car down.

'We don't have set hours, it is up to us to have the car ready. Normally we start between quarter past eight and half past. We have an hour for lunch between 12.30 and 1.30, usually go down to one of the nice local pubs in Chessington, so I would usually have a cooked meal with the people who work with me on the car.

'Charley will start doing the gearbox as soon as he can get it out of the car. That is the longest job. So he tends to stay longer than anyone else in the evening: it take him about four days to strip and rebuild. Then there is the attachment of the suspension to the gearbox, so he is mainly concentrating on the rear suspension and the gearbox.

Opposite: BRABHAM'S HERBIE *Blash lifts his ear muffs to listen to Cuoghi. Lauda sits impassively awaiting the chance to fire up the BT48 with the aid of the air-starter operator poised behind the wing*

Below: IT QUALIFIED *right at the back, and lasted eight laps at the Argentinian opener to the 1979 GP season. However the BT48's problem was race reliability, not speed, and it was replaced by a Ford-engined BT48 before the end of the year. Here is Lauda in Argentina at the start of that poor season*

Tough times at Brabham

'Every race we change the fuel pump, and filters, but everything is lifed to do so many hours and then change, like aircraft. The Koni shock absorbers would be changed every other race, for example, and the titanium springs tend to collapse pretty often, so we 'ave to change them before that can happen. The titanium exhausts means we must put a new system on for *every* race (at a cost of over £1000 for the 16-piece Milanese system). We start with new, or just bedded pads, every practice and if we 'ave a chance to test at a circuit before the race, and we usually do, then we bed in one set of new pads, ready for the race. Those go in on the night before the race.

'Normally we put a fresh engine in on the Saturday night before the race too. That engine may then do some testing, or one or two practice sessions, ready for the following meeting. Autodelta bring the engines with the two men they supply at each race to look after the motor: usually Mr Manfredini is in charge. I have never been involved in rebuilding engines myself, but I am always interested to see what they are doing. Sometimes I will help with a bit of translation, like I used to at Ferrari, but my job is stay on the car and make sure Niki 'as everything he wants.

'So, after the strip down, some time on the second day we start all the cleaning work. It's always a dirty job! On the bench where we are working, it's about five metres long, we have a washing basin that is close to the airline and other parts for replacement. We use a special fluid to wash the parts down and then bath them in hot water. Then we may put a complete suspension corner to one side as we take it off the car, keep all the parts in one drawer for each corner, and wash them only together, before checking them out for wear. The rose joints last two or three races, those you can check by eye, see if there is any sloppiness coming along.

'The nuts and bolts must be changed after a strip down because, over the race weekend, they will be taken on and off again. So you start with new ones. All the nuts are the special aircraft-type K-nuts and they gotta locking device inside, but many other parts of the car have to be secured with locking wire (on the exhausts for instance).

'The chassis itself is checked in a jig about every four or five races to see if it is moving in any place, put it under stress and make sure it is strong. You anchor the chassis on the front, put on a pivot at the centre and the rear and put on so many weights with a big bar to twist it up and see if any panels have come loose.

'It is a long job to make each monocoque chassis too. It must be eight weeks or so, the chassis is very complex for any racing car: just the riveting take you two days at least. There are all the brackets and panels to actually make and then fit. The wiring loom has to be hidden away, and so do the brakes, not like years ago! All are hidden inside two tunnels within the monocoque. If a wire burns out, we 'ave to change the complete loom.

'That is the big difference from when I start. Now you change whole components—tubs, engines, gearboxes—it's a long time since I went to a race and *repaired* something . . . practically since I came in England! JW was the same, you are more of a fitter than a mechanic, a repairman. That 'appens now only when they crash . . . but then maybe you just use the complete T-car. I still enjoy making little brackets, fiddling around,' he laughed happily. Cuoghi had taken us to Wednesday following the Belgian Grand Prix then, with all the parts now fully cleaned or sent away for crack detection. 'Then we clean up all the chassis and start checking that and the steering, universal joints and so on. Get all the radiator out, flush it through and make sure it's clean.

'Then we start putting it all together again! The chassis parts first, so when the crack detected or newly anodized parts come the chassis is ready for them. So, we share the jobs. Sometimes I am on the suspension, sometimes the chassis with Kiwi, doing things like replacing all the wheel bearings: that is another job for each race.

'There are no really difficult bits . . . it is a standard procedure now. Gordon makes us a work list to check against, items to change or check. The best part is when you 'ave got the car together and start setting up the geometry. That is interesting to me.

'You must have the chassis dead square, horizontally perfect too. Start checking the castor on the front and see if it has moved: generally it does not. Then put the chassis to zero camber and zero toe-in to check all the movement. Every time we do the rebuild there are parts that could move, like the steering arm for instance. Lose one spacer and you are in trouble. Check the chassis bump steer from the static bars and see if there are any changes. Then the job list will tell you how much camber—perhaps it will be only a quarter degree—two or three millimetres of toe-in. Basically the readings are more or less the same through the season.

'Any adjustment is usually at the race track. Then there are the tyres they supply, the cars will have to be changed to suit them as well.

'Preparing a car for Monaco the problems are

the bumps. You know from the previous year the likely ride height and so on, and know that they may ground under braking, or going over kerbs! The dampers must be fairly hard and the bump stops ready for those kerbs.

'The car is set up nose-down, the others are all the same too, so you work out the diameter of the tyres, the suspension setting and the ride height linkage, so the car does not scrape along.

'It takes a week, perhaps only four days, to put the car back together from the start, so the whole thing takes about five days for rebuild and three days' strip down and washing.

'We don't have to put extra cooling on the brakes for Monaco because the brake cooling on this car is very effective compared to the 46. Of course we have used different types of brake on the cars of 46 and 48 type, sometimes running with the aircraft carbon-fibre inserts to the discs, sometimes just conventional brakes.

'Pretty often we do a short test session with the car just to make sure everything is all right before we load the cars up for the next race, and that would be right for Monaco. We do about ten to twenty laps in Brands Hatch or Silverstone. The real drivers do that: Nelson (Piquet) is only living in Chessington, and Niki does not mind coming from Austria to do this. Although he flies himself, it must be an expensive business for the team!

'For Monaco the truck set out Sunday afternoon and I went down with the other boys on the Thursday before the race. We fly down, but this time I also go to Italy for a coupla days and then went on from there with the Alfa people. Afterwards there was no Swedish race on and we managed to have a *full* week holiday. For me it was not off work altogether though... my wife, she 'as prepared 101 items for me to do at home! It was terrible. Jesus, I work very hard!

'This year we had Thursday practice (Niki was third fastest, a second in round figures behind Scheckter's Ferrari) and have Friday off. I went window shopping, had a few drinks, with the boys from Brabham most of the time, though I did manage to just go over border into Italy and eat with the Alfa people too. I had to split myself! It is such a big team that sometimes the Alfa boys are in another hotel.

'On Saturday I start work at before eight, ready for ten o'clock start to practice. The cars are all kept with the big transporter at this circuit, under the canopies and protected by security guards.

'We didn't have any crashes on Thursday, so there were no major jobs. Niki is on the second row, trying very hard to be better, keeps brushing the barriers! He was *very* brave this year, but he couldn't do any better. It is so important at Monaco to be on the front, so Niki 'as tried so 'ard it was unbelievable. At one stage of the final practice he has told us, "look if I come in with the car damaged, or I don't come in, don't blame me too much. I try and improve."

'Niki went out: did two or three laps and comes in. He has brushed the two left wheels with the barrier! We check everything, change the rear wheel and nothing else, hadn't knocked it out of line. Niki went out again, tried really hard again, exactly the same thing! This time there is marks only on the rear tyres though. So he gives up, realizes, as he said, "I can't do anything better!" He was quite happy, because he knew he had driven as hard as he could go . . . for a driver I think Monaco is a very satisfactory circuit. At Monaco a *driver* is a big part of the time,' Cuoghi concluded.

Ahead of Niki on the grid were Scheckter, Villeneuve and Depailler. Meanwhile Cuoghi and company were, 'working 'til late on Saturday night. Practice finished at two in the afternoon. It takes us an hour to take the car away and the parts, start stripping the car down. Get the engine out, change it, re-overhaul the gearbox (not like between races though!), check the crownwheel and pinion, change any damaged bearings, stuff like that. Pre-race preparation consists of checking *all* nuts and bolts, screws, wiring that is on the car. Mainly they are set on by torque readings. The driveshafts have about six hours' life, so maybe we change them too, but at Monaco and Long Beach they *must* be changed anyway because those courses are so very heavy on shafts. Then visually check the suspension for any wear, ball joint bearings, the lot.

'It was a quarter past one when we finish. We 'ave some sandwiches to keep us going during the evening, and Mr Blash 'as organized it with a restaurant to give us a meal up to two o'clock in the morning, so most of us stop at the restaurant and have a steak. So I was back in the hotel about half past two . . . six o'clock Sunday, up again . . .' he groaned, holding his head, but laughing at the apparent madness of race weekend routine.

'I stayed in the town this year. Sometimes we suffer a bit with the hotels, most are good in the Championship year though. Monaco is not very good, but it is Monaco, so you accept it. We usually share rooms among the mechs, and I prefer it that way with company. Maybe it helps you get up in the morning too!

'Finish breakfast about seven and down to the

race track half an hour or so later. The car is ready, but perhaps you have to bleed the brakes, if the weather is bad, at the last moment. If you do that in the evening the hydroscopic brake fluid will pick up the damp.

'Then check the suspension geometry again. When you fit a new engine you never *know*, it could be a very slight difference on the attachment points, the casting *could* be slightly out and that makes a big difference to a Grand Prix car.

'Then there is a nice polish job to do (and no team does it better than Brabham, the cars just gleam prosperity and care) and then on for the warm-up session. We just push the car round for that at Monaco. People used to drive their race cars on the street at Monaco, but I find you always tend to damage the clutch. I prefer not to drive it, especially a prepared race car.

'So, we push down 200 yards or so and take our own tool boxes on with us. There is also a spare parts guy and one for the tyres with their special trolley. It is really fantastic, the Brabham trolley with a little snowmobile motor and it takes everything we need. I have a small tool box myself with everything I need for these occasions, a miniature version of my big box. It is small enough to just put on top of the car when we are pushing.

'It's nice to have the big box, but on the starting grid, you cannot have everything with you, without it is too heavy to carry. In there I have two sizes of adjustable spanner (not a very good thing to have, but in an emergency it's perfect!), then two sets of spanners; pair of pliers, screwdriver in three sizes; crowbar...' he laughed again and added, 'of course I 'ave my hammer too! That is soft-headed on one side and hard the other and I have a dolly to beat things out. Actually the crowbar made one of the Brabham boys, Stanley is his name, a very funny guy, say to me "hold it with that Ferrari bar", always they are taking the piss.... Also I have masking tape, wire, scissors, tin snippers practically everything for any emergency.

'There is very little chance to do anything in the race, unfortunately. They have to be in and out very quick if they are to score points.

'For the race itself we push the car up again. Sometimes I help Niki into the car, maybe Charley and Kiwi do it, I like to look around, see if we have left anything on the car. Is there anything else we can do? Perhaps I will help connect up the breathing tube (for the special medical oxygen supply in case of fire). If I do that myself Niki does not complain. Somebody else puts it on, Niki starts moving his head, telling us something is wrong!

'Normally the engine is started by a spare person on the team, the guy on the T-car, so at that moment there are four mechanics per car. That man is ready as soon as Niki gets in. Meantime the T-car is ready to go as well, on the side. It is set up for Niki, but Nelson can drive it in a hurry: really he needs to have the pedal box adjusted and his own seat.

'So it is all fired up at Monaco, the streets filled with noise and I stay close until he moves from the pit area for the warm-up lap. I meet him again when he comes back. Maybe I talk to him, not very often. If it is fifteen to twenty minutes before the race starts, then we talk. At Monaco he did not say anything, he just make a sign or look if he needs me: he never has to call.

'When I am too nervous I make remarks and jokes, Niki is telling me to shut up. At Monaco there was no problem. He was pretty confident, just upset to be at the back of the Ferraris.' After just twenty-two of seventy-six laps Niki was third, trying to hold off Pironi's Tyrrell as the Brabham burned its heavier fuel load down, when the young Frenchman could stand to wait no longer and flew over the rear of Niki's Brabham in an effort to overtake. It eliminated both the Anglo-Italian Brabham and the blue Tyrrell and that was Niki's race run. 'He was very disappointed,' Cuoghi recalled, 'but he was already relaxed by the time he had come back from where the accident had happened. "He just run over me," Niki said. Funnily enough Niki and Pironi had been joking in the morning and Niki had told him to keep away from him!'

The car was not too badly damaged and the long gap between Monaco and the French Grand Prix, caused by the cancellation of the Swedish Grand Prix that year, was more than enough to repair it. Cuoghi was very happy with the other mechanics at Brabham and the general working atmosphere. In testing sessions or at home, or in the heat of the races, the atmosphere was 'very good', Cuoghi felt. Ermanno added that he had already told the Ferrari boys half-way through the season that 'it's time to let me win some races with our car!'

Opposite, top: CUOGHI'S FELLOW *workers on the BT48, Charlie Whiting (brother of saloon car racer Nick) and 'Kiwi' with the immaculate BT48 at Monaco, where it was going well before an aerial attack from Didier Pironi*

Opposite and below: LAUDA SETS *off in the second of two 1979 BT48-Alfa V12s in Argentina, while the team push Piquet's 1978 BT46. Nelson was involved in a first lap crash and Lauda was quickly out too*

Tough times at Brabham

'You can do it this way or that way, but if it won't work it won't'. Ermanno and Niki discuss development work at a Silverstone test session not too much before Lauda's retirement

11

Lauda on Cuoghi

BRANDS HATCH has an almost peaceful air as a few of the major Formula 1 teams prepare in the Saturday sunshine for the 1979 Race of Champions on the morrow. The weight of the Sunday crush is absent, the drivers and their cars almost accessible within the concrete conclave that is reserved for the Formula people within the central pits.

This non-Championship event has special meaning in 1979. An enormous donation is expected, and is received, toward the Gunnar Nilsson fund. Here to help towards doubling the sum raised for Charing Cross Hospital's fight against the cancer that killed the young Swede is Nilsson's team-mate in 1977, Mario Andretti. Fittingly the 1978 World

Champion takes a Lotus descendant of the type of cars Nilsson drove to fastest practice time.

It is an achievement that the commentator almost overlooks as he concentrates attention upon an almighty dust-up between the Brabham–Alfa Romeos of Niki Lauda and Nelson Piquet versus the single brighter red Ferrari of Gilles Villeneuve. The Brabham–Alfas are showing real speed at the hilly Kentish track after a day that has been as busy as ever for the mechanics. Niki was stranded out in the country when a driveshaft constant-velocity joint broke, and Ermanno with the other Parmalat-identified Brabham mechanics have to fit another body permutation for test evaluation during the untimed session.

Out on the track I hear with unaccustomed clarity the thrilling ring of the Ferrari engine as Villeneuve flashes through gearchanges with unbelievable speed, defending the Maranello machine's honour against the Anglo-Italian hybrids from Chessington and Milan. The Brabhams, numbers 5 (Lauda) and 6 (Piquet), are both beautifully turned out, the polished red of a more orange tinge than that of the Ferrari, their drivers bending into the corners almost like motorcyclists, crouching towards darkly tinted screens.

A WORKING *relationship that lasted from 1973, albeit at the close of the season, to 1979. Then it was prematurely closed with a non-Championship win, the only victory for the BT48. Lauda and Cuoghi in their last season together*

The new Alfa V12 engine for the 1979 season rings out almost as convincingly as that of the Ferrari, but Lauda's is definitely pausing as he occasionally has trouble getting fourth gear home. I try and picture the scene inside the cockpit, thinking how much more at ease Lauda must be with the circuit unreeling in front of him and the Alfa engine howling away at 12,000 rpm and more behind. More at ease than he was this morning talking to this writer, one of hundreds he will deal with every year.

I look at the flags fluttering in the windy sunshine and hear that the Brabham-Alfas are reaching up to 146 mph on the short burst of speed that carries them along the start and finish straight like brightly coloured toys flung from a huge catapult. The battle draws to a close with Lauda and Piquet sandwiching Villeneuve, all of them divided by scarcely tenths of a second, Lauda only two-tenths away from Andretti's fastest time.

I see out over the green surroundings, register the motorway that bisects the countryside beyond the track and look through binoculars at the wire netting and the line of low concrete lock-ups. Lauda steps out of his world of flashing images and enormous cornering forces to greet the team that keep him out there. Brabham team owner Ecclestone is here today, so is designer Gordon Murray, and few interrupt when they are talking to their number 1 driver. I reflect back to my lunchtime interview with Lauda, contrast the man with the fresh-faced youngster I remember from his touring car and lesser formulae racing days. Even meeting Lauda at the annual Ferrari press conference had left me unprepared for the complete brutal honesty and torrent of short epithets that shower our conversation about Cuoghi.

The Lauda I had remembered was the Lauda prior to the Nürburgring accident. When enthusiasm and dry wit sparkled over the obvious determination to succeed. A man who has literally been through fire and the media's best attempts at hell in persecution and cruel photography is a very different individual, though the basic qualities surfaced again as soon as his concentration could be turned to the relationship between himself and Cuoghi, 1973–1979.

'I got Ermanno his first F1 car at Ferrari. They gave him to me because he speak English. This was good for him: improved his position within the company.

'In four years at Ferrari he made only two mistakes. Once a wheel came loose. I realized in time. Once a screw came out of the shock absorber: he did not put it on, but he was the chief mechanic so I blame him.' Lauda's face is grim, the grey eyes with their wounded lid on one side surveyed his interrogator quickly. He seemed to wonder whether it was worth going on? The same statement, but referring to three mistakes, the other at practice for the 1977 Austrian Grand Prix when the water system was apparently unchecked, has been made in Lauda's book about his years with Ferrari.

Then Lauda visibly relaxes, leans a little more against the stark and shiny shelving within the cavernous transporter trailer and grins with all the benevolence and humour that earned him his adopted nickname King Rat. 'So, only two mistakes I count in those years—I did many more than that!' He laughs at the quip that sharply reveals his charm, totally undiplomatic directness balanced by a basic honesty about his own mistakes.

I asked what Cuoghi's most valuable quality was to Lauda? 'Ermanno is the best mechanic there is,' that was the terse reply.

Lauda amplifies a little on their relationship. 'This is a tough job you know: there is always pressure. I am better with pressure on me, so I put it on *all* who must work around me. Grand prix racing depends on everyone giving their maximum all the time, *all* together.

'I say Ermanno has a bit of gipsy in him. His family are at home and he is living here. He is an emotional man: we are *not* winning at the moment and so it is difficult to talk to him about the future. Every year I have to persuade him to stay, and that's tougher this year.

'With his own blokes on the car he is really good at the team job. Making sure everyone is happy and working at their best—but I don't think he is so good as a complete team man . . . Ermanno keeps trying to make sure his car beats the other one: to screw the others by being better than them.

'People working with him have to share some responsibility or he may do everything. They all do the same job for me, but Ermanno is the man for the people [the man people recognize—J.W.]: to me it is *my* group.

'But the spirit comes out of Cuoghi,' Lauda concluded.

I asked about their working relationship under

MEN AT *work. Lauda's eye view from* Colin Taylor Productions *of the partnership at work on the 1979 BT48. The car was always beautifully presented, its cockpit growing switches and levers enough for Lauda Air. The 14,000 rpm tachometer is in the centre, behind the Momo steering wheel, while the 120° C water temperature gauge is visible on the right*

racing conditions and Lauda told me, 'so far as the impressions of the car go, I always work through the designer. He has to know everything. The instructions are passed from there to the mechs.

'Before the start I am always nervous. On the grid he is often more nervous than me. Then he always talks rubbish, whistles and talks such big rubbish ... it's complete shit what he is telling me. Then I say shut up you bloody Italian with this crap and we can laugh.'

Some of the journalists specializing in the sports car scene felt that Cuoghi's experience in such long-distance racing was a great contribution on the Ferrari Formula 1 team when sudden changes had to be made as the weather changed in mid-race. I asked Lauda if he felt this was so in fact? 'Sometimes he is not even involved ...' Lauda thought hard for half a minute or so, 'no, it's hard for me to really tell. I was not at Ferrari before Cuoghi was on Formula 1, so it is impossible ... but I think this could have been useful to them, yes.'

Finally we talked about the contribution a chief mechanic makes to a top Formula 1 driver's success. Niki stressed, 'It is most important to have confidence in the car. About 80 per cent is mechanical confidence that every nut and bolt is *tight*. Cuoghi's reputation is such that I believe that everything is all right. All is tight, so I have confidence.'

Ecclestone enters as we finish and the two trade insults in exactly the same way as the mechanics. Bluntness is almost exaggerated in a team full of people who genuinely seemed to like working together at all levels during the seasons I watched them. Some of the comments are extremely funny, but I retreat under some stern glares when I suggest that the huge interior of the Parmalat transporter could take in a hospitality function for journalists and others on the Formula 1 scene.

That transporter is the base for serious racing operations to be directed from, not frivolous publicity exercises, besides neither of them like the press too much, and with good cause!

The difference in manner between the industrious Italian mechanic and his world-famous master takes some absorbing. Cuoghi talks of Niki with pride and care, almost in the same way as Ermanno will discuss his son, Roberto. Of course he is aware of the faults, but Cuoghi's modest manner and gentle humour supply the complete contrast one often finds in successful marriages.

The following interview was obviously conducted before Lauda's sensational retirement two races from the close of the 1979 season. I have left in most of what was said about Lauda's decision methods as an example of their relationship. [In fact, when Lauda stepped out of Brabham, Cuoghi had already stopped working on Brabham cars and was solely working for Alfa Romeo in Italy. It would have been Lauda's first Grand Prix without Cuoghi since 1974 ... if he had not retired in practice. ...]

Talking of Niki after half a season without a win—something neither man is accustomed to—Cuoghi told me, 'Lauda is a very methodical person in his work. Logical, he can go back through the times, see how a car was behavin''—Lauda has a fantastic memory for that kind of thing.

'When you see us working together on a grand prix, it is really something, I tell you. Tic! Tac! Boom, isa all done in no time, because each one know what the other want. Usually, 'e don't 'ave to ask for anything, we *know* what must be done. It is almost bound to 'appen after so long together,' Cuoghi shrugged dismissively.

Lauda has a reputation that almost amounts to legend concerning his test abilities, so I asked Cuoghi what he thought of Niki's testing prowess? 'Always he wants to go progressively, not jump from this thing to the other. There must be a positive answer to one test before we go to another. Where he is really good is going back to something we have done and picking it out afterward.

'He did test very hard, but not so much now. That is because we do not have the facility like Fiorano—I think he would do the same as at Ferrari if we had this kind of facility.

'He is a funny guy though: if he has in his mind that a test will do us no good, he will not try. That is not true of his races—there he takes what comes. Give him something he thinks is silly to test and he will not do it, or say he has done it before and that it is not necessary.

'He *always* says what he thinks. If he has something to say he says it. No back route ways, just straight out, which is what I prefer.

'The things I liked about him when I first met him were things like his courage in the wet when 'e was driving BRM. That Lauda was completely unknown, a nice person who would try his best. He did learn Italian while he was at Ferrari, now he speaks it very well, though at that time he and Forghieri were speaking English all the time. Really he did everything during the time at Ferrari to make the best possible chances for himself.

'I don't think the criticism he had from the Italian press made him harder. Although those people who attacked him have to use a very respectful method when they approach him, otherwise he does not answer back! He has learned at Ferrari to deal only with people who do their own job properly. Even people he does not respect he will answer, if the questions are not silly: if they are, then nothing!

'I don't think he has any really bad qualities. As a driver he is consistent and one of the real top men. He is always playing jokes on me, but I don't mind that. He is always reminding you of his mistakes and your mistakes!

'Any time he has made a mistake he tells you straight away. Like he has spun it a few times . . . you ask, what happened? . . . and he tells you it was a brain failure. So far as I know nothing is hidden away.

You see Lauda was *used* to winning! It was not the money at all that made him move to Brabham: it was to achieve *something* with some other team, the same thing he has achieved at Ferrari. To prove and develop a car as much as winning races. Not only the car makes the driver win . . . it's the driver too, that is what he says.

'If we don't win races Brabham will lose him, but I still 'ope that we 'ave the chance to win a few and stay where we are. It would be very nice if this 'appened.

There were a lot of rumours, but I don't ask him anything at all. I never do ask him: when Niki is decided what he will do he will tell me at the same time he tells everyone else . . . Niki does not tell me before because he is looking at too many possibilities without talking to me as well!

'I do not say that I will go wherever he goes. I am employed by a big company: I can 'ave a job for life with Alfa Romeo. If I want to retire from motor racing I can have a very high standard job inside that company. So I would sacrifice a lot if I left Alfa Romeo now, but Ferrari is closer to home! No, I don't think this could 'appen, but I am getting on in age and know I cannot go on forever with this life . . . it's a bit tiring I must say!

'I still like motor racing, but perhaps I am enjoying it too much. One day or another I have to give up. When I do I must have some positive work to do.

'It is easier now that we usually know what he wants. What Niki doesn't want is to stop on the pit during practice time. He does *not* like that, so Gordon is telling us quickly what we must do and we get him away fast. He will not sit just in the car for no reason. He must 'ave something done fast so he can go!

'If I was not to work with Niki again I would remember everything. Lauda has been such a part of my life, the problem would be to forget.' Cuoghi laughed before summarizing his Lauda recollections as 'a very, very strong personality. A brilliant person who is always doing his best in business on the track.'

LAUDA AND *Cuoghi muffled up against the raw weather of the Silverstone International meeting in 1975. The April fixture, sponsored by the* Daily Express *as ever, resulted in a win for Niki with the then new Ferrari 312T making its first appearance in Britain*

12

Cuoghi on Lauda and others

THE OTHERS, drivers that is, are listed in alphabetical order, not in the order of importance to Ermanno. We have not included 'Pedrito' Pedro Rodriguez (the nickname meaning like a small parrot!) as this was felt to be best suited in amongst the 917 material. I should say that Rodriguez' memory was by far the strongest and most affectionately felt by Ermanno Cuoghi, but that did not prevent him seeing the best in Joseph Siffert and other contemporaries.

I am sure we have left some out (references to Paul Hawkins are within the GT40 chapter), but here is what Cuoghi recalled. I have provided some notes as to the drivers' status at the time, where appropriate.

The first man to come up for discussion was America's first World Champion since the days of Phil Hill at Ferrari, **Mario Andretti.** Cuoghi worked with him during the Ferrari sports car team's assault on the World Championship in 1972, the year they steamrollered the opposition more effectively than even Mercedes-Benz managed in their heyday. Then the naturalized American of Italian birth was thirty-two years of age, had his World Championship to come, but had already been a treble USAC Champ, Indianapolis 500 winner, and the victor of his first grand prix, for Ferrari, at Kyalami the previous year, 1971.

'I was more a consultant at that stage so far as his Ferrari sport car was concerned. I collaborate on the car rather than working on it personally.

'I reckon Andretti is another fantastic test driver. He knows quite a lot: for development he and Niki are about the same. Then it just that they have different personalities in their work. The result is the right one at the end.

'As a race driver he is a pretty hard man. There's a lot of will, a lot of fire in him. He drives a different way to most others and unfortunately he is making some mistakes.

'In a race he may not be the fastest, but he has a lot of experience—you must remember he was winning races a long time before he came to Europe. When he came here he was fully prepared—and that experience is why I say his development use is about the same as Niki.

'Although I worked with him superficially I found him a very good person to work with. From talking to the Lotus boys and the old Ferrari chief mechanic Giulio Bosari I hear that he is a very helpful person to work with, always capable of progressing the car.'

Dickie Attwood did four seasons in Formula 1 and put in a fine second place for BRM at the 1968 Monaco Grand Prix, though the Englishman was better known for driving sports cars. Cuoghi felt, 'a gentleman of motor racing! I met him when he was still racing a Formula Junior Lola: in fact I was working next door at Ford Advanced Vehicles and he was coming round to see us pretty often.

'A very, very nice guy, I did a few races with him on the JW sports cars. He was not a professional, but a gentleman from a past era that you don't see very often now.

'But he was very gentle on a car, especially the gearbox, and this is the reason he is making such a fine long-distance driver: he was pretty smooth. That was also why he was bringing results at Monaco I think.

'A nice guy to spend an evening with as entertaining company.'

Derek Bell from the Sussex seaside was a former Ferrari-contracted driver who found it harder to get a break in grand prix racing than he had in Formula 2 and sports car events. Derek was twenty-eight when he drove the JW Porsche 917s, graduating to an effective number 1 driver after the Rodriguez tragedy.

'Beautiful Derek! Another guy who want to win ... to prove what he can do ... unfortunately he never quite reached the very top.

'I don't know if he was not quite good enough,

Opposite: CUOGHI SERVES *as T-bicyclist to Peterson (left) and Lauda. Cuoghi was always happy to show the GP drivers a thing or two about life on two wheels powered by twin legs, but here (Argentina 1978) it looks as though the drivers are still telling Ermanno what to do!*

HAPPY RACING *anything: Derek 'Dinger' Bell*

or there were not the right opportunities, not much luck. When he had managed to drive for JW-Porsche he has proved he is *fast*. That pole position time at Spa and his speed at Watkins Glen show this.

'Perhaps he has the right car on the wrong moment?

'I don't really remember how he was on the car, though Porsche said Derek was hard on gearboxes and Derek said he was not! Derek did share with Siffert, and there were no doubts that Seppi was hard on the box!

'I did work with him on the open version of the Mirage and I remember,' pause for laughter, 'we were at Silverstone testing in the summer on the open version of that car and Jesus Christ, he went into a cornfield! We couldn't see him at all! When we recovered the car it was full of corn . . . it was terrible . . .' more laughter.

Cuoghi went on to point out, 'it was not Derek's fault, something broke anyway.

'I would remember Derek as a real friend of motor racing, a real enthusiast. Even now he is very friendly, and always say hullo very happily, nine years later.

'It is a shame for "Dinger". Now it is too late, but I will always think of him driving with pleasure.'

Lucien 'Luciano' Bianchi, Cuoghi starts talking straight away about his career, 'poor Luciano. He was a mechanic for Olivier Gendebien, starting his racing career gradually after that.

'He knew the car, and this Belgian was Italian-speaking too, very good. We were communicating very well. Bianchi was gentle on the car, a very good driver but never make it, he just died too early. I think he was about twenty-six–twenty-seven, not very young, but he started driving late, that is why I say he was taken too soon: but he was already a very good driver, I admire him very much.

'When you are with a guy who knows about the mechanical side of the car it is a good help. Like the drivers who are in there, watching you: if you don't see something, maybe they do. It does not bother me to be watched in this way, not at all. If Niki and everyone is around looking I do not get upset.

'I did not do many races with Bianchi, just that Le Mans and some GT40 races for Ecurie Francorchamps, but his smoothness was the best quality. He knew what could happen to the car if it was not treated well.

'We were very close to each other, more than the other drivers I would say. Not the same as Pedro, but a good friend for me.

'I liked it that Lucien came from nothing and worked his way on top. In a sports car I think he was as good as anyone I worked with.'

Of **Ian Burgess** the expatriate Briton who introduced him to Shelby, Cuoghi commented, 'he was very unlucky at the beginning of his career. In Formula 3 he was pretty good and then he had a great accident on the Avus track, Berlin, when he flew off the top of a banking. So that was six or seven months in hospital and his leg was not very good after that. I think he lost his chance there.

'He was not a bad driver when I worked first in England, more of a British club driver I think. He and Tony Settember were very much like each other so far as driving a car went.

'A very nice person, a friend to me and my family. I have not seen him for a long time now, and that is unfortunate, I would like to see him again.'

Also from that period was the young **Campbell-Jones**. 'I only worked with him once, and that was the race at Solitude where he crashed on the infield in practice.

'I saw him racing a coupla times in England, and he was faster than Tony at Solitude. Maybe there was a talent in him, but it was difficult to tell in that car!'

One of the most popular drivers ever to come

from America to Europe was **Dan Gurney**—even at home they had bumper stickers made up asking people to vote him in as president at one stage! Gurney was a real enthusiast for the European road racing scene, though he could have earned a handsome living at home, being adaptable to saloon cars as well as Indy cars. In Europe his career spanned a variety too, for he drove for Porsche in Formula 1 in 1961 and only reluctantly left the grand prix scene after a spell with McLaren in the early seventies. In between he had tackled some of the top sports cars, Cuoghi meeting him in 1964 on the Cobras before Dan went on to win Le Mans with A. J. Foyt for Ford.

'I was just one of the mechanics to him at that time, and the communication I had with him was with me a long way down the order. As a driver I remember him best with the Porsches in Formula 1: I think he was a very good driver, but in those small cars there is another thing to consider: with those 1500 type of cars to put twenty kilos extra in, with a big man like Gurney, was a real handicap from the beginning. In Formula 1 that was the only handicap he had at that time. In sports car races, like at Reims, he was always fast in the big cars. When I saw that Bonnier was as fast as Gurney in a Porsche, I knew there had to be a reason.

'As a person he was very easy to get along with, but he never struck me as being a very American character.'

We discussed the few races Cuoghi did with **Jo Bonnier**, driving in Scandinavia, inconclusively and moved on to a great favourite on two and four wheels. The man who emigrated to New Zealand at the end of his career, only to hit winning form in the Isle of Man TT in two consecutive comeback years before announcing his final, final, retirement. 'Mike the Bike' had then returned to UK residence and ownership of a motorcycle shop. Of **Mike Hailwood**, Cuoghi said, 'To know a man like Mike, a character who was many times a World Champion on motorcycles (Italian as well as Japanese) was an honour.

'As a driver I cannot say much about him, though he did a pretty good job. His advantage was a big 'eart: if he made a mistake it was a big one, but his courage ... and he was not much problem to look after.

'After all anyone who wins on MVs is a good person!' was Cuoghi's patriotic summary.

Phil Hill, the 1961 World Champion for Ferrari, was thirty-seven when Cuoghi worked with the Shelby men on the American's Daytona Cobra at Spa in 1964. Cuoghi reported, 'I was a little guy when we work on that fuel problem at Spa, but he was very quick that day: he was genuinely a fast driver, but I got the impression he was a bit of a moaning type of driver. He was a World Champion once and I got the feeling it made him want to be superior than anyone else, and less communicative.

'I met him again the last few years at Long Beach, but he does not remember that I was working at one time on his cars, I think.'

David Hobbs, an experienced Englishman who lives most of the year in America these days. Hobbs combines long-distance racing in saloons and occasional sports car outings with his broadcasting commitments and is the kind of articulate driver it is very easy to get along with. David was twenty-eight years of age and a driver recognized for his sports car achievements, though he was to go and complete seasons of Formula 5000 single-seater racing with success, as well as venturing into Formula 1.

Cuoghi affectionately said, 'He was one of the boys. I worked with him very often and enjoyed my work with him. It was always a pleasure, even when something went wrong. He was not a guy to moan, always smiling and a big joker.

'It is good to know something about the man you are working for, and it was because David used to bring his wife and family that I thought I knew a bit more about him.

'Today it may be not his will that he is not one of the very top drivers, but he has adapted himself well. He was a good driver, but I never thought he would be one of the top five.

'He was often paired with Hailwood and they were comparable: madmens together! A good pairing for racing and off the track, I think.'

One of the most interesting and enigmatic characters on the tracks was Belgian **Jacky Ickx.** A man with more sports car international victories to his credit than anyone, Ickx was also such a talented single-seater driver that it is puzzling he never was able to secure the World Championship. He was only twenty when Cuoghi met him, driving an Essex Wire GT40, team managed by David Yorke.

Cuoghi commented, 'He was so young looking that you wondered if he should be driving a car at all! I knew him through the magazines though and it was easy to realize that here was a good boy!

'I was very happy working with him. Good to work with, but not a fantastic test driver. As a personality and a driver I find him very, very nice, *provided* you know 'im. Jacky is a guy who says good morning sometimes, and others he does not. When you know him, you don't worry about it, but if you don't know and you try to talk with him when he is not willing to talk, you are wasting your time.

'What stopped him being a World Champion? He was very fast, but when he had that accident in the Ferrari that time it took the best chance he had away. Then seems everything went wrong, though he was fast again in the Brabham in 1969 too.

'In the World Championship and when he was very young I think, in the beginning on formula cars, he was overshadowed by Jackie Stewart. He did make mistakes, but they were very little ones. Having Jackie Stewart on the same team with Tyrrell in Formula 2, Jackie Stewart was taking the big role.

'Another thing was that Ickx was a fantastic driver in sports cars, prototypes, any types, but not *so* good in a single seater. That was my impression, but still he was one of the best, but in a sports car he was dominating the field.

'To see him driving today I would say he likes the sport more than most drivers. When he has a chance he is doing it for fun.

'From the mechanics' point of view we had to thank Jacky for the bonus schemes he introduced. He was a generous person, and understood the job we were doing, and how much it was worth in this kind of long-distance racing.

'I have a lot of admiration for Jacky—I think he was undoubtedly the best sports car driver there has ever been. To me he was even better than Siffert and Rodriguez at their best in 917s. He was not in such cars of course, but to see how he was driving the Ferraris and other sports cars, I think it was true to say this.'

The next character is well known through his own book, *All Arms and Elbows*, and his journalism, but **Innes Ireland** was a top-grade Formula 1 driver with Lotus, winning them the Watkins Glen World Championship round in 1961. Cuoghi dealt with him in 1965 in his early GT40 days and asked, 'Innes—is he from Ireland or Scotland? I think it must be Scotland because he likes the Scotch very much!

'He was always a nice amateur driver. Good, but never takes it seriously. Never liked the professional way. He was not a hard driver on the car and he does not have the crashes he had in other cars. The sports car was more predictable.

'I admired him for doing his driving for the sport. Bad or good, whatever the race was, Innes would always have a drink afterwards.'

Gijs van Lennep, who won both Le Mans (1971) and the 1972 British Formula 5000 single-seater championship, left little impression on Ermanno. 'He was the second driver in the cars I prepared sometimes, one of many drivers and I did not get to know him as a person.'

The fiery Belgian **Willy Mairesse**, Ferrari F1 team member and a master of Spa before Ickx, could never be forgotten. 'Mairesse was a good driver in Spa and in the races like Naples he did for Ferrari. So quick in that it was unbelievable!

'In sports cars? Fantastic, but unfortunately he had to race against Jacky Ickx. He never have an idea of his limit, so he has many accidents, even in Spa. He was older than Ickx and should have learned more.

'We could never convince him the suspension was OK, for the Goodyear tyres were not so good in those days!'

Next character assessment was for the controversial former Ferrari-contracted sports and Formula 1 driver **Arturo 'Art' Merzario**, whom Cuoghi encountered at Ferrari. Born and bred near Lake Como in the extreme north of Italy, Merzario was then twenty-eight. Cuoghi grimaced thoughtfully and broke into Italian. 'You know, he is the kind of guy who sells ice cubes and ice cream in America! When he is joking they are cool jokes. . . .

'Merzario is another good driver . . .' sighs . . . 'but he want to be bigger than he will ever be. I remember having *wonderful* times with Merzario at the different races with Ferrari, especially Targa Florio.

'He ran quite a bit in the sports cars, but always he was so *fussy* about steering. He has a funny way of driving, his precision comes from the steering. If the steering wheel is a 16th of an inch out one side he cannot drive the car anymore. Always he is complaining, even when it was straight, he find it was not!

'He wants the steering straight, but he does not know if he has one tyre bigger than the other! Sometimes we put the steering straight, change a set of tyres and it was not straight anymore, but he does not know.

'Arturo was especially good on the road courses: Targa, Mugello, or in the rain. A nervous driver like that, you would not expect it. But he had a very sensitive way of driving.

'He was a difficult person to fit in a team because of his driving. He has a different way of driving, but does not admit it: consequently when the other driver was in the car and not doing well, Merzario says it is the driver, not because the car is set up his way.

JACK OLIVER *in Team Lotus GP days*

CARLOS 'MOCO' *Pace, talent tragically terminated*

'There was trouble with him going past Ickx at Nürburgring, but that was because he want to be on top; always he has something to prove, to be a big man.'

Back in 1964 **Jochen Neerpasch**'s name did not mean much in motor sport. By 1972 he was an acknowledged team manager for Ford and went on to mastermind the rebirth of BMW's competition aspirations. Jochen's sports car career included Shelby Cobras, Ford GT40s, saloons and a variety of Porsches.

In his twenties when Cuoghi worked with him, Neerpasch is remembered as, 'a very correct gentleman. I didn't see so much of him to work with as driving against us too well in Porsches! I met him on the Cobras and I remember he had a good chance at Le Mans before we had camshaft trouble . . .

'He was getting better all the time, but he has a big accident at Spa. I think it has kept him out of racing a bit, but even then he was good: better than as a number two driver, a bit faster than Redman I think: a good man, but not with a good car at the right time.

'In some ways perhaps he did retire a bit early to go and manage at Ford . . . but he has a nice family, sometimes you have to sacrifice that if you stay in the game too long. The experience of driving had helped him in management too I think.'

We discussed briefly how Gerard Larrousse was another good example of sports car driver turned manager, Larrousse managing Regie Renault's grand prix efforts from 1978 onwards.

Jackie 'Jack' Oliver drove for Lotus in 1968 and went on to appear in grands prix for BRM and Shadow, but he will probably be best remembered for winning Le Mans with Ickx in 1969, and for his involvement with the Arrows Grand Prix team on the managerial side. Oliver was twenty-seven when Cuoghi first worked on his cars. 'He did get fired after that CanAm business when he was in the 917s, but did some other races for us with the Mirage I think.

'As a driver I think he was OK in a sports car, but not in the hard world of Formula 1. Oliver was quite effective as a test driver, but he didn't have much patience. Though it may have been the management at JW who did not give him the time. Jackie was getting upset because they did not act quickly on what he said. Straight away, he wants to have things done. Everything was so slow, it was not suiting him well.

'JW were not generally slow in acting, but Jackie was always driving with somebody else. If you are driving with a guy like Siffert, they are tending to believe him more. Siffert was a little quicker than Oliver, but perhaps Oliver was right because Siffert never was a very good test driver.

'Oliver was a pleasant guy to work for.'

Of **Carlos Pace** it can be said he had only a short time with Ferrari, some sports car rides in 1972 and a fuller season in 1973, and that his death in an aeroplane crash took him from the racing scene before we could see if he was able Championship material as fellow-countryman Emerson Fittipaldi.

'I remember only that he was very fast and had a very funny driving position. Right close up to the steering wheel, I was always asking him how he could drive like that because I could not have turned my arms in that position. I never see that style before, especially for such a big boy with great big shoulders.'

The angelic-looking, demon-driving, Swede **Ronnie Peterson** was also a member of the Ferrari sports car squad. Ronnie was perhaps the largest asset the March factory ever had, but his talent was frustrated often, even at Lotus in his final year when he had to sit behind Andretti acting on team orders. He had been European Formula 2 Champion, but his death at Monza in 1978 prevented us from ever seeing if the man many regarded as the fastest thing on four Formula 1 wheels would ever put a complete year's success together.

Cuoghi simply says, 'Jesus Christ, that was a *really* quick driver. Unfortunately he was a disaster as a test driver. . . . This is funny though, because with him and Schenken in the same car they were talking, talking, and getting the same results as the others.

'Some way the two of them could produce a good car. They managed to produce a good chassis. Always running at the front, score a couple of wins. I didn't understand it, they were talking so deeply about the car's behaviour.

'Of course Ronnie did drive Lola and Alfa Romeo sports cars before. We could slow him down to a pace . . . but it took some time before he would settle down "on rails", then he would do six or seven laps at *exactly* the same speed: Amazing! To slow him down to that was a real hard job though. . . .

'I liked him very much—we always used to call him the big Viking. Easy to get on with and nice to talk to.'

Next came the very experienced and successful sports car driver **David Piper**. Cuoghi explained Piper's life simply: 'He always worked very hard, going along with not *too much* money . . . dealing, always dealing, a fine trader.

'He was a fill-in driver for JW, but a very good sport car privateer with an excellent record of wins. Working on a private car he often made it better than the factory!

'Another gentleman to be with socially.'

A big change as we came right up to date with **Nelson Piquet**. The quiet Brazilian who looks uncannily like Emerson Fittipaldi, and who also won a British Formula 3 Championship convincingly before flashing straight into Formula 1 with Brabham. Emerson at least did a Formula 2 apprenticeship before showing some of the F1 hotshoes the way around.

'Nelson has a big sense of humour, always making jokes. Always poking fun at my hair . . . you know the hair I have not got: it pisses me off, I can tell you!

'What makes his success nice for us is that he has worked very hard to reach F1. Nelson has been around with a truck, done a bit of mechanic work, had not too much money and so on. I tell you he even has his own tool box!

'He comes around at the factory [Brabham—J.W.] very, very often, four or five times a week from his home nearby. But he does not come often because he lives close—it is because he *wants* to be there, he is so interested.

'He is very interested in preparation. Not long ago, we have some play on a throttle shaft linkage on Niki's car. I didn't know it because I have not reached the rear of the car. So he calls me over and show me . . . I say "thank you very much, a very good job you find it!" The other day it happened to his car, so we do not have to tell him what the problem was.

'He is not gentle on the car, but his brake-pad wear is good and I think he is a bit like Niki in some ways. Very determined and learning quick. . . . A definite World Champion if he carries on at the same rate. I hope so, he will have deserved it because he tries so *hard*.'

Next to Jacky Ickx, **Brian Redman** is the most successful of international sports car drivers, though he has also won Formula 5000 races and Championships in the USA and Britain, and put in some polished Formula 1 drives despite his comparative dislike of grand prix racing.

Cuoghi worked with him on a number of occasions, but Cuoghi chiefly worried that, 'Brian is still driving now. He should give up because he has hurt himself so many times and maybe that can hurt his family too. Every time you have an accident, it is not only you.

'I remember when he was driving the Nick Cusson's GT40, but to work with he is a nice, easy, sympathetic personality. He makes funny faces when things go wrong, but a terrific man.

'As a driver I think he started a bit late on formula cars, then you have little chance. In sports cars, one of the very best.'

Alan Rees, today also of the Arrows F1 management, is succinctly recalled. 'He was not long on our JW team, David did not give him a chance, but from what I know in Formula 2 he was pretty good.

BRIAN REDMAN, *Lancashire's pride*

STILL WINNING *in 1979: Gianclaudio 'Clay' Regazzoni*

A hard worker, but they did not give him a chance.

'I still see him regularly and always enjoy talking with him. Very quiet, but a nice person.'

A professional since 1968 **Gianclaudio 'Clay' Regazzoni** is a Swiss-born, Italian-speaking driver who has outlasted many contemporaries, despite a controversial career punctuated with incidents and accidents. Twice a driver for Ferrari in grand prix racing, Cuoghi encountered the man the mechanics nicknamed 'Breakazzoni' in 1972 sports car racing and subsequently as Lauda's team-mate in Formula 1 Ferraris.

'A fantastic character, with a big personality. Very good company and I wish I knew what the girls see in him, so I could have it too. . . .

'As a driver, years ago, he used to have so many accidents, practically every race. Then he had a big accident in Kyalami and Hailwood pulls him out and Regga has hurt himself pretty bad, puts a big lump on his chin.

'Since then I think Clay hardly has accidents like he did before.

'As a test driver he was getting to the same development points as Niki, just taking a little longer that is all.

'In sports cars you could make Clay a team man any time. He has a funny temper, but that does not affect the job: a real professional, not a player.

'He likes all sports, but racing cars give him the most pleasure. He trains himself, gets really ready to drive.

'Some people criticized Clay for the start line crashes at Ferrari with Niki, but it is hard to 'ave team rules at such moments! You find yourself there and it is a question of who 'as the guts to go in!

'Niki did not seem to blame Clay too much for these things. They got on very well together—socially they have a completely different way of life—but work-wise. I think it was the best team Ferrari ever had.

'In England especially, Clay is not as highly regarded as he should be. My view is that Clay is very good in anything: in the Williams in 1979 I think we 'ave seen this . . . right with the Ferrari at Monaco and so on. In the right car he is as good as anybody.'

Another with what Cuoghi describes as 'Latin fashion' appeal to women has been a Grand Prix winner with a vengeance for Brabham (in their

Ford-powered days) and Ferrari, leaving Maranello for a 1979 season with Lotus. **Carlos Reutemann**'s ejection was pretty curt from Maranello, considering that he won four Grands Prix for Ferrari in their 1978 first season on Michelin.

Cuoghi was never directly responsible for Reutemann's chassis in the Argentinian's sports car outings (Antonio Bellantini was), but he did have overall responsibility at that time and recalled, 'we used to call him Tarzan with his long hair and Johnny Weismuller build.

'Sometimes he can be moody and cannot cope with situations, but I don't think it makes *that much* difference when he is sitting in the car. It was more upsetting to his social life.

'As a driver I really did rate him as one of the very best.'

Another sports car name from Cuoghi's Ferrari days was the other half of the Berkshire Residents' Association, **Tim Schenken**. The young Australian who blazed across the British Formula Ford and Formula 3 scene to great effect was beginning to lose Formula 1 momentum a little by 1972, leaving Surtees half-way through a grim season.

'To get to know Tim was very hard, he was always joking. I liked his sense of humour and his way of life.

'Perhaps because he was a mechanic he understood what Ronnie was saying [Schenken formed Tiga, a formula racing car construction firm with Howden Ganley in the late seventies].

'Ingegneri Caliri was telling me what they were wanting in the car. As I said, they were talking deeply and made a good car, so one of them must have been able to test a bit better than I thought!

'Tim fell in love with a German girl and settled down in his life and his driving. To be a Formula 1 driver at the time was very hard: either you were paying for your drive, and there was not much money available at that time, or you had to be one of the top drivers.

'Unfortunately Tim never managed to prove himself. He was not driving often enough to improve himself. Then you have always to begin again each time you race. Undoubtedly the testing and constant driving helps you get to know the car and yourself properly. But when you 'ave the experience and the talent like Niki, it is not necessary. Niki gets into the car and he is on top of it, turning the best time, in two laps.

'It was not always easy to match the speed of Tim and Ronnie in the Ferrari days, but it would be 'ard to find two nicer men to work for.'

Frenchman **Jo Schlesser** was killed at Rouen in 1968 driving a new Honda V8 in that year's French Grand Prix. Cuoghi met him in his Cobra days and later racing GT40s. 'To me he was one of the old-fashioned drivers. Not for his driving position but because he liked the racing life.

'To me he was a good driver and person. I admired what he was doing and was very sad when he died.'

Tony Settember we have talked about earlier, but Cuoghi added on a personal note, 'I have been lucky in meeting a lot of really nice people in my life and Tony was one of them. We were sharing flat when we were building the cars in Goldhawk Road. We were not a driver and a mechanic, more friends.

'I enjoyed my life with Tony and he taught me so many things. When we have dinner, going in Greek restaurants all the time, we were, always he was making a mess of the table cloths. Drawing suspension, showing me how it all works, the basic principles.

'I think I could call him my teacher.'

Joseph 'Seppi' Siffert was thirty-five when he was killed at Brands Hatch in a BRM. As with Rodriguez's fatal accident, Cuoghi was not there and frankly admits he does not think he could have stood the shock if he had been in either case. Siffert was a German-speaking Swiss who worked his way into motor racing from a career on two wheels. Everything he had, right from the start, was the result of his own working and competition abilities, for he came from a very poor background: yes, there are such things as poor Swiss, or at least there were in Seppi's childhood.

Cuoghi knew Siffert through sports car racing, of course, and it is worth pointing out that Porsche thought so much of Joseph that they even bought him a ride in a Formula 1 March (1970) in preference to his accepting a Ferrari offer that would have led Siffert into opposing Porsche in the sports car world, as well as an obvious formula commitment.

'Siffert, Siffert, he was very, very quick. Unfortunately he was gone too early, not too young, but too early. I see one of his mechanics who worked on his Lotus Formula 1 car (with which Siffert won the 1968 British Grand Prix) and I remember with him how fast Seppi was.

'He was reaching his peak, and he had a good car when he was killed ... by good I mean fast. I really think he would have been a World Champion.

'He had the discipline. Siffert was hard, very hard on a car, but he has finished quite a lot of races in front, sports cars too, so he was not *that* hard on the machinery. In sports cars, when you have two good drivers, one always try to beat the other: unfortunately Siffert wanted to prove all the time that he was quicker than Pedro . . . and he was quicker. Very often he was faster than Pedro, especially in the long run—but when the weather was bad Pedro was better than Siffert, though Seppi would still keep trying and there was not much difference. He was a fighting guy, all the time.

'Like David Piper he was always dealing cars.

'As a person we could talk easily because he spoke Italian, but it is difficult for me to say I learned a lot of his character, even though he was with us for a long time. He would come and have a drink with us in a hotel bar, and he was entertaining company. But he was always early to bed; Seppi would be with us in the bar, but not for long . . . he was there to be polite. He had tried hard all his life, so he was taking care to go to bed and be ready in the morning.

'At the time there were professionals like Stewart and others who wore suits and did everything in a business way, and I think Siffert was more like them so far as his off-track manners were concerned.

'In setting the car up we often had to copy the settings from Pedro's car for Jo. Seppi would know he was not happy in the car, but not the exact reason why he was not happy. Often he would just drive around the trouble in the car! Pedro knew how to set the car up, all the little details on the suspension.

'Siffert was a hard man on the brakes because he was always braking later than anybody else . . . I think they called him the "last of the late brakers" in some magazines! Regazzoni is the same, both Swiss, both brave, and always 'aving the higher wear because of it.

'I must say he was not rough again: look at the Porsche gearbox. It had a synchronizing system. A slow change, if you try to rush it, you ruin the synchromesh. Bye, bye! Seppi was used to formula cars and motorcycles, quick changes.'

Peter Sutcliffe, the British sports car driver was summarized quickly, 'he always look like a kind of Sherlock Holmes character to me! Very sophisticated English gentleman. I liked him as a person, pleasant to work for, an amateur driver who enjoyed it. When racing did not make him happy any more he just gave up.

'In a sports car he was quite a good driver.'

Dr Dick Thompson was an American club racer who appeared in the Gulf team through his contact with Grady Davis. Cuoghi thought, 'It's very hard, he bent so many machines for us. He was trying hard, unfortunately making mistakes because he is trying too hard. . . .'

After James Hunt's mid-season decision to retire in 1979 **John Watson** from Ulster, domiciled by the Sussex seaside of England, wore the uneasy mantle of being Britain's only hope of Grand Prix honours . . . but the McLaren he took over from Hunt at the start of the 1979 season was a disaster.

John made his name in Formula 2, particularly with Brabhams, before a number of false starts in F1—even the Penske team, for whom he won the 1976 Austrian Grand Prix, folded under him!

Watson was Lauda's 1978 team-mate at Brabham, having led the team following Pace's death and also having suffered more ill-luck while leading than anyone since Chris Amon.

Cuoghi commented, 'People tell me he is an Irishman and this is the reason for his troubles!' Cuoghi grinned and continued, 'John is a very good boy and a good friendly person to deal with.

'Unfortunately he is making a lot of mistakes. I don't know how . . . last year (1978) he could have won so many races, you could not believe it. Before that even more, but he never has the winning result for us.

'It must be because of his way of driving, or of thinking. On the gearbox, he is the same as Niki, changing straight for the gear he wants on a tight corner after a straight. So, he comes from fifth to say second . . . Nelson at the moment is not doing this, he is changing gear by gear.

'That is not hard on the car the way Niki and John do it. There is less wear on the gearbox, no surge on the driveshafts and there is less chance for a mistake: miss one gear and you are in trouble. Change two gears and you are on the brakes, a more positive and slower change. From fifth to second in one go may be slightly harder on the engine, but on the transmission it is better.

'John is a true fast driver, faster than Niki sometimes, especially on practice times. Niki in a good car is unbeatable, but anything less than good car, and the Brabham was such a one, and Niki is not so good. In a 99 per cent car Watson is quicker, he will stick his neck out.'

Generally Ermanno is so co-operative that I think the comments are kinder than one would find from most other regular Grand Prix mechanics. Experience and age lend a tolerance and an insight that I found invaluable. Thanks Ermanno. Ciao!

Index

Ahrens, Kurt 70, 71
Alfa Romeo 136, 162
Amon, Chris 32, 41, 52, 57, 65, 68
Anderstorp 120
Andretti, Mario 65, 78, 81, 103, 106, 125, 142, 144, 146, 158, 160
Aston Martin 2, 4, 44, 46
Attwood, Richard 40, 50, 56, 72, 80, 91–93
Audetto, Daniele 127, 129, 130

Bailey, Len 60
Belgian GP 28, 29, 30
Bell, Derek 83–88, 91–94, 106
Bellucci 22, 21
Beltoise, Jean-Pierre 83, 108
Bianchi, Lucien 27, 30, 61, 62, 64
BOAC 500 57, 60
Boffa 21, 22
Bondurant, Bob 40, 41, 48
Bonnier, Jo 27, 58
Bowes, John 39, 42
Brabham, Jack 32, 112
Brambilla, Vittorio 126
Brands Hatch 57, 60, 74, 78, 79, 87, 94, 98, 120
BRM 26–32, 45, 66, 83, 87, 115, 162
Burgess, Ian 30–36, 51

Caliri, Ing. Giacomo 98, 103, 106, 110, 117, 120
Campbell-Jones, John 27, 28
Cevert, Francois 107, 108
Chiti, Ing. Carlo 29, 136
Clark, Jim 27, 28, 30, 60, 112
Colombo, Ing. 114
Coltrin, Peter 19
Cosworth 30
Cunningham, Briggs 24

Cuoghi, Maria Grazia 19
Cuoghi, Roberto 19

Daytona 33–38, 51–65, 74–78, 83, 107
Delage 18
Depailler, Patrick 118, 153
Donohue, Mark 83, 86

Ecclestone, Bernard 82, 136–138, 146, 148, 160, 162
Edwards, Guy 129
Elford, Vic 75–79, 81, 91, 104, 142
Emery, Paul 23, 25, 28
Emeryson Cars 23–27, 33
Ertl, Harald 129
Etheridge, John 46, 48, 50, 51, 59, 61

FAV 4, 7, 44, 45, 46, 50–52
Fiat 19, 38, 75, 102, 127
Fittipaldi, Emerson 117, 119, 121, 124–127
Forghieri, Ing. Mauro 106, 110–116, 124, 162
Francis, Alf 8
French GP 30, 33

Gendebien, Olivier 24
German GP 26, 32, 121
Ghedini, Sante 136
Ginther, Ritchie 28
Giunti, Ignazio 83
Goodwood 41, 45
Gregory, Masten 50
Gunnar Nilsson Fund 158
Gurney, Dan 27, 41, 57

Hailwood, Mike 30, 64–68, 81
Hawkins, Paul 58, 60–64
Herrman, Hans 68
Hill, Graham 24, 112
Hill, Phil 24, 26, 40, 57
Hobbs, David 60–68, 81, 83
Hockenheimring 60, 131, 132
Horsman, John 4, 52, 55
Hunt, James 118, 125–131

Ickx, Jacky 54–82, 91, 98, 103–120
Imola 70
Ireland, Innes 32, 40, 41, 50, 52
Italian GP 28, 32

Jaguar 24, 38, 40
Jenkinson, Denis 19, 40, 57

Karlskoga 58
Kinnunen, Leo 75–81, 104
Kyalami 50, 53, 59, 64, 102, 124, 148

Index

Lamborghini 12
Larrousse, Gerard 68, 91, 108
Lauda, Niki 6, 8, 10, 12, 111, 115–122, 124–163
Le Mans 7, 23, 24, 36–67, 75–92, 109
Lotus 19, 23–28, 83
Lyons, Pete 129

Mairesse, Willy 27, 52, 55
Marko, Dr Helmut 91–98, 104, 115
Maserati 12, 19–33
Mass, Jochen 115
Matra 42, 67, 82, 83
Merzario, Arturo 98–129
Mille Miglia 19
Monaco GP 30, 120
Montezemolo, Luca di 115, 125, 127
Montlhèry 41, 59
Monza 50–56, 61, 79, 87, 106, 114, 115, 121, 126, 127, 132, 148
Moss, Stirling 8
Muir, Brian 56, 61
Munari, Sandro 98, 103, 104
Murray, Gordon 138–163

Naples GP 20, 22, 26
Neerpasch, Jochen 40, 41
Nurburgring 38, 40, 52, 56, 61, 66, 80, 81, 91, 108, 109, 121–130

Oesterreichring 70, 72, 79, 82, 93, 98, 126
Oliver, Jack 61–68, 83, 84, 87

Pace, Carlos 98, 106–109, 118, 138
Parkes, Mike 40, 83
Parton, Jim 39, 40
Patrese, Riccardo 146
Pescarolo, Henri 108
Peterson, Ronnie 98, 103, 106, 118, 120, 136, 144, 146
Piech, Dr Ferdinand 72
Pilette, Andre 27
Pink, Bill 46, 53
Piper, David 50–56
Piquet, Nelson 149–160
Pironi, Didier 154
Powell, Hugh 23, 25, 26, 32
Pryce, Tom 131

Ramirez, Jose 51
Redman, Brian 59–66, 72–78, 80–83, 91, 98, 103, 107
Rees, Alan 54, 55
Regazzoni, Clay 91, 93, 98, 103, 114–131
Remington, Phil 4, 39, 41
Reutemann, Carlos 108–142
Rindt, Jochen 50, 52, 76, 114
Rodriguez, Pedro 53, 57, 61–94
Ross, Gordon 28
Rouen GP 27

Salvadori, Roy 24
Scheckter, Jody 117, 120, 121, 132, 142, 149, 153
Schenken, Tim 98, 103–109
Schetty, Peter 93–110
Schlesser, Jo 40
Sebring 33, 38, 51, 52, 60, 65, 77, 78, 86, 87
Settember, Tony 6, 19–44, 112
Shelby, Carroll 4, 7, 33, 36–44, 57, 112
Siffert, Jo 30, 55, 61–94
Spa-Francorchamps 39, 42, 48, 54, 55, 61, 66, 80, 88, 103, 109
Spence, Mike 57
Stafford, Arnold 42
Stanguellini 19, 20–26, 33
Stewart, Jackie 57, 58, 107, 108, 112
Stuck, Hans 138
Surtees, John 80, 112, 127
Sutcliffe, Peter 52, 53
Symons, Ernie 39–41, 51

Tambay, Patrick 150
Targa Florio 23, 36–66, 75–91, 103–110
Tedeschi 23
Thompson, Dr D. 54, 55–57
Tour de France 42
Trintignant, Maurice 33

Vaccarella, Nino 23, 109
Vallelunga 107, 108, 140
Van Lennep, Gijs 91, 93
Villeneuve, Gilles 142, 146, 149, 153, 159, 160

Wadsworth, John 20, 22, 23
Waterman, Bob 40
Watkins Glen 61, 70, 82, 93, 94, 106, 121, 130–135
Watson, John 138–149
Whitmore, Sir John 48, 50
Willment 39, 43, 53
WRE 20–23
Wyer, John 4, 42–45, 52–54, 60, 61, 74, 78, 82, 94

Yorke, David 4, 50–59, 62, 82, 91–96, 109

Zandvoort 120, 125